# DOROTHY EINON'S
# learning early

# DOROTHY EINON'S
# learning
# early

Facts On File, Inc.

# Contents

A Marshall Edition.
Conceived, edited and designed by:

Marshall Editions Ltd
The Orangery
161 New Bond Street
London W1Y 9PA

First published in the UK in 1998 by Marshall Publishing Ltd

Copyright © 1998 Marshall Editions Developments Ltd
Text © 1998 Dorothy Einon

Checkmark Books
An imprint of Facts On File, Inc.
11 Penn Plaza
New York, NY 10001

Cataloging-in-Publication information is available from Facts On File.

ISBN: 0-8160-4013-3 (hc)
ISBN: 0-8160-4014-1 (pb)

Checkmark Books are available at special discounts when purchased in bulk quantities for businesses, associations, institutions or sales promotions. Please call our Special Sales Department in New York at 212/967-8800 or 800/322-8755

You can find Facts On File on the World Wide Web at http://www.factsonfile.com

Printed and bound in Portugal by Printer Portuguesa

10 9 8 7 6 5 4 3 2 1

This book is printed on acid-free paper.

Originated in Singapore by Master Image

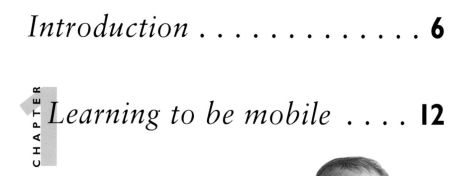

# Introduction

As parents, we have a vital role to play in our children's development. By the time we hand them over to teachers at the age of five, most of their basic learning skills are in place. A happy, confident child who knows that learning is fun will breeze into school ready and willing to participate. Children who enter school confidently are more likely to sail out with their self-esteem intact and enhanced. Whether a child can add two and two or write her name is less important than developing her confidence in her own skills and abilities. Helping a child to realize that learning is one of the great pleasures in life is among the most important lessons we can teach our preschoolers.

If a child knows she "can" she will learn. If she thinks she "can't" she won't. Nobody gets it right all the time, but the child who believes that she can do it will persevere. Self-esteem is the key and that is much harder to measure than prereading skills – and infinitely more important. Your child

develops self-esteem through the knowledge that there are people in her life who will always love her, not for what she can do but for who she is. A child who is told every day in words and deeds that, of all the "Suzys" in the world, she is the best will gain such esteem. And, if she has self-esteem, she can retain confidence in herself and in other people's love for her in spite of making mistakes. A child who believes that she is only loved for what she can do will be undermined by failure and may become too frightened to try. A child who has unlimited love, support and praise has the knowledge and confidence to find solutions. She can take the knocks, feel the despair of failure, yet retain the confidence to try again.

## Understanding how children learn

When children are born they can perceive little of the world around them and understand even less. Because their senses are not focused, they look without understanding what they see and hear without comprehending what the sounds mean. In the first few weeks they do not even realize that they are separate from the world around them. Why should they? They cannot control either their body or the world. In this respect, their previous life within the womb has not fitted them for life outside it.

Before a child can discover her world, she needs to find out where her own body stops and the rest of the world begins. To do that she must first realize that she can make things happen, which would be easy if she could control what her body did. As she cannot, it is no wonder that she needs a guide. In fact, she has two guides. One is an inborn development "package," which tells her when and what to be curious about and how best to induce those around her to help her find out. This package is described in the first section of each chapter. The other guide is her parents or caregivers. The more sympathetic, understanding and consistent they are, the easier her task is. The second part of each chapter provides practical ideas to help you steer your child toward learning.

Underpinning each chapter are the keys to understanding and helping your child reach her potential – love and knowledge. The well-loved child grows and blooms, and the caregiver who understands how she develops will provide her with the best possible start.

## The ways that children learn

At first, children learn by trial and error: this is what all that exploring, poking and messing around is for. What motivates them is their delight in their own action and their parents' or guardians' pleasure in watching and encouraging them to learn. Later they also learn by imitating adults, copying actions and then intentions and interests. A child who watches you interacting with friends will want to develop her own social skills; one who sees you reading will want to explore books.

As children grow up and can understand what you tell them, they start to learn more formally by taking in what you explain to them. But however they learn, all children have their own personal mountain to climb. Not all of them scale the peaks, but with parental guidance they can set off from the best possible base camp. How far a particular child goes ultimately depends upon her individual ability, personality and determination, and more tangible factors like confidence and self-esteem – as well as a little luck.

### The rhythm of development

Children grow in fits and starts. Although your child will gain 10–12 inches (25–30 cm) in the first year of her life this does not mean she grows at a steady rate of ¼ inch (0.5 cm) each week. She may gain a whole inch in a night then not grow at all for a month or so. Children absorb knowledge in the same way. They go on a learning "binge," then need time to consolidate their findings. They put their ideas together and work out how the new facts modify what they thought they knew.

Parents need to match this rhythm. Life should not be one huge cycle of activities. Children need quiet and busy times, routines and challenges, sensible and serious tasks balanced by games that are silly but fun.

## How this book is organized

You give your child the best start by understanding how her knowledge of the world develops and knowing what you can do to challenge and help her. The first 11 chapters of this book discuss the skills a preschooler has to develop in different areas, such as moving, using her hands, communicating and getting along with others. The final two chapters specifically address those skills that your child will need in order to make a smooth and happy transition to school, notably independence and self-esteem, as well as the building blocks for reading, writing and math.

Each chapter charts the milestones you can expect to note in your child as she develops, and gives an indication of when you can expect to see them, then shows precisely how your child builds her knowledge. This is followed by a set of activities that will help her to learn, explanations of what they teach her, tips on toy-buying and advice on dealing with the most common problems. To a child, playing is learning; the goal of the book is to make that learning fun, both for you and your child.

## Note

Most parents share the care of their children with others for varying amounts of time, and the influence of other caregivers on a child's development can be great. Although the term *parent* is used for simplicity throughout the book, this should be taken to mean "parents or other major caregivers" – all those who love and interact with children for several hours a day. The terms "he" and "she," used in alternate chapters, refer to children of either gender, unless a topic applies specifically to a boy or girl.

# Your growing baby

*All babies are different, but a child's gains in height and weight follow a general pattern in the first couple of years*

There is nothing smooth or steady about the way a child grows. Between conception and birth, a baby grows 19½–20½ inches (50–52 cm) in length. After birth the rate of growth slows and continues to slow throughout childhood. Your baby will grow 10–12 inches cm (25–30) in his first year, and 5–6 inches (12–15 cm) in his second, at the end of which he will be about half his adult height. On her second birthday a girl is slightly more than half her adult height.

Weight follows a similar pattern. The average child doubles his birth weight by the age of four to five months and triples it by 12 to 14 months. After that it increases by about 6½ pounds (3 kg) a year. Some children grow faster than this, others more slowly. Nutrition is one obvious factor that affects growth, but genetics, race, love and stimulation also play a part.

A baby's body does not grow at a uniform rate. The head grows quickly to begin with, and the rest of the body then has to catch up. A toddler's head is about a quarter of his total height, an adult's is approximately an eighth. The head grows quickly because it has to be big enough to house the brain. At birth, a baby's brain is only about a third grown, but it develops rapidly in the first year of life and by the time a child is two years old it is not a great deal smaller than an adult's brain. (You can check this rapid growth by comparing the size of a baby's bonnet with a two-year-old's hat.)

By the age of two, a child has all the brain cells he needs to control breathing, sleeping, digestion, seeing, hearing, tasting, feeling, walking and balancing, as well as the basic allocation for talking, remembering, thinking and skilled movement. Skills (and the brain) continue to develop over the next 14 years, but this is more a case of putting on the finishing touches than laying down the basics. At two years of age, the body still has a long way to go.

## GROWTH TIMETABLE

**At birth**
- The average baby girl is 19½ inches (50 cm) long, the average boy is 20½ inches (52 cm). Both grow about 1 inch (2 cm) in the first 6 weeks and another 1 inch (2 cm) in the next 12 weeks.
- The average baby weighs 7 pounds (3.2 kg) at birth and gains about 5 ounces (150 g) a week. Boys take about four months and girls five to double their birth weight.
- The head is large and the limbs relatively small.
- The bones are soft and pliable and, like the muscles, have a high water content. Some "bones" are still composed of cartilage.

**6 months**
- The average boy is 22½ inches (57 cm) long, the average girl about 21½ inches (55 cm).
- The bones of the hand and wrist have begun to ossify.
- The legs and back are still pliable (which is why a baby can suck his toes and place his foot behind his head).

**1 year**
- The average child is 29½–32¼ inches (75–82 cm) in length.
- The average girl triples her birth weight by 13 months, the average boy by 11 months.
- Children have only 3 bones in the wrist (adults have 28), which is why small children are more clumsy than adults and they cannot place things precisely.

**2-4 years**
- A child is about half his adult height and grows 2–2¾ inches (5–7 cm) a year.
- Weight increases by 4½–6½ pounds (2–3 kg) a year.
- The head is still relatively large for his body.
- The muscles are stronger and his bones are less flexible.

**5-6 years**
- The body is now growing faster than the head, which gives a child more adult proportions.
- He has more bones in his wrist and ankle.

| HOW GROWTH AFFECTS DEVELOPMENT | HOW TO HELP PHYSICAL DEVELOPMENT |
|---|---|

The brain is immature, so a baby can do very little for himself.

- A baby who uses his legs will walk earlier than one who doesn't, so always support him in your lap and encourage him to push with his feet.
- Kicking exercises the muscles used in walking. Regular playtime when he wears a light diaper, or none at all, helps walking, especially if you play games that encourage kicking.

Physical growth is a reasonably good guide to how quickly a child's skills develop.

- Make your baby stretch to reach some of his toys.
- If he is not mobile by eight or nine months, a bouncer or walker may be useful (see p. 26).

A baby grows at night and it can hurt; teething is not the only reason for disturbed nights.

- One-year-olds love to push things as they walk. Within a few months of walking, she can manage a pushalong (movable toy propelled by pushing) or a sit-and-ride.

Within the general pattern of growth, a child makes sudden leaps and bounds. He can grow ½ inch (1 cm) overnight, then not grow at all for weeks. You can sometimes spot this growth in a sudden need for bigger shoes.

- Toys to expand his skills include toddler monkey bars, swings and slides.
- Good activities include chasing games and dancing to music.

The gradual development of the wrists and ankles enables children to begin to dart and dodge, manipulate objects and use the hands with greater skill.

- Consider formal lessons in swimming, dancing, gymnastics or skating.
- Resist the temptation to overload a child with classes; skills also need to develop in informal ways.

# 1 *Learning to be mobile*

A newborn baby's muscles are weak, his bones are soft and pliable and his nervous system is neither fully formed nor developed. Over the first 18 months of a baby's life his muscles become stronger, his bones ossify and the parts of his brain that control movement mature. The pace of this development is largely built-in. Children who sit early not only walk early but they also reach for a toy sooner. This does not mean they are more intelligent – they have simply inherited genes that quicken their development.

While speed of development runs in families, parents and caregivers can also play a part. Children nourished with love, attention and food develop sooner than those who receive little. If you encourage your baby 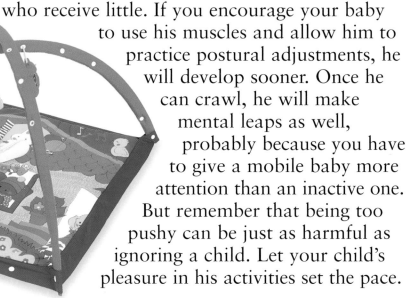 to use his muscles and allow him to practice postural adjustments, he will develop sooner. Once he can crawl, he will make mental leaps as well, probably because you have to give a mobile baby more attention than an inactive one. But remember that being too pushy can be just as harmful as ignoring a child. Let your child's pleasure in his activities set the pace.

# Milestones in becoming upright

| | **WHAT YOUR BABY CAN DO** |
|---|---|
| **At birth** | ● Held with the soles of his feet on the floor, he moves in a reflex walking pattern. Without practice this skill soon disappears. |
| **8** *weeks* | ● He kicks and waves his arms when he is excited (by 6 weeks). This uses the same movement as stepping. It is easier to lift heavy legs when lying flat.<br>● He briefly holds his head up when pulled into a standing position, but is floppy if pulled beyond a sitting position. |
| **24** *weeks* | ● If you hold him under the arms he holds his head in line with his body and supports most of his weight.<br>● He begins to push against you with his feet and may try to raise his bottom as you pull him up.<br>● When he moves he holds his posture and adjusts his balance. |
| **30** *weeks* | ● His postural adjustment is improving.<br>● He can support his weight and stand if he holds the furniture.<br>● Some babies can pull themselves up and may tool around the furniture, clinging with both hands.<br>● He looks more erect when you hold him in a standing position.<br>● If you put him down, he lowers his legs and flexes his knees. |
| **36** *weeks* | ● He pulls himself up to stand using the furniture and adjusts his posture as he moves.<br>● He may need to hold on with only one hand to keep his balance. |
| **48** *weeks* | ● He walks around the furniture, holding with one hand and exploring with the other.<br>● His stepping and postural adjustment is more obvious and he can stand with little support.<br>● He pulls himself up and sits again with confidence.<br>● He can stand on one foot if he holds onto something. |
| **12** *months* | ● He can stand for a moment without help, and his body is erect when he stands against the furniture.<br>● By 13 months, about half of all babies walk, but most still fall over if they lose momentum. |
| **18** *months* | ● He can walk forward, sideways and backward.<br>● He can pull a toy on a string, manage a pushalong and sit and ride on a truck.<br>● He may run but still falls often. |

| **WHAT IS HAPPENING** | **HOW YOU CAN HELP** |
|---|---|
| This is a reflex movement; stepping is automatic if his feet touch the floor. | • Practice develops the leg muscles. He will walk earlier if you play walking games. |
| Kicking uses the same muscles as stepping but does not require the foot to touch the ground. Once the automatic step response is overridden, he can stand still if you support him under the arms. Stronger neck muscles enable him to hold his head up. | • Kicking helps him to coordinate breathing with movement. Encourage diaper-free playtime.<br>• Bounce him up and down, letting him "feel" his feet. |
| The ability to control his body has begun. This comes from the head down, and center outward from his shoulders to his fingers and hips to toes. If you watch carefully you will see the neck, then the shoulders and back, strengthening. | • Use a sling or a carrier when out shopping: learning to adjust to your body sway is very beneficial, as is matching your breathing as you move. |
| As his brain develops, he gains the ability to control the fine muscle movements necessary for these small adjustments. | • A baby walker can help, but only if used in moderation (see p. 24). |
| Early control of muscles runs in families. If either (or both) of his parents walked late, then he is likely to do so too. | • Games in which he sits and rides on your knee or bounces on the cleft of your foot help him learn to adjust his posture when moving. |
| Plump babies are often slower to walk because it is more difficult to pull up a heavier body. | • Check that it is safe for him to pull himself up. Store any wobbly furniture until he is steady on his feet. |
| Babies of African origin mature a little sooner than other babies, sitting and walking earlier on average. Some babies stand for a few weeks before they start to walk; others take off at a run before they can stand still or walk. | • He is likely to fall often over the next weeks; make sure there are no sharp edges he can hit.<br>• If he is slow to start walking, move the furniture apart so he has to "bridge" a few gaps. |
| Children who "bottom shuffle" may still not be walking at this age — when you can move and carry objects at the same time, there is not the same incentive to walk. | • Pulling and pushing toys help him to improve his balance.<br>• Sit-and-rides let him judge how to twist and turn to avoid obstructions. |

# How babies grow

*Understanding the factors at work as your baby grows will help you to make the most of his early months*

*Toys
that move when
hit or encourage periods
of sitting to play give
your baby a chance to
develop mobility skills.*

Babyhood is short and full of small achievements, each of which quickly follows the one before. By the time your child is two years old, he will have more in common with his adult self than with himself as a newborn.

As long as you respond to your baby, offering the help he needs when he needs it, your baby will grow and develop at his own pace. Try not to wish his babyhood away: take the time to cherish him as he is now, rather than watching eagerly for the next milestone, thrilling though that will be.

### The influence of the brain

The brain develops in a predetermined way. The parts that control breathing, sucking, digestion, blood flow and other basic survival mechanisms are fully functional before birth. Those parts that control voluntary movement appear in the first few years of life and those that control intellectual development (language, memory, perception,

thought) mature throughout childhood. A tiny baby does not move or think like an adult; a toddler moves and thinks more like one. By the time a child starts school, adult and child ways of moving and thinking differ only slightly, and by the teenage years they are virtually indistinguishable.

Skills develop from the top down and out. The mouth and tongue are skilled before the neck muscles can hold up the head or turn it from side to side. The upper back can support itself before the lower back can, the arms are controlled before the legs, and the arms and legs before the hands and feet. In practical terms this means that a child can swipe at objects with his entire arm before he can grab them with his hand, and grab them with his hand before he can explore them with his fingers. He can sit before he stands and use his hands quite skillfully before he can adjust his ankles and feet to maintain his balance as he walks.

### Breathing and movement

There are two different systems of breathing in adults. The first responds to the chemical needs of the body and is automatic, the second is voluntary and overrides the first. This voluntary control is the one we use when we talk, sing, run, swim or carry out any complex action, and is the one which enables us to carry out a long conversation without running out of breath or to talk as we walk or jog.

The breathing patterns of the two systems are different. Automatic breathing uses a slow breath in and fast breath out. The voluntary system uses a fast breath in and a slow one out. Babies begin to switch over from purely automatic breathing at 12 weeks of age. At this time they practice taking a slow breath out when they kick, jog or babble. By the time a baby is four to five months old you will hear that sustained breath control in his crying. Later this voluntary technique will accompany skilled movement and speech.

### How love makes a child grow

Babies have a set developmental plan that depends on caregivers providing the tools and stimulation to stretch the child's abilities. If you do not provide your children with what they need they will not develop as quickly or as smoothly as they should. In extreme cases they may even stop growing. A baby who is happy is receiving what he needs and parents who are sensitive to their children's happiness are almost certainly providing all the right inputs. Fortunately caregivers do not need to know much about child development to communicate well and make the correct responses: if you make him smile and keep him amused, you are getting it exactly right.

### A good enough parent

Good parenting is always a compromise because families have to balance the needs of each of their members. In the real world we all have to know how to cope with coming last. No one should expect to always be first in line. Remember this when you put finishing your cup of coffee before picking him up. It's OK. Of course it would be wrong always to put your baby last, but equally it would not be right to make yourself a slave to your children. Children do not need endless stimulation or constant attention.

Part of being a successful adult is having the ability to motivate ourselves and function when we are not the center of attention. Children need the time to discover things for themselves. They learn as much from getting things wrong as they do from getting them right. Everyone (and that includes small children) needs the space to reflect on what they have learned. Time to rest is important too.

### How you can help

All children kick, but a child whose parent responds to that kicking by tickling his tummy kicks harder and longer. All babies reach out toward things that interest them. The child whose caregiver has arranged things so that he hits a toy easily will reach again. If things keep happening the child soon learns "I did that."

*A child's control over his body progresses from the top and center of the body and moves systematically down and out along the limbs.*

*Babies love kicking and it helps develop leg muscles. At about 12 weeks old they adjust their breathing to their kicking, learning to breathe voluntarily as well as automatically.*

# Activities for immobile babies

*Even before your baby is mobile, he will respond to games and activities if you play with him*

An immobile baby likes and needs to feel movement to strengthen his weak muscles, help his bones to harden, learn how to keep his balance and interact with you.

## Sitting upright

Tiny babies have no control of their backs. If you pull your baby up from a lying position with his arms he curls forward but his head lags behind. Until a baby can tuck his head in while he is being pulled up into a sitting position, his back should be supported at an angle when he sits. Use a chair with a gentle slope. Sitting in a bouncy chair or propped up on cushions is the best way to view the world and your baby will be less sleepy than when he is lying flat.

## Diaper-free playtime

Diaper changing is an important event in a baby's day. He loves to see your face and hear you coo as you change him and shows this by smiling, gurgling and kicking. These interactions rapidly develop into turn-taking "conversations" which lay the basis for language (see pp. 150–172). You can extend diaper-free periods (and so increase the practice) by laying him on a bath towel on the floor. Some babies like to have a light shawl thrown over them as they kick.

## This is the way we ride the horse

This is a game to play once your baby can hold his head up and his back is firm.

Sit your baby on your knee and gently bounce him up and down as if he is riding a horse. Support your baby by holding him under the arms. There are lots of rhymes you can sing as he bounces, but most involve the rider falling off the horse at some stage, "down in the ditch" where he falls between your knees.

An older child may like to ride on the crook of your foot. Cross your legs, place him on the crook of your feet and bounce him up and down by swinging your upper leg. Now uncross your legs, swinging him high in the air. After this swing him back by crossing your legs.

## Carrying the baby

One way to balance household chores and time with your baby is to attach him to your body with a sling or carrier. He will adjust his balance as you move. You will probably not notice until he stops – it is the lack of postural adjustment that makes sleeping babies seem heavier.

## Take a walk

If a newborn baby is held in a walking position with his feet on the floor he instinctively takes a step. This reflex movement usually disappears after a few weeks. Recent research suggests that this is because most babies' legs become too heavy. Babies with light legs continue to step, as do those who have lots of practice standing and walking in the early weeks. Such children walk a little sooner. There is no evidence that this makes a child "bowlegged."

## Swing high, jump low

Putting a baby into a bouncer or freestanding swing is another way to amuse him while you continue with the chores. Even very small babies like to be in the deep stirrup seat of a bouncer for short periods because it gives them such a good view of the world. Once they find their feet they will jump up and down by kicking against the floor.

### WHAT YOUR BABY LEARNS

**• Sitting upright**
A chair that rocks as your baby kicks teaches him "I can make that happen," a simple but important lesson.

**• Diaper-free playtime**
Kicking exercises the muscles and joints and gives the movement sequences that he will use when he walks some practice.

**• This is the way we ride the horse**
Action games like "This is the way we ride the horse" – and the many variations on it – help develop balance. It is a wonderful social game, helping your baby's communication skills. Through such games your baby also learns to anticipate going "down in the ditch." Later he can "ask" by his action. He may, for example, lift his bottom to say "Now, please."

**• Bouncing and being carried**
The swinging and swaying movements of bouncing or of being carried as you work improve your baby's balance and have the added bonus of calming minor irritation. Swinging is also an excellent way of encouraging a slow exhale of breath since both adults and children naturally match their breathing to the ebb and flow of a swing.

**Milestones in learning to crawl**

| | **WHAT YOUR BABY CAN DO** | |
|---|---|---|
| **At birth** | • If you pull your baby up by his arms into a sitting position, his head lags behind his body.<br>• His back is rounded and his head flops when supported in a sitting position. | |
| **6** *weeks* | • His back is still rounded but he is beginning to support his head.<br>• If placed on his stomach he makes crawling motions using the arm and leg on the same side.<br>• Turning his head does not affect his body. | |
| **12** *weeks* | • His head does not lag so much when he is pulled toward sitting.<br>• He can raise his head and flex his knees.<br>• His back is straighter and his head more upright when he sits; he can sit for about 10 minutes if his bottom is wedged. | |
| **20** *weeks* | • He may try to pull himself up when you take his hands; his head lags slightly.<br>• He can look around without toppling.<br>• Propped and supported he sits for 30 minutes.<br>• He rolls from his tummy to his back.<br>• On his tummy he pushes with his hands and flexes his feet. | |
| **24** *weeks* | • He lifts his head when you take his arms and pulls against you to move into a sitting position.<br>• He begins to tuck his head into his chest as he comes up.<br>• Once up he needs only slight support and may sit briefly unaided. The strength is there but not always the balance. | |
| **30** *weeks* | • He can push himself into a sitting position and sit briefly without support (by 28 weeks).<br>• He can turn to the side and look behind.<br>• When lying on his tummy he creeps forward.<br>• He rolls from his back to his tummy.<br>• When placed on his hands and knees he rocks. | |
| **36** *weeks* | • He sits alone and stretches to reach a toy without toppling over; he pivots from side to side on his stomach (by 32 weeks).<br>• He rolls intentionally and uses this and stomach pivoting to move about.<br>• He may push on to his hands and knees and rock for some time before he crawls. | |
| **48** *weeks* | • He can lower himself into a sitting position from standing (by 40 weeks).<br>• He rolls intentionally to be in a sitting position.<br>• He leans forward and crawls; when he stops, he sits.<br>• He is less likely to roll off a bed or crawl down stairs or steps. | |

## HOW YOU CAN HELP

- A baby who is pushed around all day does not practice postural adjustments in the way he does if he is carried. Spend some time each day carrying the baby.

- Lying on the tummy is safe for babies who are awake; this position makes it easier to move and to reach.

- Propping gives babies a better view of the world.

- He can now spend more of his time propped up; keep plenty of cushions around him in case he slips.

- He will manage to sit inside a large playring or a car inner tube and if propped will need fewer cushions.

- As he begins to creep across the room, make sure that nothing can hurt him as he rolls.
- He will sit and play but may still need cushions to protect him when he falls.
- If he is still not moving, encourage him by placing his toys where he has to stretch to reach them.

- Take care when you put him down in a chair or on the bed because he can easily roll off.
- If he is creeping, he may soon crawl. Babyproof your rooms and buy a stair gate.
- Encourage him to move by calling to him, placing toys some distance away and putting him on the floor to play.

- As soon as he starts to pull himself up, ensure that any sharp edges are covered and that you have removed unstable rocking furniture. One solution in a small home is to buy a big playpen and alternately put your child and the dangerous furniture into it. A child who keeps hurting himself will become understandably cautious.

## WHAT IS HAPPENING

Four separate elements are at work over this period.

First, your baby's brain is growing and connections are being formed. This growth and development begins with the area of the cortex that controls the face, then moves down to the neck, shoulders, upper and lower back. Once control reaches the shoulders it moves down the arms to the hands and lastly to the fingers. The control of the legs starts with the hips and then moves to legs and feet. The last areas to come under control are the bowel and bladder.

Second, your baby is learning to adjust his posture as he moves. Postural adjustment is a complex skill which depends on practice. Putting children on the floor rather than in chairs and carrying them instead of transporting them in car seats and buggies provides more practice.

Third, the safe environment and gentle coaxing of caregivers give the child the confidence to take the next step. Feeling loved and secure always helps a child to learn.

Finally, an interesting and challenging environment motivates young children. A child who receives little attention does not return much or strike out to explore as readily as one who has plenty to look at, touch and lick.

## SAFETY FIRST

A consequence of the speed with which an immobile baby becomes a sitting, rocking and crawling one is a constant need to update safety arrangements. While a child is immobile you can leave a hot drink on the coffee table or the cat's dish on the kitchen floor. Once the child can move you have to be more careful. Don't wait until he shows signs of crawling – most children can pivot across the room before they can crawl.

# Activities for sitting and mobile babies

*Strength in the neck and upper back greatly increases your baby's capacity to learn about the world*

Carrying your baby calls for frequent postural adjustments from her as whoever is carrying her walks, bends and sways. But modern ways of transporting babies make few demands on their ability to adjust balance with each movement. Likewise, strapping a baby into a chair to play with toys on the tray makes none of the postural demands that sitting propped up on the floor and reaching for distant toys does. Without a harness the baby sometimes topples and becomes more motivated to avoid doing so. If you don't have a carrier, you can make a simple sling from a beach sarong. Fold it in half horizontally and tie the lower edge around your waist and the upper edge around your neck.

### Sitting in a box

There is something about small confined spaces that seems to attract most young children and sitting in a supermarket box is the simplest answer. A toddler may like such additions as a cushion for a seat and a steering wheel, but a baby will be happy simply to sit. Toddlers may also like you to put the box behind the sofa, throw a cloth over the top and keep peeking inside.

### TROUBLESHOOTING

**My daughter is 15 months old and still not walking or crawling although she is an efficient bottom shuffler. I have been told that children who bottom shuffle are often late walking. Is this true?**

Bottom shufflers can move around while they learn to walk, which is probably why many of them are reluctant to take to their feet. Don't worry. Your daughter may be shuffling for another two or three months but will eventually walk. Encourage her to stand up by placing toys on the sofa, and on an adjoining chair so that it is more efficient for her to stay on her feet to gather her toys together. By gradually widening the gaps between the furniture you will encourage her to walk across.

### Lying on her tummy

A car inner tube, inflatable life preserver or imporvised play ring makes an excellent tummy support, encouraging your baby to keep her head up and improving her view of the world. Cover an inner tube or preserver with a towel and lay the child face down so the inflated section is under her waist and her legs rest on the floor. A play ring may have integral toys but, if not, put your child's favorites into the center. Later she will like to sit inside the ring and play with her toys. A toddler may just like to sit inside the tube and pretend it is a car or boat.

## An uphill crawl

This is a good game for the patio or any other area that is a little hard on the knees. You will need a wide shelf or a length of countertop. Prop this along one edge to make a wide slope. The child crawls up the hill, then lies flat to slide (or be pushed) back down. You could make a permanent hill by hinging two countertops together, but put a piece of rope in the joint to prevent fingers being trapped. A steeper hill will need a textured section for climbing (a towel would do) and a smooth section for sliding.

## Encourage walking

By far the easiest way to encourage a baby to walk is to stand or kneel with your arms wide open to invite her to walk into them. If she is still going strong as she approaches, you can always take one step back while she takes another two steps forward.

## Barefoot babies

Even the softest shoes are stiff for babies in the early stages of walking. If you feel her feet will get cold, socks are better than shoes unless there is a danger that the baby will slip on a waxed floor.

## Arranging the furniture

Once your baby is pulling herself up and starting to walk around the furniture, increase the fun by pushing sofas and chairs close together to provide a good run. When she can support herself using one hand, draw the chairs apart so she has to bridge a small gap. As soon as she can take one step, encourage her to take two by moving them even farther apart.

### HOW YOUR BABY BENEFITS

**• Sitting**
In addition to improving your baby's view of the world and interaction with it, sitting helps her to perfect the ability to hold her head up and move without falling over. This ability is the cornerstone of later movement: from crawling to reaching and walking.

**• Lying on her tummy**
It is difficult for a baby who is lying on her back to raise her head high enough to look around, spot a toy and try to reach it. When she is propped on her tummy she has a good view of everything that might interest her and has some support if she wants to reach for a toy.

**• Encourage walking**
The more practice your baby has at walking, the faster her balance and confidence will improve.

# Toys to aid physical development

*Your baby will walk in his own time, but walkers and other toys can help him to perfect his skills*

There are two basic types of baby walker: those that otherwise immobile babies sit in and those that cruising babies toddle behind. The toddling kind include heavy-based trucks and sit-and-rides that the baby uses to pull himself up and then clings to as the truck moves forward.

### Types of walkers
Neither type is an essential piece of baby equipment, and many health professionals feel that the disadvantages of sit-in walkers, in particular, far outweigh their advantages. Used cautiously, however, a sit-in walker can satisfy a baby's frustration at his lack of movement. If you use one for your baby, remember that a walking baby can sit if his ankles hurt, while one trapped in a walker cannot. There have been reports of ankle damage in babies who used walkers excessively. Also choose a model that has some integral toys: many do not give a baby something to do with his hands.

Pushalong walkers do not harm the ankles or curtail exploration so, if you can only buy one type, this is the one to choose. Remember that only toys specifically designed as

*Sit-and-rides are the best value toddler toys. A horn on the steering wheel adds an extra dimension.*

walkers are suitable for small babies (other toys may not be stable enough).

Make sure that neither type of walker tips if it is pushed hard against the furniture and that stairs, steps and fireplaces have guards installed.

### Pushalongs
Before a baby can walk alone, he needs a sturdy pushalong with a heavy base that will not tip if he uses it to pull himself into a standing position. In the early weeks after he starts to walk these remain the best choice. Once he is steady on his feet small animals, bells or rattles on the end of sticks, vacuum cleaners and brooms are good. While he still needs to pull himself up into a standing position avoid lightweight wheelbarrows and doll carriages.

### Sit-and-rides
As a toy to sit on, move and steer, most parents choose cars, fire engines and animals rather than smaller three- and four-wheeled cycles. However,

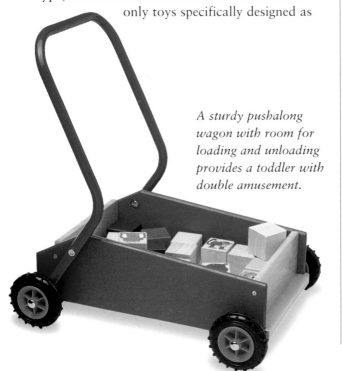

*A sturdy pushalong wagon with room for loading and unloading provides a toddler with double amusement.*

cycles are easier to maneuver inside the house and take up much less room in a small apartment or backyard. There is a wide choice and most have plenty of added features, such as toy storage or a horn.

## Pullalongs

Before he can manage a pullalong a child needs to be able to walk and do something else at the same time – such as carrying toys or calling to you. The best pullalongs are noisy and active. Pullalongs tend to have less universal appeal than pushalongs so take your child to a toy store and let him try them out before you buy.

## Crawl-through

You could buy a long flexible tube or play tunnel for your child to crawl through, or you can easily make one from a series of cardboard boxes opened at both ends. Select about six boxes of the same size. Open the bottoms and tops and tape them together to make a tube. Toddlers manage better if they play with older children who can show

them what to do. If your child is on his own, you may have to play too, so make sure the tunnel is wide enough. You could also make a crawl-through by throwing a sheet over the backs of four or six chairs lined up back to back.

## Rockers

These come in a variety of shapes, sizes and price ranges, from the gentlest rockers which move only a few inches to the full swing of a classic rocking horse. Before spending a great deal check that your child likes rocking and don't be tempted by an "heirloom rocker" for a young child.

## Household appliances

Children start imitating grown-up actions at about the same time that they start walking. It may happen only fleetingly at first but by 18 months most children enjoy miniature versions of household appliances. Brooms and vacuum cleaners are probably the all-time favorites, but a small feather duster or dustpan and brush are also ideal and in the summer months your child may like an imitation lawn mower.

*Tunnels invite curiosity and exploration. Bought ones flatten for easy storage when not in use, or you can improvise.*

# CHAPTER 2

# From standing to jumping

Once they are on their feet, children make rapid progress, although they vary enormously in how they approach physical challenges. Some are cautious and always need parental approval, while others have no fear and continue climbing, for example, without a thought of how they might get down. Even before she can shout "Me do it," a fearless child may want to tackle activities that you think are unsuitable, unsafe or even impossible.

Although minor bumps and bruises are common, few children have serious falls in the first couple of years. Their low center of gravity and flexible bones mean they are unlikely to fall far and hard enough to break any bones. If you find yourself saying "Be careful" often, try to remember that children like an audience – your child may have found a good way to grab your attention. Providing safe outlets for exuberant behavior and turning a blind eye to all but the most dangerous activities are the best ways to deal with this. The easiest way to invite children into safe activity is to provide them with playmates and an open space.

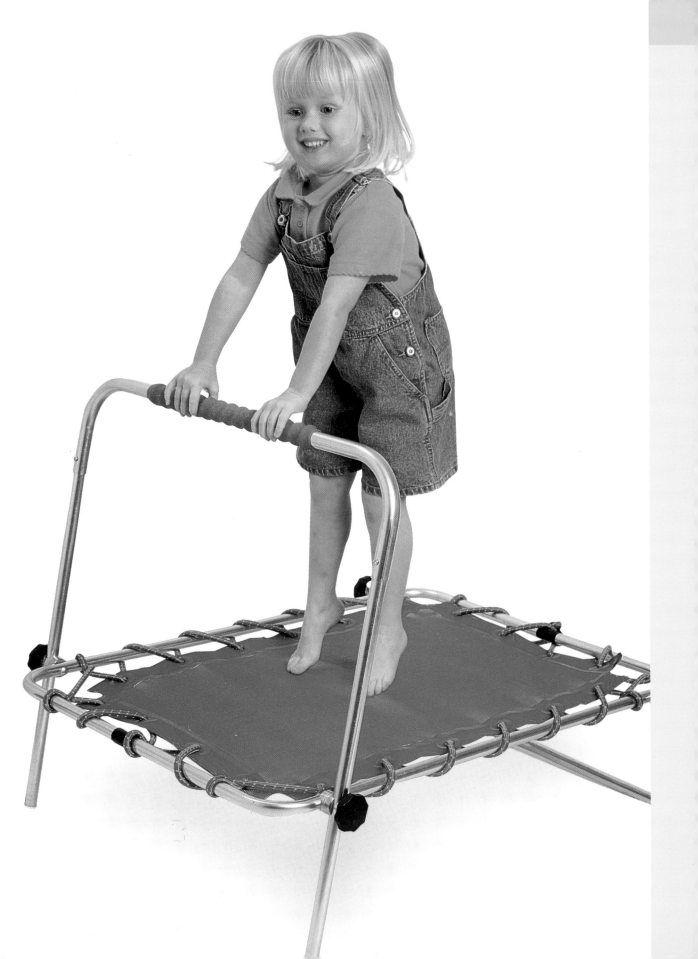

**Milestones from standing to jumping**

## WHAT SHE CAN DO

### 18 months

- She can stand on one foot with support and walk with a wide-legged waddle.
- She can use her feet to scoot along on a cycle.
- Most children find it difficult to carry anything large while walking.
- All but the most cautious may go up and down stairs on hands and knees.

### 24 months

- She climbs on a chair, runs and climbs up the stairs holding onto the banister.
- She can play on a simple climbing frame, push and pull wheeled toys, and stop to pick up a toy without falling over.

### 2-3 years

- She jumps and hops, and walks up and down stairs one foot at a time without necessarily holding the banister.
- She knows what is safe and what is dangerous.

### 3-4 years

- She runs, starts and stops without falling, suddenly dodges, runs and skips.
- When she jumps and hops she raises her feet high and bends her knees as she lands.
- She walks up and down stairs using alternate feet.
- She throws a ball for a short distance. She catches a large ball thrown directly into her arms.

### 4-5 years

- She can walk along a curb, climb up the steps of the playground slide, use a standard monkey bar, ride a bicycle, dodge when chased and carry large toys.
- She can learn to swim, skate, ski, dance and use a trampoline.

## HOW YOU CAN TELL

- Because the "go" mechanisms of the brain develop before the "stop" mechanisms she tends to launch herself from place to place and sinks to the ground when she stops.
- Her center of gravity has altered by 18 months, so that her legs are less widely spaced. Most children can stop, start and change direction as they walk.

- As her balance improves she walks with less of a waddle and can talk and carry things as she walks.
- She may try to jump but does not yet leave the floor.

- Social play becomes more important. If other children are around she may "explode" into activity.

- She loves running and chasing, and always wants to race to the next tree.
- She is reluctant to be still.

- She moves in a more grown-up way although she lacks an adult's strength and foresight.
- She is still a little clumsy and unaware of the consequences of some of her actions (for example, swinging her backpack could knock the glass off the low table).
- Her fine motor movements are improving but they still lag far behind the skill of an adult.

## HOW YOU CAN HELP

- Let her walk by the side of the stroller occasionally to make her feel grown up and give her a chance to explore.

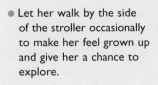

- Give her pushing and pulling toys to improve her balance and coordination and her ability to plan movements.

- Walking along inclines, swinging, climbing, sliding and rolling all improve balance.
- Running, jumping off the stairs and stopping and starting as she is chased around the backyard develop muscular strength and skill.

- Ball games such as volleyball, catch or kickball (use a beach ball) improve her balance and coordination.

- Chasing and dodging other children improves the planning of movements, as do climbing, cycling, skating or rollerblading and throwing and kicking balls.

# Playing safe

*The average home is full of potential hazards for a curious, mobile baby, but safe areas are easy to provide*

Most accidents to under fives happen in the home. As babies become mobile, those who care for them have to look carefully for potential danger zones around the home and backyard. This should not be a once-and-for-all look; as your baby's skills develop, continually update safety precautions.

### • Electrical equipment
Hide electrical wires and make sure a child cannot pull appliances (or their contents) on top of himself. Install a video guard. Put safety plugs in empty outlets.

### • Countertops and tables
Never walk away from a baby you are changing on a table or countertop. Bouncy chairs move when the baby rocks (or an appliance such as a washing machine vibrates), so keep watch. Never leave her unattended in a chair on a high surface, or near the sink or stove, even if she is asleep. Do not use long tablecloths once babies can crawl, and put utensils and appliances at the back of the countertop once a child can walk. Never put a high chair where a baby could grab a wire, knife or anything sharp or dangerous.

### • Cabinets and doors
Replace glass in low cabinets and doors with safety glass, or cover with plywood or Plexiglas. Close doors and desk flaps so that your child does not walk into them. Install safety locks to low cabinets. Keep drugs, chemicals, alcohol and tools locked away out of reach.

### • Furniture
Soft furnishings should be fire resistant. All furniture should be stable and heavy enough not to tip if a child uses it to pull himself up.

### • Low tables
Cover sharp edges and remove small objects and ornaments. Cover a glass top with Plexiglas.

## TOY SAFETY

Don't give a baby anything that could be poked in an eye, swallowed or stuck down the throat. A toy labeled "unsuitable for children under 36 months" probably has small parts on which a child could choke. Anything labeled "This is not a toy" is unsafe. Buy from reputable stores, and check for special seals and safety marks.

### • Windows
Install window gates, but make sure that these are easy to remove in case of fire. Make it difficult to pull furniture up to a window and do not place anything that could be used to help a child climb onto a sill nearby. Tie curtain and blind cords out of reach.

### • Bookcases
Make sure bookcases are stable (tall ones should be anchored to the wall). Wedge books so that a child cannot pull them down. Make sure that ornaments cannot be pulled down and will not fall if the bookcase is pushed.

### • Doors
Wedge doors ajar so that babies cannot get stuck behind them, and to avoid trapped fingers.

### • Floors
Avoid throw rugs on waxed surfaces, and make sure carpets are properly fitted, particularly on stairs.

## AROUND THE HOME

### • Baths
Never leave a baby alone in the bath. Make sure the surface of the bath is slip resistant and always put cold water in first, then add hot. Shield the faucets. Once your baby can pull herself up on the furniture, install a toilet lock.

### • Beds
If you leave a baby on the bed or sofa make sure there is a soft landing if she rolls. Do not leave a baby asleep on your bed unless she is well tucked in. If you leave her on the sofa, place cushions on the floor just in case.

### • Stairs
Install safety gates at the top and bottom of stairs. Check that the child's head cannot get stuck in banisters and that small babies cannot crawl through them.

### • Heating and fires
All fireplaces should be shielded by a fixed guard. Turn the hot water thermostat down to no more than 120°F (50°C). Install a smoke alarm and make sure it can be heard all over the house. If it can't, install more than one.

### • Poisons
Keep cigarettes and alcohol out of reach. Do not store chemicals under the sink unless you install a proper lock and use it consistently. Keep all medicines locked away.

### • Stoves and Ovens
Install a burner cover and keep saucepan handles turned toward the back of the stove. Use the back burners only if you can. Choose an oven with a "stay-cool" door.

# The importance of mobility

*Mobility enhances your child's other skills, including her spatial awareness and social interaction*

Children need to move about for themselves to grasp the concepts of distance and direction. To understand distance you must have some idea of how long it takes to go from one place to another and how fast you are moving, both of which are more difficult if you are strapped in a stroller.

A child acquires an idea of direction when she finds the best way around obstacles or, after moving from the family room to the kitchen, thinks about the route she has just taken. It all seems straightforward, but how do you learn that your bedroom is above the family room? You never take the direct route through the ceiling. How do you know that a shortcut will end up in the next street when you have never been that way before?

*With her newfound mobility, your child will enjoy running across the room and climbing into your lap. Sometimes a cuddle in front of the television is just what she needs.*

The skills needed to understand space build slowly. They come about through practice at planning routes, cutting corners and fitting pieces of a puzzle together, as well as building and running around. They are also helped by considering whether it is possible to squeeze a bicycle through a small space, how to reach someone in a game of tag and judging which balls are going to be close enough to catch. Some people are much better at spatial thinking than others (just as others have more aptitude for language); understanding space is thought by many to be related to mathematical competence. The average man is better than the average woman, although there is little difference between the sexes before about nine years of age.

### Why mobility improves other skills

Once a child becomes mobile those around her must interact and watch her constantly. You rush to her aid, talk to her and interpret and praise what she does. Her life is full of new experiences and she also has your running commentary. It is not surprising that with mobility children take a sudden jump in competence. They seem smarter and more grown-up because they are. Children grow in leaps and bounds, not in measured steps. This is one huge bound. Even without adult input the leap that gave her mobility was probably accompanied by a bound in memory and understanding. Your input builds on this.

Excitement helps learning. When you walk down the road on a dreary wet day you do not think beyond the journey, but on the first sunny day of spring you notice leaves coming into bud and the birds singing. Arousal (and light increases arousal) makes an enormous difference to learning. A child's excitement at her new abilities opens the way to progress in all areas.

### Social interaction and mobility

Even before they know how to interact with other children, toddlers love being with them. At first they cannot cope with their own age group, but older children make allowances for the toddler's lack of social skills. Older children – especially siblings – know how to build up the excitement until the toddler screams with delight. Of course there will be tears before bedtime, but what fun they have first. The only snag is that the older child usually tires of the game first. Much of the laughter and glee is based on physical rough and tumble. The toddler is chased, caught, pushed, pulled, hidden and found. As she passes her second birthday a child begins to play with peers.

## Caution and curiosity

Accidents happen because young children lack the foresight to see when an activity will lead them into danger. So, for example, a toddler does not remember she could slip on the wet floor. She does not imagine that a car might come around the corner even if the street is presently clear.

*All children combine a degree of curiosity with a sense of self-preservation. A toddler does not willingly put herself in danger. But she does not think about finding the route down before she climbs up the tree.*

*Look at how your child interacts with objects to see what attracts him and absorbs his attention. It may be as simple as a piece of wrapping paper – often initially seen as more interesting than the present itself.*

When a child can see the cars speeding along the road or see how she could fall, she proceeds with great caution. It is when her view is blocked that problems arise.

Finding the courage to let an adventurous child discover the consequences of some of her actions is extremely difficult, and few parents get it right all the time. It is worth remembering that shouting makes a child continue with an ongoing action with added vigor, so yelling "stop" is likely to have the opposite effect and make her go. A soft and urgent voice is more persuasive.

## Helping to develop her skills

It is easy to select exactly the right games and activities for a child; you simply watch carefully with empathy and love. Ask yourself "Will this make her laugh?" or "Will it capture her full attention?" or more basically "Will it keep her absorbed for 10 minutes?" If the answer is yes, that is what she needs. It may be a cardboard box, a toy or a game of peek-a-boo. If it feels right and she is content, it was the right choice.

# Activities for mobile babies and toddlers

*Capitalizing on her ability to walk and run broadens the scope of your interaction with your child*

Once your child can walk, she will probably demand to do so constantly, which can make it difficult for you when you want to hurry. But the ability to walk is important as a baseline against which skills can be developed. Once she can walk, she refines the skill to enable her to sit down and stand up when she wants to, bend down to pick up a toy, walk in a circle, climb, run and jump.

### Pick it up

This simple activity stretches the ability to start, stop, bend down and pick things up without falling over. All she needs is a little bag and something to collect. It could be pebbles, large beads or even the grass after you have mowed the lawn.

### Stamping in puddles

Toddlers cannot jump or skip but they can stamp their feet. What better place to stamp than in a rain puddle? Put on your waterproof boots and slicker and head for the nearest puddle.

### A simple slide

You can buy special baby slides that are not too high and therefore easy for a child to climb by himself. If the floor is hard, make a soft landing with some cushions.

### Circle games

In circle games children make a ring by holding hands and dancing around. Games such as ring around the rosey where children simply dance

### TOYS TO BUY

• At a year old, your child will enjoy a swing and a low slide, even if she is not yet fully mobile.
• The only pushalong she should use in the early stages are heavy-based push-and-rides or walkers specially designed for this age group. Once she is walking steadily she will be able to manage a lightweight pushalong, such as a dog or roller on the end of a stick.
• A doll carriage or wheelbarrow takes a little more coordination, as do pullalongs.
• At 18 months most children can manage a simple slide of a few steps up and a slide down. Look for one that you can build in various configurations to gain maximum use from it.

then fall down are easy enough for toddlers and can be played with just two or three people. You need more people for the farmer in the dell, but you could always use stuffed animals and dolls for some of the characters.

### Tunnels

Even after they can walk children love to crawl through a tunnel. There is something about being enclosed that pleases small children. In the backyard you could throw a large sheet over the clothesline (lower the line if necessary) or the branch of a tree. It doesn't matter if it is a tight squeeze – that is part of the fun.

### Climbing and jumping

At 18 months, a child who climbs on a chair then jumps into your arms will fall unless you are in exactly the right place to catch her. By 30 months, however, she is able to leap more accurately to you. As she grows bolder she will also want to go higher, but make sure she understands that someone has to be ready to catch her. Always say "One two three – ready? – jump!"

### Wheelbarrow

If you take her out in the stroller she may well want to walk, but if you offer her a ride in the wheelbarrow she can't wait to climb in. Take a trip around the yard tipping her out carefully if

---

## HOW YOUR BABY BENEFITS

**• Stamping, pick it up and walking**
Once a child can walk, she needs time to perfect her skills. These activities, as well as being fun and therefore keeping her interested in doing them, help her mobility, encouraging her to move, start and stop.

**• Sliding, climbing and jumping**
These activities help a child to gain confidence, as well as balance and motor control.

**• Circle games**
These games and many others like them help your child to start and stop, weave and dodge. It is also good social play: children still play more sophisticated versions of circle games in the school playground.

---

she wants you to. In the house you could attach a string to a cardboard box or pull her along on an old curtain. It helps if the floor is waxed.

### When to walk

It is often difficult to keep a walking child in her stroller. Because parents think that agreeing to a child walking will lead to constant demands of "Me walk," they are understandably reluctant to let her out of the stroller. The way around this problem is to let her walk in certain places. So, for example, she could always walk the last block on the way home, or between the park gates and the swings.

### Looking

When you want to keep your child in the stroller, watching for animals or cars is an obvious activity that works, especially if you draw it out: "Let's see if there any cats around this corner … are there any?… can you see?… YES!" The second is even simpler but usually works: ask her to carry one item of shopping such as a can of peas or a bag of cookies. Finally, this is the most tedious for grown-ups but greatly loved by children: tie a pullalong toy to the stroller or let her hold the string so that it follows behind the stroller. This works best when the seat and child are facing you so that she is facing the toy.

# From toddling twos to schoolchild

*As she develops a taller, slimmer body, your child builds on her basic mobility skills*

The major characteristic of a two- to three-year-old is her independence, coupled with a readiness to demand what she wants. These demands are often unreasonable, especially if she is tired and you are distracted. It may seem as if her favorite words are "No! Me do it" and her ideal game is pushing your buttons. But although this period is often called the terrible twos, it is also a magical time.

In the first year or so of her life you passively watch as your child develops, but in the preschool years you listen to her commentary on what she is doing. "Watch me jump," she tells you as she lifts her heels off the floor or "See me take off" as she pedals furiously around the yard. In many ways boasting about seemingly small achievements sums up these years. The big physical leaps are behind her and language, thought and social skills move center stage. That is not to say that nothing physical is changing. A look around a playground full of preschoolers shows how much of their play is intensely physical and that two- and four-year-old children move quite differently. But the most striking changes are happening in other spheres and, because they concern the mind rather than the body, adults seem to have greater input.

## Changing body shape

The short square body of a baby gradually gives way to the longer, leaner build of a child in which the head and body are less dominant. There is more leg and relatively less body. Children have a longer reach and stride and are capable of greater speed and endurance. They no longer need to be carried as often and can walk quite lengthy distances if encouraged to do so.

## Stopping and starting

The physical abilities that develop in the preschool years modify basic skills such as walking at different speeds and standing up from a crouching position without the need to hold onto anything. They involve perfecting balance, developing flexible movement, the capacity to deal with different terrains, gathering speed, stopping and starting and doing more than one action at a time.

Dodging and darting and stopping and starting are major components of all these late-developing skills and their practice is central to many games. You will see your child stop and start on her tricycle, dodge and dart when she races around with the kids at playschool and later use all these elements in games of football or tag.

## Balance and coordination

As children dodge and dart and bend and twist, their balance and coordination improve.

*Traditional games such as hopscotch refine mobility skills: changing direction while moving, stopping and starting without falling over and bending down without sitting.*

*With practice, walking along fallen tree trunks or low walls, riding bicycles, jumping off the stairs, swinging, cartwheels and* *rolling down grassy banks all activate and make children aware of their ability to remain in balance.*

But running around is not the only way to perfect these underlying skills.

As their muscles strengthen, children add jumping, hopping and skipping to their repertoire. They bounce on the beds, jump off the step and skip down the road with obvious delight. Being with other children seems to magnify it all and their games are accompanied by whoops of delight and wild exaggeration.

### Falling over, getting up

As their center of gravity moves farther from the ground children fall less. But since they often fall off, trip over or bump into obstacles when running fast, they are more likely to hurt themselves than when they were younger. Their bones are still relatively soft (although hardening) and are only occasionally broken, but grazes, cuts, scrapes and bruises are all common.

### Planning activities

The other obvious characteristic of older preschoolers is their ability to plan an activity in advance. They can follow a predetermined sequence of movements, plan which route to take and think about coming down before they climb a tree. However such skills are in their infancy. A three-year-old's plan is for a few actions and she is easily distracted from it. It is more a case of having a plan to get there and thinking what to do next after she arrives.

### Adding imagination

Planning now infuses a child's games. She is never simply riding a bike: she is Batman in the Batmobile or a police officer chasing robbers. She knows where to park the Batmobile and which part of the yard is the landing strip. The closer children get to school age the more elaborate the story lines of these games become. At first each story has a small "window"; they are neither sure where it is going or where it has been before but gradually the flow of the story is sustained and they are able to talk it through with other playmates. Listening to stories enhances this skill. Watching popular videos and TV programs helps children play these games together. When you do not have the verbal skill to explain properly what you mean, it helps if you all know the same stories.

*Providing a mini-trampoline will save your beds and sofas being used as convenient bouncers. If two children jump around together, the fun will be doubled.*

# Activities for twos and threes

*Improved balance and coordination and natural exuberance pervade many activities for preschoolers*

Most of these activities require the minimum of equipment and are quick and easy to set up.

## Footprints

This is a summer outdoor game. All you need is an area of paving and a bowl of water. The children get their feet wet then walk on the paving, leaving footprints behind. If you are feeling indulgent and don't mind the mess, you could add some water-based paint to the bowl and let them walk on a roll of wallpaper or newsprint.

## Walking the line

This is surprisingly difficult for a small child to do. Draw a chalk line down the driveway. The task is to walk along it. On a hot day she could draw the line herself by squeezing water from a dishwashing liquid bottle. Inside the house a length of twine could be her guide.

## A balance beam

You could set this up in the house but it is probably easier to do in the backyard. You will need a plank of wood (the kind used for bookshelves is ideal) and some cinder blocks. Support the plank on the blocks and see if she can walk across without falling off.

## Stepping-stones

This is a version of the balance game, which works better indoors. You will need a package of paper plates and a little imagination. Scatter the plates around the floor so that the child can step between them. Now imagine the carpet is the sea and the sea is full of sharks. Only the plates are safe. Can she cross the room to rescue teddy and get back safely? A foot in the water means she loses a toe. (You may have to give the smallest children a hand the first few times you play.)

### WHAT YOUR CHILD LEARNS

All these activities enhance your child's ability to balance, which is central to such activities as dancing and gymnastics. They also enhance her planning skills as she decides where to put her foot next.

## Bubbles and balloons

Sometimes the simplest toys can give hours of fun. Balloons and bubbles are obvious examples. Children love chasing bubbles around the yard or keeping balloons off the ground by batting them.

## Jumping off the stairs

Put a pile of cushions on the floor and let your child jump from the stairs onto them. Make sure she uses only the bottom couple of steps.

## A boogie before bedtime

There is a period just before bedtime when reasoning seems to have passed, leaving you with a child who is silly, rather wild and for whom the phrase "tears before bedtime" seems to have been invented. This is also a busy time in most households: the baby has to be fed, the dinner cooked and parents are tired. What better time for a boogie? It drains their energy, keeps them amused and can be followed by the calming routine of a bath then a story. All you need to do is put on some suitable music, then let her kick off her shoes and dance. If you feel like joining in she will be even more delighted.

## Bouncing on the beds

If you don't have a trampoline, jumping on the bed is fun, but an old sofa is even better because the child can use the back as a support. If you have furniture that you don't want her to jump on, make it clear that only the sofa is a "trampoline."

## Sleeping lions

This is an excellent game at the end of an exuberant period. Sleeping lions lie completely still. They do not move a finger, answer questions or laugh. If there is more than one child, you can have a competition; if not, play against the clock: can she stay sleeping for longer than yesterday?

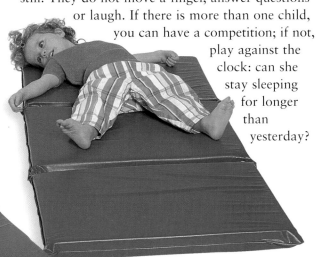

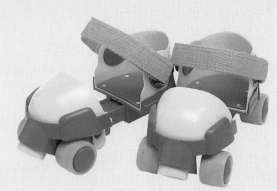

# Activities for older children

*Physical play becomes more sophisticated, purposeful and sociable as children grow older*

By the time they are three or four years old, most children are more sociable, playing with – rather than simply alongside – their peers. This adds sophistication to their games.

### London Bridge is falling down

There are lots of variations on this basic theme in traditional games and dances. Sometimes everyone passes through a single arch; at others, couples pass through and form a second arch alongside the first until everyone is making arches and there is no one to go through them. Although the words differ, these games were once played all over the Western world. The simplest variation is with one arch and children passing through one at a time. All is safe until the song reaches the point where the child is caught between the arms of the arch-makers.

> "*London Bridge is falling down,*
> *Falling down,*
> *Falling down.*
> *London Bridge is falling down,*
> *My fair lady.*
>
> *Take a key and lock her up,*
> *Lock her up,*
> *Lock her up.*
> *Take a key and lock her up,*
> *My fair lady....*"

### The big ship sailed...

This is a wind-up game, played to the chant of "The big ship sailed through the alley alley oh." Everyone holds hands in a long line. The last player makes an arch against a wall or tree and the leader takes the line through the arch so that the last player's arms are crossed. The leader then takes the line through the arch between the last and second to last player, and so on. By the end of the game, all players have their arms crossed.

### Tag

Young preschoolers need to be organized, and play best if an adult or two play too because allowances have to be made for the youngest children's poor planning and dodging abilities. When children are chasing and being chased adults need to judge how bad they can let a child be without seeming condescending and how good the child can be and still be caught. By the time children start school they will be able to play with their peers. It is in the middle school years that children enjoy this game most.

**My son has a birthday coming up and I cannot decide whether to buy him a bicycle with stabilizers or a tricycle. What do you think?**

It depends where he is going to use the bicycle. If he has the opportunity to ride quickly he will get more fun from a bicycle, but bikes are difficult to ride slowly so you need plenty of space and a long run without corners. If you live near a park or in an area where a small child can safely ride on the pavements choose the bike. A trike is easier to turn at slow speeds so suitable for most yards the child can stop and sit on it while playing. It is a better choice if there is no obvious place to ride safely, or if the route to the park is busy. Because trikes can be ridden slowly they are easier to take out on walks if you are looking after more than one child. Choose one with a pushing handle. Trike riding is tiring (especially if the trike does not have a chain). Without a pushing handle you might find yourself carrying the trike home.

## Don't touch the floor

This is a more advanced version of stepping stones, which can be played in the garden using inverted flower pots or in the house using furniture supplemented with inverted dishpans and paper plates or indeed anything else that will keep a child off the floor. The child's task is to move from start to finish without touching the ground. Set the course out so there are a number of routes and a few challenges, so that the child learns to plan the route in advance.

## Paint-can stilts

You will need two old paint cans with lids for each child (two thick plastic flower pots each).

Make two holes in each can – they should be on opposite sides of a closed end – and pass a thick piece of string between the holes. Take the loose ends and loop them up to make handles. Adjust the length of the handles to suit the child.

## Swings, twisters and rope ladders

It is often difficult to find room for a swing in the garden, but if you have a large tree you can attach a monkey swing that has a small seat on a single rope. The swing could also hang in a door frame of the garage. Attach it with a firm hook, so that it is easy to remove when the garage is in use. Small children use rope ladders much like swings, climbing on to the bottom rungs and swinging or twisting. As they grow older they climb further up. Twisters are T-bars suspended on ropes. They hang so that the child grabs the bar and swings or twists by her arms. These can be suspended from trees or door frames too.

**• Rhyming games**
Rhyming games improve memory and coordination, social skills and the physical ability to bend and weave.

**• Tag**
Tag gives a child ample practice at dodging and darting and at planning where to go next to avoid being caught.

**• Don't touch the floor**
Depending on what you use as your stepping-stones, this may improve your child's ability to balance; it will also help her spatial awareness and planning abilities.

**• Paint-can stilts**
These improve your child's balance and coordination.

**• Swings, twisters and rope ladders**
Swinging and climbing improve spatial awareness. They also build a child's confidence.

# How the senses develop

Compared with most animals, human babies are immature at birth. Physical and intellectual immaturity is obvious, but that of the senses is less apparent. Most parents know their baby cannot focus at birth but don't realize just how little he can see – he can't make out the mobile on the bedroom ceiling, for instance. But he is skilled at listening to language, swaying in time to words and expecting an adult chatting to him to pause for him to answer. Hearing games teach children to pay attention, a valuable skill for school. Smell is probably more acute now, and more important, than at any other time in his life. He knows you first by your smell, next by your voice and last by your face. Babies use their mouths to explore the world by touch, children their hands. The sense of taste evolves, too, from surprisingly sophisticated preferences to a desire for sweets.

# Milestones in sensory development

| | SIGHT | HEARING | |
|---|---|---|---|
| **At birth** | • A baby can focus on an object 8–10 inches (20–25 cm) away, but does not see detail.<br>• He will follow an object slowly with his eyes, but may often lose it.<br>• His pupil reacts to bright light and he blinks. | • He hears high-pitched noises and is quieted by low-pitched sounds.<br>• He can locate sounds in front of him.<br>• He is startled by a loud or sudden sound. | |
| **4** *weeks* | • His eyes now work together, he focuses and can spot things out of the corner of his eye.<br>• His visual acuity is still poor and he sees things better if they move. | • He prefers female voices and high-pitched sounds.<br>• He moves in time to the sound of your voice and can distinguish simple sounds, such as "p" from "b." | |
| **12** *weeks* | • He is interested in faces and recognizes his mother.<br>• He prefers moving objects to still. | • He watches you when you speak and turns toward a sound. | |
| **20** *weeks* | • Stationary objects are now much clearer but he still prefers strong contrasts, sharp edges and bright colors. | • He quickly turns to a sound and recognizes the voices of people he knows.<br>• He can tell more complex sounds apart, such as "baba" from "baga." | |
| **28** *weeks* | • He prefers to look at complex objects and changes position to seek a better view.<br>• His visual acuity is 8,000 times better than it was at birth. | • He looks toward sounds from above and below.<br>• He recognizes voices and his name and tells tunes apart. | |
| **44** *weeks* | • He can perceive depth and if he crawls, does not attempt to go down steps head first.<br>• He begins to look for things he drops. | • He responds to one or two commands.<br>• He may know when the surprise happens in a song.<br>• He recognizes the names of people, familiar objects and places. | |
| **52** *weeks* | • He searches for things he has lost and can follow a rapidly moving object.<br>• His vision is almost as good as an adult's. | • He responds to simple commands.<br>• He understands half a dozen words. | |
| **After the first year** | • He remains a little short-sighted until the age of nine or ten years.<br>• His visual memory is excellent and he may find things an adult has lost. | • His musical abilities improve.<br>• The ability to hear high-pitched sounds decreases. | |

| SMELL | TASTE | TOUCH |
|---|---|---|
| • His sense of smell is keen: he recognizes his parents' scent within days.<br>• At one week old, he can distinguish his mother's breast pads from those of other women. | • At first he prefers salty tastes, but that rapidly changes to a preference for sweet. | • His hands are closed.<br>• He turns his head and opens his mouth if his cheek is touched.<br>• He cannot control his hands but will reach to a noise or light. |
| | | • He begins to lose the ability to reach toward a sound. |
| • He turns away from a foul smell. | | • He no longer reaches for a sound or light.<br>• He knows if something is familiar. |
| | | • His hands are open and he reaches out to touch and grasp.<br>• He uses his mouth to explore objects. |
| | • He begins to accept different tastes, even quite bitter ones.<br>• He shows likes and dislikes. | • He strokes and starts to poke and prod.<br>• He picks things up to explore with his mouth. |
| | | • He pokes, prods and explores with his hands.<br>• He laughs if tickled. |
| | | • He strokes and pats and turns objects in his hands. |
| • A child's idea of a good and bad smell is the same as an adult's. | • Most children prefer sweet, salt and fatty flavors. | • He stops using his mouth to explore as his hands become more skilled. |

# What babies can see

*A baby's sight is immature at birth, but his ability is rapidly refined over the first year of life*

Seeing the world is low on the list of a baby's priorities: your baby recognizes you by your smell before he knows your face. Like the brain, the human eye is immature at birth. The cone-shaped cells in the center of the eye (which process color and fine detail) are few and widely spaced, but the surrounding rod-shaped cells are plentiful. These analyze movement and work better in dim light. The best way to imagine what a baby sees is to sit in a dim room. Let your eyes grow accustomed then look around. There is a slight indication of color and little detail, but the edges are clear when they contrast with the background. A dark chair is outlined against a pale wall, a tree against the sky and the movement of a cat is easy to spot. Imagine this amount of detail and color without the darkness, which is what a newborn baby sees.

### In focus and in the picture

There are other limitations on what a baby can see. In the early weeks a baby's eyes are focused at about 8–10 inches (20–25cm), or about the

*A baby's vision is blurred at one month (top left). It becomes progressively clearer at two and three months until it achieves the clarity of an adult's sight (bottom right).*

distance from his eyes to his mother's chin when she feeds him. Outside this bubble everything is blurred. There is evidence that babies do not see the world as a continuous picture as adults do. Initially, at least, they may see it item by item. They are not, for example, disturbed if a face has the mouth on the forehead, nor do they look at things in a systematic way. All this comes later.

### Getting used to the world

Babies and children can see what they need to see. Initially those needs are confined to their mother's face and outlines of the rest of the world. As a baby's horizons expand, so does his ability to focus and resolve detail. By the time he is ready to reach out he is able to see the objects in range. Once his hands are ready to explore, his eyes make sense of what he can hold. By the time he is mobile and wants to be across the room his vision is almost as good as an adult's.

## VISUAL PROBLEMS

Most serious visual problems, such as blindness, are recognized in the early weeks although occasionally it may take a little longer. Less serious problems are harder to detect. Because the visual system is flexible in the early years and somewhat rigid later on, the sooner treatable problems are detected the more likely it is they can be corrected. If cataracts and squints are corrected in the early years vision may be normal in later years. But if they are still uncorrected by the time the child is about six years old, the operation may be little more than cosmetic.

Most developmental exams do not pick up problems such as near- or far-sightedness, so you should be alert. Have all the vision exams as reccomended and consult your doctor or an ophthalmologist if:
• your baby's eyes are not focusing together at six months to a year
• he seems to go up close to objects and stare at them
• he seems not to notice you
• you are in any way concerned

*Puzzle books in which characters are hidden in a landscape or teddies or toys have to be found in various situations are perennial favorites.*

### The eye is not a camera

Regardless of the angle from which an adult looks at a bucket, it almost always looks bucket-shaped – the sides are straight and slightly tapered and the top opening is round. But in a photograph, the shape of the bucket depends on the angle of the shot. From directly above the bucket, the opening is round but from any other angle it is oval. The sides remain straight but the taper varies depending on the angle of view. In a photograph the size of the bucket might vary dramatically, depending on how far away the photographer was standing when he took the shot.

In real life, none of these factors are apparent, yet the image that is focused onto the retina by the eye's lens is exactly the same as that focused on the film by a camera's lens. The difference is that, unlike a camera, the visual system interprets the image. This interpretation means that objects remain a constant size, shape, color and brightness. Babies are probably not born with this facility, but by about seven months they are interpreting what they see just as adults do.

### Seeing depth

As in a photograph, the image that falls on the back of the eye is two-dimensional, although the world we see is in three dimensions. The dimension we "see" but which is not in the visual image is depth. Babies almost certainly do not see depth at first, although they clearly can by the time they are crawling at around seven or eight months. Children who crawl early – by about five or six months – may crawl over the edge of a step as if they do not realize the step is there. However, if you lay a baby face down on a clear plastic surface with a drop below him, his heart rate goes up and he cries, which suggests he does see it.

Perhaps the earliest crawlers do not know they should stop when in danger: they lack caution rather than depth perception.

### Ignoring the background

The key to solving the puzzle books where the baby has to find a face in a crowd is learning to ignore the overall picture. Some people find this difficult (psychologists call them field dependent); others easy (field independent). Children are more field dependent than adults and gradually become more independent as they grow older.

Those who can ignore the background tend to be good at manipulating and building; those who take more notice of it usually have more intuitive social skills – they pick up the cues that signal someone is unhappy or telling lies.

*While children who find it easy to ignore the background in a picture build a house of multicolored blocks, those who find it hard sort the blocks into shapes, call them types of animal or make color-coded structures.*

# Putting on a show

*Almost from the start, your baby's eyes will respond to your attempts to engage his attention*

The fact that your baby's ability to focus is limited does not mean that there is nothing you can do to train his developing visual skills. Remember how much time your baby spends lying on his back one way or another: hang a mobile above the changing table and over the crib. If he has a bouncy chair, try to find a toy to fit across it (see also pp. 64–65).

## Making mobiles

Mobiles make pretty decorations for a baby's room. But if you intend it to be more than an adornment you need to remember that babies look at mobiles while they are lying flat on their backs. This means that the pieces need to be horizontal rather than vertical so that they face the baby. Remember too that a baby has little color vision and poor acuity. If your ceiling is pale, make the mobile from large, dark, noisy, shapes that move. Alternatively, let the mobile reflect the light.

Your baby will also find metallic balloons, light reflected onto the ceiling from moving water, a set of wind chimes (the sound will attract his attention) and white lace curtains blowing in the breeze of a fan worth watching.

## Buying mobiles

There are two kinds of mobiles for young babies, the traditional hanging type and those that throw light onto a screen or the ceiling. If you attach a traditional mobile to the crib, you either need a wobbly crib (which will not be a good idea when the baby is older) or a motor to make the mobile move, although in summer an open window or fan will produce enough breeze to make it turn. Since babies can locate sounds, a music box attached to the mobile makes it easier to find.

Most mobiles that throw light onto the ceiling also have music boxes. These probably appeal to the parents more than their babies, since if a baby looks toward the sound he will not be watching the light show.

## Face me

If your baby could tell you what he wanted to see most he would say "faces." Everything else is really just a substitute for those moving heads that turn to face him, come in close and whisper endearments in a high-pitched voice. Mobiles are attractive but the real thing is better. As you pass the crib or wherever else your baby is lying, always pop your head into view.

## What should we look at now?

Until your baby can reach and grab, you can tie all sorts of objects to his crib for him to look at. You may attach them to the bars but keep his safety uppermost in your mind. Cut all strings shorter than the circumference of the baby's neck and remember that, in the unlikely event of tangles, wool (pure, rather than a synthetic mix) breaks more easily than string. You also need to make sure that nothing has a sharp edge or points which could hurt the child if it fell into the crib.

## Mirror, mirror

Once a baby starts to kick, a mirror placed near his head will reflect not only light but also his moving image. You can buy special baby mirrors that are safe to put inside the crib or fix a mirror or mirrored tiles to a wall beside the crib. A large cardboard box lined with aluminum foil makes a good kicking tunnel. Cut off the top and bottom to make a tube and line the inside with foil. Lay the baby so he can see his movements reflected in the foil. Mirror tiles firmly stuck to the underside of the kitchen table make a safe and interesting "den" in which to settle an immobile baby while you prepare meals.

## Pictures around the room

Children like to see the same items again and again. Simple pictures of familiar objects make a fine collage. Pointing and naming lays the basis for language skills, and saying goodnight to them can be part of a calming bedtime routine.

## Watching the wash

Babies love to look at moving images. If you have a front-loading washing machine or dryer with a glass door, your baby will love sitting in front of it in a bouncy chair. A clothesline full of wash blowing in the breeze is even better.

## Let's go out

By the time they are a few months old, children are beginning to reach out to touch and explore for themselves, but that is no reason to stop showing them objects. Outings offer a visually stimulating world that is beyond their reach and that will excite their interest. You could try visiting any or all of the following: a level crossing to watch the trains pass; a bus depot to see all the buses parked; the fire station to watch the engines; the pond to feed the ducks; the zoo; the display at the local garden center; a street of stores in late evening when the windows are lit and streetlights are on.

## Under the trees

In the days when everyone had a large baby carriage, babies where routinely taken out in the "fresh air" for a morning sleep. It is well worth reviving this habit in the summer months, since trees in full leaf make the most magnificent mobiles – a moving, rustling canopy of dark shapes against a bright sky.

### WHAT YOUR BABY LEARNS

All these activities train your baby's ability to focus and use both eyes together. Moving images train him to concentrate and follow them, and he will later learn that they exist even when they are no longer directly in his line of sight. Looking at familiar objects is also comforting, and it helps the development of memory.

# Hearing sounds

*Your baby can hear well at birth, although his ability to detect the direction from which a sound comes is limited*

Babies start to tune into language almost as soon as they are born. In the first hours they pick out a voice from the background, swaying gently in time to its rhythm. When they start to make bigger movements, the kicks and arm waves also keep time to a voice. Babies turn in the direction of a voice (although they may not be able to locate exactly where it comes from) within hours of their birth. They seem to be particularly happy if the voice has a high pitch, such as that of an older sibling.

It could be said that they have heard it all before. The womb is neither a dark nor a silent place. Some light enters through the stomach wall, especially on bright days, and their mother's body makes a large number of sounds. The ears are functional for months before a baby is born (as are the eyes) and he will hear his mother's heart beat, her blood pumping, and her chest sucking in each breath, as well as stomach rumbles, conversations, passing sirens and coughing fits. All these sounds are muffled by the amniotic fluid which surrounds the baby. His mother's voice will not sound the same when it comes through the air as it did when it echoed around her body and entered through his fluid-filled ears, but it will have enough in common for him to be able to pick it out as familiar. There is even evidence that the voices of fathers who talk to their babies through the mother's abdomen are recognized sooner than those of fathers who don't.

### Comforting sounds

You can buy teddy bears that give out a reassuring "heartbeat" sound which is supposed to remind the baby of being in the womb. Without the breathing, blood pumping and stomach churning the sound is probably not very womb like, which may be why the vacuum cleaner, washing machine and car engine work just as well at soothing a fretful baby or sending a wakeful one to sleep.

### High-pitched sounds

Children prefer high-pitched sounds to those with a lower tone, and most adults – and even very small children – instinctively raise the pitch of their voice when they talk to a baby. It is almost as if babies train grown-ups to talk in this way by smiling and laughing more when they do. That response does not, however, explain why people also talk to their dogs in this way. It may be that humans have an built-in tendency to talk in this way to loved ones who cannot understand.

## RECOGNIZING HEARING PROBLEMS

Deafness often slips "through the net" of medical checkups because it is difficult to detect problems in a newborn. Profound deafness may be noted by parents before it is discovered by developmental exams at four or five months, but selective deafness (deafness for a range of sounds rather than all noises) is rarely discovered until formal tests can be carried out.

Ask that your baby's hearing be checked if:
• he does not startle to loud noises (this is a reflex action at birth, which is lost and replaced by more childlike expressions of surprise)
• he turns when he catches sight of you rather than when he hears your voice
• he consistently turns in the "wrong" direction when trying to locate a sound (but remember that his ability to track noises behind him will be poor until he is about six months old)
• you have any other reason to suspect a problem
There are ways of testing even tiny babies, but these are often not used until a problem is suspected.

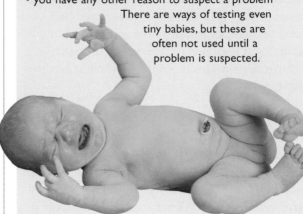

*Babies can locate frontal sounds at birth. They can also tell whether a noise is coming from right or left – but not exactly where. Locating sounds behind them is the last skill to come.*

## Locating sounds

Sound waves travel relatively slowly, much more so than light waves, which is why you can see the lightning before you hear the thunder. A sound coming from the right reaches your right ear slightly before it arrives at the left and vice versa. These minute time differences enable you to locate where a sound is coming from with great accuracy. It is easiest to locate a sound from directly in front because not only does the time that the sound reaches both ears coincide, but also you usually have the visual clue of seeing what is making the sound.

If a sound is sustained or repeated, small movements of his head often help a baby to pinpoint it more exactly. When you call to your baby from across the room, waiting for him to turn in your general direction then calling again provides exactly the sort of training he needs.

## Music right

In most people language skills are controlled by the left-hand side of the brain (in some left-handers and a tiny percentage of right-handers these skills are controlled on the right). Music is generally controlled by the opposite side, that is, the right in most right-handed people.

If you are talking to a baby he slightly prefers you to talk to his left ear; if you are playing music, he may like it to be closer to his right ear. This may or may not have something to do with why adults always instinctively cradle children in their left arm (even left-handed adults do) and why they often put them onto their left shoulder to sing to them. When you cradle the baby, his left ear is closest to your words, when he is hugged against your left shoulder his right ear is nearest your voice.

*Most young children find the novelty of hearing the voice of an invisible person on the telephone thrilling. They breathlessly blurt out news rather than having a conversation.*

# Helping your baby to hear

*Numerous games and activities help your baby to locate sounds in space with accuracy*

Newborn babies have a crude system for locating sound, although with practice this becomes sophisticated in quite a short time. Most of the skills a tiny baby learns are based on trial and error. He starts off as if he has a rough idea of what to do and then fine-tunes the new skill by trying it out, getting it wrong and then trying it in another way. Even when caregivers help they show rather than tell what to do. As he grows up, however, more and more of what he must learn depends on listening. Adults tell children how to do tasks; even if they show them, they are also explaining as they go. Good listeners learn faster, are less frustrated and make fewer mistakes, but most children need to be trained to listen.

## Hey baby!

Call to your baby from across the room, and wait for him to look. Reinforce where you are with a few words then move and call again. Talk as you approach him to pick him up, and always chat as you change him. The small movements you make as you throw away the dirty diaper, pick up the cloth to wipe his bottom then reach for a clean diaper and fasten it help him to fine-tune his location skills.

## Rhyme and reason

To recognize words children have to listen to little sounds, both the sounds of individual letters as in c–a–t and sounds like "ba" and "co" and "ing" that make up syllables. Rhymes draw a child's attention to these sounds, telling him which parts of strings of sounds are the same and highlighting the differences. Songs and poems, especially those intended for children, emphasize rhyme. Familiarity with rhyme also helps with the early stages of reading. Some studies suggest that early exposure to rhyme could minimize the problems of dyslexia. If dyslexia runs in your family it is worth giving as much practice as you can.

## TROUBLESHOOTING

**My son is 18 months old and does not say anything at all. Not even "Mommy" or "Daddy." Is this normal? When should I start to worry about this?**

Does he respond to your voice and understand a few simple words? Are there no other obvious developmental delays? If the answer to both these questions is yes, you probably have nothing to worry about. Some children find it much harder to produce words than understand their meaning. Eighteen months is a little late for a first word but is still within the "normal" range. If your son has had recent developmental and hearing exams and these showed no obvious problems, I expect he will be starting to say one or two words in the near future. If he has not had these exams you should arrange for them. Sometimes there is a simple explanation – such as excessive wax – which is easily treated. If he is still not saying anything by 24 months you should ask for another exam, whatever the earlier results.

## Taking turns

Caregivers seem to know instinctively how to talk to a baby. They ask a question, wait for an answer then tell him what they think he said. "Do you want me to pick you up?" pause "You do?" pause "I bet you're ready for some dinner now?" pause "Yes, I bet you are." In time he will fill those pauses with smiles, coos, signs and words.

## Comforting sounds

Unvarying sounds seem to comfort young babies. This may or may not have anything to do with remembering how it was in the womb. The motor of the vacuum cleaner or washing machine and the hum of the car engine work very well, as does a radio tuned slightly off station. Putting a crying baby in a carrier while you vacuum the carpet is not a cure-all, but it may calm a moderately unhappy baby.

## Listen

Stop and listen to what you can hear. The rumble of distant traffic, the hum of a bee, a plane overhead, water dripping from the faucet. If you both sit still you can hear the clock ticking, the birds singing or even a distant fire engine. First listen, then talk about it, then listen again.

As your child gets older he will like games like Simon says, which train him to listen for a sequence of words to initiate an action.

## Under the bridges

Putting on music works well when you are at home, but is not so good when you are out shopping with a tantrum-prone child. Allowing him a good shout is worth a try, especially if he has had to endure the frustration of being cooped up in the car or strapped into the stroller. As you pass under the railway bridge, or through the dark trees or over the top of the hill, let him shout or scream. (You pick the place, especially if you are driving, so that you are not distracted at an inappropriate moment.)

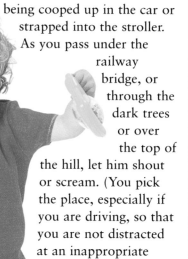

## Listen to music

This activity needs no explanation. Whether he just sits and listens, claps or jiggles in time or dances in his own free and easy way, practice listening skills by listening to the music.

## Just noisy

Why is running around shouting raucously fun? Why do children need to screech when the wind blows or they are rolling down a grassy bank? Perhaps the nearest adults get to this impulse is at the amusement park or when battered by large waves on the seashore. The point is that there are certain activities which would be altogether less fun if children (and adults) had to do them in silence. Japanese day-care centers sometimes have a special tune to play during times when the children can make as much noise as they like, in the belief that periods of "letting off steam" seem to help them stay calm at other times. If you feel there will be tears before bedtime, this is an idea worth trying. A shouting song has the virtue of squeezing out the silliness in one glorious binge.

### WHAT YOUR BABY LEARNS

• **Hey baby, find it and listen**
These improve your baby's ability to locate a sound precisely, and to differentiate one sound from another – can he hear the bird above the rumble of traffic, for example? He will also learn which sounds are closest and which farther away.

• **Rhyme and reason**
Rhymes improve a child's memory and anticipation skills and help later with prereading and reading.

• **Listen to music**
From a young age music may calm a fretful baby – move slowly and rhythmically with him in your arms; he will like it even more if you hum as you dance.

# Smelling, tasting and touching

*The secondary senses in adults are far more important to your baby's understanding of the world*

In adults sight and sound are the dominant senses, with touch playing a secondary role and smell and taste less important in the pecking order. For small babies touch, smell and taste play a much more central role. Touch remains an important sense well into the preschool years. Fiddling is endemic in children. If it is there, they will touch it or pick it up.

### Changing priorities

The early reliance on smell and touch happens because the eyes do not function well and, until the child understands language, sound is less informative. Later, children concentrate on touching because they have to put all the pieces together. They want to discover not just how things look but how something with a particular appearance feels and smells.

*Older children are often far more adventurous about new tastes than many adults and will try anything. Some even like guessing games, such as when you blindfold a child and let her try to guess what is on the spoon.*

*For a baby, having a teddy introduces a new texture into his world. When he is a little older it makes an excellent comfort toy to cuddle at night or in nerve-racking situations.*

### Learning about smell

Although smell is important to small children, they are not good at doing it to order. If asked to smell a flower, a child is more likely to blow through his nose than to suck air in. The easiest way around this is to teach him to blow out through his mouth, so that he automatically breathes in through his nose.

Children seem to have much the same preferences and dislikes in smell as adults. They wrinkle up their noses in distaste at smells that adults think are foul, and seem pleased with smells that delight us. The only exception perhaps is their fascination with the contents of their potties – which they do not seem to find the least bit offensive.

### Smell and memory

Because smell is an important sense in childhood, odors in later life may evoke powerful memories. My grandfather grew chrysanthemums and as a child I used to help him weed the flower beds. I adored him. For me the smell of chrysanthemums always elicits that feeling of utter security and high self-esteem I had when with my grandfather. Other smells have different meanings: pine cones mean Christmas, burning leaves autumn, and so on. Smells, like emotions, are difficult to put into words, which is perhaps why they stir up nostalgia so powerfully.

## The tasting mechanism

All omnivores have built-in mechanisms that prevent them from eating too much of a new food before they have tested whether or not it will harm them; humans are no exception. If you come across a new taste, you probably take the tiniest bite. If 24 hours later you are still feeling all right, you try a bigger piece, and if you remain well even more. If somewhere along the line you are sick, your first thought may well be "What have I eaten?" or, more especially, "What new or unusual thing have I eaten?" You then avoid that new food in the future. Most adults and many children have had a bout of sickness after eating a certain dish and found that they could not face that food again.

## Weaning children

Children have this mechanism, which is partly why they are sometimes extremely difficult to wean. The problem is not only that parents often give them lots of new tastes, but also that solid food sometimes upsets their delicate stomachs. The best way to introduce solid food is to work with the mechanism. Start with milk – which they know and trust – and add something bland, such as a small amount of potato. When they are happy with this, add the tiniest amount of carrot to the potato, and when they are happy with this add something new. Always start with the smallest amount of a new food and mask it with something they have eaten before. If they refuse to eat the concoction don't force them. They don't need a particularly varied diet while they are still taking plenty of milk.

## The sense of touch

It is probably possible to train a child not to touch anything that does not belong to him. But it would take a great deal of effort and have the negative effect of repressing the child's drive for discovery. It is always better to move dangerous and precious items out of your child's way.

Small children fiddle because this is the way they explore the world. Once they have the necessary hand skills they touch, stroke, poke, bang and prod anything and everything within reach. They do this not only to find out what different objects are like, but also as a means to build up a full picture.

## Discovery and knowledge

Children have to discover how things that feel a certain way look, and banged a certain way sound. There is no other way to discover that a handful of uncooked rice will flow through your hand like sand, but that cooked rice sticks to your fingers, than to try it out. The only way to discover all the properties of different materials is to gather information actively from each sense and combine it all. How do objects look and feel if they are going to be able to bear his weight? What sort of items are comfortable to lie on? What manner of things float or sink? The list of discovery is endless.

*Reliance on touch is one reason why small children are so much better than adults at "feely" games: place a handful of familiar objects in a bag and let him try to decide what they all are.*

# Making sense

*Games and activities to foster your baby's skills at touching, tasting and smelling*

Because sight and hearing are so important to adults, it is all too easy to ignore touch, taste and smell in babies. But babies and children like games that stretch their abilities in these areas, and actively enjoy tactile experiences.

## Making perfume

It does not really matter to two- and three-year-olds what they collect: they simply like to pick something up, put it in a bag and take it home. In the summer months, a child can put a collection of flower petals into a jar of water to make "perfume." A few drops of essential oil or rosewater will enhance the perfume, but most children are quite happy with the game whether or not the smell is worth the effort.

## SIMPLE ICE CREAM

Almost all children love ice cream, and most can manage many of the stages involved in making it for themselves. Add 4 ounces (125 g) sugar to ½ pint (300 ml) heavy cream. Whipping the cream beforehand gives the finished ice cream a lighter texture, but is not vital. Heating the cream a little helps the sugar dissolve. Add a few chopped strawberries, a mashed banana or some small pieces of chocolate. A three-year-old could pour the cream into the mixer bowl, measure out the sugar and turn on the beater. A younger child could be given the whipped cream and the fruit or chocolate to mix together. Pour it into a container and put it in the freezer. You will need to take the mixture out of the freezer a couple of times and stir it to break up the ice crystals that form as it freezes.

    If you don't want to bother with the crystal-breaking, start with an Italian meringue base. You will need to make this in advance because it involves melting sugar. However since it is used cold it can be given to the child as one ingredient. Melt 8 ounces (225 g) sugar in ¼ pint (150 ml) water. Bring this to the boil, then boil for five minutes. Add the syrup to two stiffly beaten egg whites, whisking all the time until it is glossy and well mixed, then add a couple of tablespoons of lemon juice and leave to cool. Whip ½ pint (300 ml) heavy cream until stiff. Now give your child a large bowl and let him stir together the cream and meringue, adding whatever flavorings you choose. Try rosewater and chopped organically grown rose petals or nasturtium flowers, chocolate chips, broken cookies or any combination of fruit. Then just pop it in the freezer.

## Tactile books

Collect five or six fabrics with a different "feel" and stitch them together or fix them into a small loose-leaf folder to provide your child with a tactile book. You could have a page of fake fur, one of satin, a carpet sample, some interfacing, a strip of Velcro and a piece of corrugated cardboard. Sewing some buttons on to some cloth gives an interesting feel, as does a small piece of burlap carpet or some tiny lengths of string stuck to a piece of cardboard.

## Touchy feely

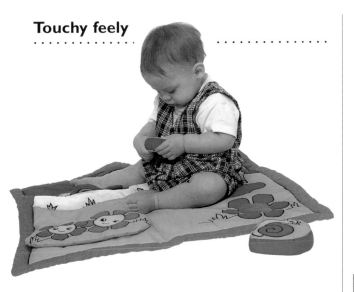

At about seven to eight months when children first start to use their hands to explore (having used their mouths up to now) they love to examine different textures. They like things that can be stroked such as silk and fur, prodded or squeezed like a sponge. There are lots of toys that harness all these elements, such as play mats, soft play activity centers or dolls or animals with special "feely" areas.

## Comfort objects

At about seven months children begin to realize that you exist when you are not in the room with them, which means they can miss you. Before this stage it was pretty much out of sight out of mind. The ability to miss his loved ones coincides with the development of the ability to stroke surfaces, and many children find comfort in the satin ribbons around blankets or the soft fur of a teddy bear. Studies suggest that attachment to a comfort object is a positive advantage for children, especially if they learn to use it to "psych" themselves up and give themselves confidence. A child who is used to using a dummy as a comfort object may not take to a blanket or a teddy, but it is worth trying. It is easier to take a teddy to a sleepover when you are older! Don't be concerned by attachment to comfort objects: research suggests that in new situations even 13-year-olds fare better with them than without.

### WHAT YOUR CHILD LEARNS

• **Making perfume**
Children like making things, and enjoy having an end-product. Through this he will learn about different flowers as he gathers them and how they float or sink in the water.

• **Tactile objects, touchy feely**
These enhance his tactile skills, enabling him to discern the sometimes minute differences between materials.

• **Comfort objects**
These give a child something familiar at a time when everything else may be new or different. A comfort object may give a child confidence.

# CHAPTER 4

# Developing hand-eye coordination

Even if she could see them clearly – which she cannot – a newborn baby would not realize that her hands belonged to her. Because the world inside the womb is constant, before birth she had little reason to discriminate between her body and the rest of the world. As she begins to uncurl in the first few weeks of life, her arms and hands sometimes move into view. She probably does not notice them when they are stationary, but she can see them when they are moving. This helps her to recognize them as belonging to her. When her arms move, signals from the joints are sent back to the brain. Gradually she realizes that the feeling of her arm waving and the sight of the arm are part of the same phenomenon. She begins to realize that she can make her arm move. Once she has learned "I can" she just has to wait for improvements in muscle control for her skills to develop.

**Milestones in hand-eye skills: the first nine months**

| | WHAT SHE CAN DO |
|---|---|
| **At birth** | ● The hands are predominantly closed.<br>● If something is placed in the palm of her hand, her fingers roll over it to clasp. |
| **12** *weeks* | ● Her hands are still usually closed, but are now sometimes held open.<br>● She does not deliberately reach, but may swipe at objects and if they move will swipe again. |
| **16** *weeks* | ● Her hands are now usually open and she clasps her hand around objects she touches.<br>● She watches her hands and is distracted by them if they come into view.<br>● She will not look for anything she drops. |
| **20** *weeks* | ● She reaches out with open hands to touch, glancing away just before she grasps so that she is not confused by her hands.<br>● She deliberately brings her hands together.<br>● She still cannot grasp an object until it touches the palm of her hand and does not use her thumb to push things into her hand. |
| **30** *weeks* | ● She uses her eyes to help her reach out to touch, adjusting the position of her hand under visual control.<br>● She grasps by cupping her entire hand around an object. She takes the things in her hand to her mouth to explore them.<br>● She is beginning to use her thumb to push things into her hand (by seven months). |
| **36** *weeks* | ● She can catch a suspended object or a ball rolled directly to her.<br>● She uses her hands together to reach for large objects but can also use them separately – reaching with one hand, storing the object in the other.<br>● She passes toys from one hand to the other.<br>● She begins to use her fingers separately and may poke, prod or use her flat hand to stroke.<br>● The palm grip develops and her thumb moves around in opposition to her fingers.<br>● She reaches directly and accurately for objects, even small ones.<br>● She may look for things she drops.<br>● She can poke and prod, pick up peas or other small objects between thumb and forefinger.<br>● She anticipates how she will grasp, moving her hand into a horizontal or vertical position before it reaches the object. She can now reach an object from above, not only from the side. |

## HOW YOU CAN TELL

## HOW YOU CAN HELP

- Shake a rattle: even a newborn reaches toward a rattle directly in front of her.

- Stroke her palms so that she clasps your hand.
- Loosely tie an object in just the right place for her to hit it.

- Suspend a soft toy that she can hit while she kicks. The movement will excite her and she will kick all the more, hitting it again as she does so.

- Put well-balanced objects into her hand.
- Stretch her abilities by encouraging her to reach a little farther every week.
- Reward her by putting the object into her hand if she finds it too difficult. Balance letting her try with avoiding frustration.

- Coordinating looking and reaching is difficult, but she can manage if she gets a lot of help from you.

- Provide her with a variety of objects to reach for. Secure them so they do not swing out of reach.

- She will grasp objects if you offer them to her. At first you need to place them almost into her hand but gradually she will start to reach toward them.
- If offered a toy, she will look back and forth between the toy and her hand, laboriously adjusting the position of her hand.

- Roll a ball to her to encourage her to use both hands.
- Pass her one small toy then another to encourage her to use her spare hand to store the first object.

- Grasping anything that moves is still difficult but she is beginning to reach out more directly.
- Her skills improve rapidly. She will soon be able to reach and grab.

- She starts to use her thumb, cupping her hands and moving her thumb around to secure the object in her hand.
- Her hands are more skilled and her movements are more deliberate and varied.
- She begins to treat objects in different ways. It is not enough to chew or bang it, she also wants to poke, prod and stroke it.

- Let her feed herself with tiny pieces of bread, peas, raisins or banana.

**Milestones in hand-eye skills: 12 months to school age**

| | **WHAT SHE CAN DO** | |
|---|---|---|
| **12** *months* | • She learns to let go.<br>• She uses objects in appropriate ways to achieve her own ends, rather than as extensions of the hand to bang or suck. | |
| **15** *months* | • She is beginning to twist her wrist so that her hand turns independently of her arm.<br>• She begins to put sequences of movements together, such as pointing, holding and turning, opening and closing. | |
| **18** *months* | • She combines wrist-twisting movements with letting go. | |
| **24** *months* | • She begins to control objects which are distant from her hand, such as the toy at the end of the string.<br>• She can manage simple puzzles and will move chairs to climb up and reach what she needs.<br>• She can build a tower of many blocks. | |
| **2-3** *years* | • She begins to use a crayon.<br>• She can build quite elaborately.<br>• She begins to dress herself.<br>• She can feed herself. | |
| **3-6** *years* | • She draws recognizable pictures, prints her name, does elaborate puzzles, dresses herself (although she may still have problems with shoelaces and small buttons).<br>• She can assemble models with small pieces. | |

## HOW YOU CAN TELL

- She drops things from the high chair.
- She likes to hold her spoon.

- At first she can put only round shapes in her board, but as her wrist skills improve she can cope with more complex shapes.
- She points to objects and pets.

- She can put any shape in her sorter and throw a ball.
- She can put one block on top of another.

- She plays by herself, fitting the pieces into her puzzle board.
- She feeds herself (still somewhat messily) with a spoon.

- Not all children like to build, but you should expect to see comparable skills such as being able to tuck teddies into bed or put on simple garments.

- Children tend to be as independent as you let them be. Some boys are still waiting for you to dress them although most girls are putting on all their clothes.

## HOW YOU CAN HELP

- If you are tired of picking up all the things she drops, attach one of her toys to the side of the highchair on a short length of elastic. When she drops it over it will bounce. She will soon learn to pull it up.

- Select toys carefully. Things which are too difficult for her to use will frustrate her. By the time she could use them she may have already lost interest.

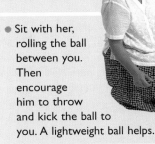

- Sit with her, rolling the ball between you. Then encourage him to throw and kick the ball to you. A lightweight ball helps.

- Do not rush in to help too quickly: she wants and needs to be able to do things which she cannot yet manage. Try to make the tasks simpler rather than saying no.

- Children make better progress in small steps. If you start with a two-piece puzzle, then go on to four to eight and 16 pieces, she will manage a surprising number of pieces at a young age; if you take too big a step, she may stop trying.

- Encourage your child to dress and feed herself.
- Let her draw and paint, and display her pieces of art.

# The hand as a tool

*How the hand is transformed from a clenched fist to a usable tool over the first few months*

*By 18 months old, a child can decide which item she wants from a group of similar objects, pick it up and grasp it in one hand.*

A newborn baby has a strong reflex grasp, holding on so tightly that, in theory, you could hang her on a clothesline by her fingers and toes. It is this grasp that baby apes and monkeys use to cling onto their mother's fur. Because the grasp is automatic, it is not particularly useful for exploring.

As the days and weeks pass, a baby spends less time with her hands tightly clasped. Her grasp is not as vise-like and the stimulation needed to elicit it has to be stronger; as a result she can touch an object without her hands automatically curling around it. Like her hands, her body opens up. She is less likely to be curled in the fetal position and her arms open out. She starts to move and kick, which makes her hands come into view more frequently.

### Watching

In the early weeks a baby finds it much easier to see something if it is moving. She may not see her stationary arms, but as she kicks her waving arms attract her attention. Like all moving objects she sees, she watches them. When she waves her arms, the shoulder and elbow joints send feedback signals that tell the brain that her arms are moving. As she looks at her waving arms her brain receives two separate signals, one from the eye saying she sees movement and one from her joints saying she is moving. Gradually she comes to realize that whenever a certain "eye" report comes into the brain there is always a particular feedback report and she associates them. In this way she discovers the moving limbs belong to her.

She learns next how to bring her arms in front to watch them move even if she is not kicking. She begins to learn that the eye signals she receives when she brings her hands together are matched by a brain signal. The eye signal when she moves her right hand alone is matched by another. Soon she knows more than "That's me"; she understands "I made that specific movement happen."

### Hitting

Knowing "I did it" is different from making it happen. To begin with, babies simply extend their range of "I can do it" to hitting objects. While kicking in her crib she hits the toy you have strategically tied to the crib bars or the row of teddies you have strung across her carriage or

*If you show a baby a string of teddies, first she will swipe at them, then in trying to clutch* *she may make them spin. Finally, she will succeed in grabbing one of the teddies.*

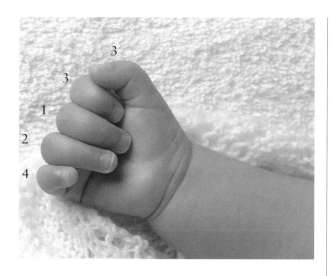

*For the first seven to eight months of life, a baby's fingers and toes close in a predetermined order when the palm of the hand or foot is touched.*

bouncy chair. The object moves. Movement excites her so she kicks harder and hits again. Then things change. As she gains the ability to control her body she begins to make the movements that will hit the teddy, without kicking as well. These are not precise at first because she has control only of her shoulder rather than her arm or hand. She has to swing the whole limb at the teddy (see p. 70).

## Reaching

When she begins to control her lower arm, the ability to hit matures into the ability to reach. As her hand comes under control, rather than reaching she is able to grab. At first her hand does not close until she feels the touch of the object on the palm of her hand, and she can only grab from a sideways swiping movement, which can be frustrating if the object swings out of reach before she takes hold of it. At this stage help her by holding things for her to reach and helping her hands close around them. She will look back and forth

between the toy and her hand, laboriously adjusting the position of her hand until she can grab the toy.

## Now I see it

Babies remain obsessed with their hands and at first are completely distracted by them. They look at an interesting toy, reach out for it, see their hand and forget all about the toy because at this stage memory is fleeting. Slowly she learns to ignore her hand. At first she does this by looking away when her hand comes into view, later by looking between the hand and the object (by this time her memory has improved enough for her to span the gap between her original intention and the distraction of seeing her hand).

## Coming together

By 20 weeks babies can see 800 times better than they could at birth and if they could name the letters would be able to read about halfway down an optician's chart. By now your baby can keep her eyes on an object while she reaches for it, no longer distracted by her hands. Body control improves and she begins to cup her hand around the object using her thumb to secure it. By 28 weeks she can pick up a pea or point at it, which uses the same movements.

*From 28 weeks on, she will use her thumb and finger to pick up raisins if she is given the opportunity.*

# Really useful hands

*Improved motor skills make the hands even more versatile tools after the first few months*

As the thumb comes around to oppose the fingers, a baby is able to control it independently which makes her hands altogether more skilled. She no longer grabs with an open hand which she then closes around the object, but reaches with her hand ready to grab, using her thumb to push the object into her cupped hand. If the object is not well-balanced in her hand, she can adjust its position with her thumb. As she begins to control each finger independently she is able to hold the object between her palm and thumb and feel it with her fingers. By now she will be able to reach out with confidence for anything she wants, even grabbing a swinging toy. Success breeds success. There is no longer anything laborious about the movement: it is instant and confident.

### Pinching, poking and prodding

The thumb can oppose one or all the fingers. When she wants to pick up something tiny, such as a pea, a baby uses her forefinger and thumb in a pinching movement. This is deliberate and precise, the finger and thumb come together slowly and accurately to take the pea without squashing it. Once she starts to use her fingers independently she pokes her forefinger into small places and prods her fingers into soft surfaces. This is the stage when activity centers, activity mats and some baby gyms come into their own, and she will also probably love an old-fashioned telephone dial.

## HANDEDNESS

In the early months a baby's "handedness" is not always clear. By the time they are about nine months old, most babies use one hand in preference to the other for reaching, stroking and holding a spoon. The consistency with which this hand is favored increases during the preschool years.

Left-handedness clearly runs in families, although the inheritance is not straightforward: if one twin is left-handed there is only a 50 percent chance that her identical twin will also be left-handed, for example. On average less than half the children of two left-handers are also left-handed.

### Patting and stroking

Once her fingers are under control and her arms are able to move gently and precisely into position, she begins to stroke and pat with an open hand. It is a general principle of the nervous system, which controls all body movements, that the "go" mechanisms mature before the "stop." A go mechanism by itself is like a light switch, either on or off. When you see her stroking the carpet you know that the stop mechanisms are beginning to modulate her hand movements. The stop mechanisms give your baby a range of controls so that she can move her hands at varying speeds: stroking fast then slow, stopping and restarting.

### Using the hands together

By about 28 weeks, a baby begins to use both hands together, holding a ball, for example, or wrapping her arms around her teddy. By 32 weeks she will catch a ball you roll to her, but only if she has her arms open before you start to roll. She will also start to hold an object in one hand while she reaches with the other. She begins to modulate her movements after they

*Activity centers provide scope for prodding, pushing and dialing once a small child can use her fingers independently.*

have started, and this makes the visual control of movements more accurate. She can use her hands in a variety of ways. One hand becomes the active one while the other is used for storing, assisting, holding and steadying.

### Dropping and letting go

At first, a baby tends to let go of an object because she sees something more interesting and opens her hand to reach for it. The "dropping" is not deliberate: she simply needs the space in her hand. By about eight months, however, she learns to let go, dropping objects deliberately by opening her fingers and letting her hand dangle so they roll out. Later she will turn her hand over before she opens her fingers.

### Looking more skilled

The combination of finger control and the ability to modify movements under visual control make a baby seem more skilled. Up to the age of six or seven months, babies either bang toys or put them into their mouths. In both cases the toy is little

*In the first year children come a long way, but they are generally into their second year before they can fit shapes on a board.*

more than an extension of the hand. From about eight or nine months all this changes and they begin to use each toy in a unique way: teddies are cuddled, hammers hit, dials are turned, buttons pressed and doors opened. Objects become tools. The food in the spoon is aimed at the mouth, and the building block in the hand rather than the hand itself is put into place.

*Your child needs to have developed her wrists and the ability to twist and turn the hands before she can place pieces in a puzzle. Encouragement from you helps, too.*

*Building blocks can be used in increasingly sophisticated games as coordination improves.*

# Wrists and twists

*The development of the wrist bones gives your baby finer control over the movement of her hands*

The wrist and palm of an adult's hand have 28 bones, those of a newborn only three. While control of the rest of the body depends on the maturation of the brain mechanisms that govern the muscles and joints, manipulating the wrist depends on the growth of the relevant bones. This is why wrist control happens "out of order." The development of the ankle is late for the same reason. The ankle bones develop late, which explains why skills that need a flexible ankle (such as jumping) do not mature until the child is about three or four years old. As the wrist matures a child begins to combine the twisting movements of the wrist with her hand and finger skills to enable her to place objects more accurately.

*As his dropping skill is perfected, he starts to stack objects and place one toy inside another.*

### Pointing

Children start to point at about 10 months. At first they use the whole arm to direct the pointing finger, but by about 14 months they are able to point using only the hand. As her understanding of language increases, your child is able to point out more and more objects to you.

### Ready and waiting

If you watch your child's hand as she reaches, you will see that it is now in position before she touches what she wants. If she reaches to pick up a block from the floor, her hand is horizontal; if she is reaching for the handle of her toy vacuum cleaner, it is vertical. In both cases the fingers are closing onto the object before she touches it. If she is catching the beach ball, both her hands are already open, with the fingers slightly curled and the thumbs spread.

### Lifting

Once she can twist and bend her wrist your child can begin to cup her hand over the top of objects as she picks them up. A small baby always reaches from the side. A toddler increasingly reaches from above – as adults do – spreading her hand with her thumb opposing her cupped fingers and then dropping it from the wrist.

### Turning, dropping and placing

Once she can twist her hand, your child learns that turning it over is by far the easiest way to drop things. A child practices this movement frequently, dropping spoons from the high chair and toys from the bath until she can build with blocks. Accurate stacking takes precise skills and her rough and ready towers will rarely be more than three blocks high. Practice makes perfect and by the time she is two years old she can place carefully enough to make a tower that is well worth toppling over.

*When she sits on your lap looking at a book her hand is now exactly in the right position to turn the page before it touches the paper, to lift the flaps or stroke the cat.*

## Throwing

Once children have mastered the turn hand and let go routine they also start to throw. Throwing, after all, is simply dropping with a little more force. Toddlers do not throw with any great accuracy or foresight, so a supply of foam balls – or better still, crunched-up paper – will protect you and your home from flying missiles. By now your child is capable of understanding "Only balls are for throwing," but you need to be firm and consistent about it.

## Using a spoon

Being able to twist her wrist also makes it easier for your child to find her mouth with a spoon. In the days when she aimed her hand at her mouth (as all babies do at first), feeding herself was a messy and haphazard business. Even though her hand skills improved between eight months and a year old, her accuracy in finding her mouth left a lot to be desired.

As her ability to twist and turn her hand is refined, she will find her mouth with increasing precision. This does not mean that she can abandon a bib or leave the table without needing her face and hands wiped, but she is getting there.

## Becoming a tool user

In their second year, children begin to be able to control an object in their hand and use it as a tool. They can push a broom and make a rounded scribble with a crayon.

By the time they reach school they can write their name, turn the pages of a book, use a wrench, knock a teddy off a high shelf with a stick, pour water from a jug into a cup, fish for metal objects with a magnet on a string, hammer in a nail, put on a shoe and paint the fence with a can of water and a large brush.

Tool-using skills develop gradually and depend on practice. It was no accident that craftsmen and -women in the past learned at their parent's knee. If children enjoy an activity it is surprising how much they can achieve: folding paper to make little birds, embroidering a simple picture, undoing screws to take apart an old engine.

*Over a year old, children can find their mouth with a spoon with some degree of accuracy, although they still need help at mealtimes – and their faces wiped afterward.*

# Hand-training activities
*Making the most of your baby's developing hand skills*

Before small babies realize that their hands belong to them, they find watching them a curious affair. When selecting activities to help your baby find her hands, keep in mind that she is better at locating sounds than objects.

## Bells and rattles

Fastening a little bell to a mitten or around your baby's wrist will help her to find her hands. It will also excite her (as all high-pitched sounds do), and this in turn will make her wave her arms. Like wrist rattles, bells on the wrists have the advantage that they cannot be dropped.

If you choose a rattle, the easiest ones for tiny babies are dumbbell shaped. The ball at each end stops the rattle slipping from her hand, she can clasp the narrow neck and the rattle is balanced and therefore easy to hold. As her muscles strengthen she will be able to manage a variety of different shapes. Added visual interest – such as liquid containing glitter or clear, deep color – will interest her too. When selecting a rattle for a young baby, try to visualize what she will see when she is looking up at the rattle in her hand.

## Reach out

Once she is able to reach and begins to grab, she will be frustrated if objects slip out of her hand. Some of the dangling dolls and pom-poms need to be replaced with things stable enough to grab.

These can be fixed across the crib or buggy, but keep her safety uppermost in your mind: nothing should be sharp or easily breakable. A row of paper cups with smiling faces drawn inside will delight, for example, but a row of expanded Styrofoam cups could be dangerous if the cups started to fragment.

You could also thread traditional wooden cottonreels on strong elastic and secure these at one end to the pushchair. If you paint them first you will make them more interesting. Another idea is to attach a toy phone using a strong short curly cable.

## Swipe it

Put a dark shape (such as a brown teddy or a dark blue pompon) on a short piece of elastic. Place it in a position where it will be knocked as she kicks in her cot. Make sure that the fixing string is too short to pass around her neck. The toy should be firmly fixed but free enough to move easily when she hits it.

## Give me

Training a child to reach needs both practice and patience. Offer her a rattle, shaking it until she can see it. As her hand comes out to swipe, "arrange" for the rattle to hit the palm of her hand. This stimulation will make her fingers close over the rattle. Shake the rattle in her hand so she knows it is there. She will not be able to reach

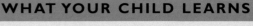

directly at first and you will need to move the rattle toward her hand, but if you always do this she will not learn to stretch out for herself. Let her try before you make her succeed. Remember that in the early stages she forgets about the rattle if she catches sight of her hand. You will need to remind her by giving the rattle a shake.

## Catch

When he can sit confidently and with his legs spread, roll a medium-sized ball to him so that his arms come together to catch it. He will soon be able to push it back to you. Older siblings can play too. When the baby can stand without toppling over, throw a larger lightweight

ball (such as a beach ball) into his outstretched arms. Start by virtually placing the ball in his arms then extend the distance you throw as he learns how to play the game.

---

### WHAT YOUR CHILD LEARNS

All these activities help your baby to fine-tune her hand skills.
• Initially she needs to learn where her hands stop and the rattle begins.
• Reaching is a complex skill and it takes some time before your child gets it right; she needs all the help you can give her.
• As her skill improves you will need to judge exactly how to stretch and practise her growing abilities without frustrating her.

---

## TOYS TO STRETCH HER ABILITIES

### • At five months
Your baby grabs and then takes things to her mouth to explore them, so toys are the safest option: new parents sometimes find it difficult to foresee all the problems that playing with household objects — keys, for example, which babies love — can produce. Toys are produced to exacting safety standards, and potential problems have to be considered by the manufacturers during the toys' design. Furthermore, if a child does find a dangerous way to use any toy it will be withdrawn from the market.

### • Five to seven months
At this stage your child needs toys with plenty of mouth interest — textures to feel, soft bits to "gum" and knobbly shapes to suck.

### • Six to eight months
Your baby will enjoy things she can bang; at seven to eight months add an activity center to poke and prod and something with textures to stroke.

### • Nine months
She will enjoy something with a button to press or a dial, something with a hiding hole, a peg board and a toy telephone: the old-fashioned ones with a dial are still the best.

# Activities for busy hands

*Children spend all day using their hands, but you can improve hand skills by choosing fun pastimes*

Wrist control gives your child countless opportunities to enjoy new games and activities. None of the activities listed here involve much expense, and most can be easily improvised.

## Building with blocks

Select blocks that are easy to stack. Large square fabric-covered foam bricks are probably easiest for babies under a year old. Traditional square wooden blocks are also good and long-lasting – they can be passed down through the family for years. Cheap plastic blocks are difficult for children to manipulate, especially if they have been pushed (or chewed) out of shape. If you don't have blocks, use cardboard cartons – the boxes from individual portions of breakfast cereals work well.

Small children love dens and at nursery school, large-size building blocks are the most popular choice for this activity. Most parents, however, have neither the space nor the bank balance to provide them at home. If you have the storage space, a collection of boxes from the supermarket can be used to build a big structure. Those used by movers are even better since they are all the same size and pack flat.

## Making roads

If there is one activity that convinces parents that boys and girls might be born different it is playing "bumper" cars. It is not that girls never "bump" or that boys always do, but there is a

definite male tendency in this activity. Toddlers are quite happy to push the cars up and down; older children enjoy laying out a system of roads. You can buy playmats with road systems laid out, but these are also easy to make from long pieces of cardboard that can be pushed together. Join the sections with masking tape to keep the road in place. Children also enjoy using roads scraped into sand with a rake. Simple wooden or plastic rails and a train, or a set of loops for cars to whizz around and a garage, will add to the fun.

## Puzzles

Children can start doing easy puzzles as soon as they are able to push simple shapes into a board. Tray or inset puzzles are easiest to begin with. Look for those that "remind" the child which piece to choose with a drawing of the same or a similar picture in the slot they need to use. Once they can manage two or three pieces they can move on to the simplest jigsaw puzzles. In selecting puzzles for small children it is more important to look for well-cut pieces than to count the number of pieces in the puzzle. Each jigsaw piece should have enough information on it to tell the child where – and in what direction – it is to be fixed into the picture.

## Bowling

You can buy bowling pins to use in the house or yard, but these are easy to make from plastic soda bottles: you will need at least six. Place the bottles in a doorway in a triangle shape. Stand back and roll a soft ball at them. You may need to

### WHAT YOUR CHILD LEARNS

• **Making roads**
This is noisy and fun, but also improves your child's spatial awareness, his wrist control and his imagination.

• **Bowling**
Bowling is a good way to use up some of your child's natural exuberance, as well as improving his aim and ability to throw or roll a ball. You can improve his visual recognition skills, too, by adding distinctive features if you make your own bowling pins from plastic bottles – stick colored gummed paper over the label and add shapes, letters or numbers.

• **Pom-poms**
Pom-poms satisfy your child's desire to make something "useful": they can be added to decorate hats or the end of scarves. Manipulating a needle demands fine hand-eye coordination and is excellent practice for later attempts at sewing or knitting.

add some sand to the bottles for stability if you are playing on thick carpet; for outdoor use, add some gravel and use a heavier ball.

## Making a pom-pom

You will need some board, wool and a bodkin. Cut out two circles of board (draw around an inverted glass or mug and egg cup or large coin). You should have two circles on each board, one inside the other. Cut around the lines so you have two pieces of board shaped like a lifebelt. Make a small ball of wool.

The child winds the wool around the board, taking it through the center and out around the edge. At first he can do it by hand but as the center fills he will need to use the bodkin. When he can fit no more wool into the center hole, cut around the rim. This is easier with sharp scissors, so do it yourself or supervise. Start by pushing the pointed blade between the two discs. Keep the blade in the gap to cut all the wool. Take a strong piece of wool and tie it tightly between the two circles so the strands hold together. Remove the cardboard and fluff up the pom-pom.

# Fun and games with paper and cardboard

*Paper and cardboard are versatile materials, ideal for countless indoor activities*

Many parents tend to think that supplying their child with unlimited paper only leads to lots of drawing or demands to be allowed to paint. But paper is also a creative tool, ideal for busy young hands to work in all sorts of ways.

## Turning pages

Children like to imitate their loved ones. A child who watches you reading will want to "read" for herself. Cloth and cardboard books are easy for small children, but they are much more limiting than those with paper pages, as well as being relatively more expensive. Children who are familiar with books do not tear them. Once your child can pick up a pea or raisin she can manage to turn the pages of a book. However, flaps and pop-up books are usually too delicate for a toddler to use by herself: save these for times when you look at books together.

### WHAT YOUR CHILD LEARNS

Reading is one of life's key skills, the foundation on which almost all formal education is based. Instilling a love of, and respect for, books in your child is one of the greatest gifts you can give her. In addition, books
• stimulate her imagination.
• teach her to listen and improve her listening skills.
• help develop her memory. She will remember key words, sequences and interesting pictures long before she can read.
• promote positive associations between books and interesting information.

## Making models

Simple models can be made from old cereal boxes, toilet roll centers, corrugated cardboard and any other scraps you have on hand. It is a good idea to collect these in a recycling bin ready for a rainy day. A bottle of glue, paper clips and binder clips (the sort that split after they have passed through the paper), a small staple gun, construction paper

and double-sided sticky pads are also useful. Children are not always realistic about the sort of model that will stay in one piece. If your child is not highly skilled, let her copy something you have made or give her clear instructions at each step.

### WHAT YOUR CHILD LEARNS

Model making improves spatial awareness, and teaches your child about the nature of different materials. Until she has tried to glue a cylinder to corrugated cardboard, for example, she cannot realize how tricky this is. Likewise, unless she uses binder clips, she cannot know that these allow some degree of movement, whereas dry glue does not.

## Folding paper

Start with a piece of good quality paper, about 3–4 inches (8–10 cm) square (alternatively use a page from a small writing pad). Help your child to fold the paper in two, lining up the edges. Then, holding the edge in place, show her how to smooth the fold. At first this is all she needs to do. If she finds it too difficult, start by working with a narrow strip of paper. This makes it easier to hold the edges in place as she smooths the fold. (The folded paper can be used as tents or animal houses for her farm.) Once she has mastered this simple folding technique show her how to fold paper along a line. It helps if you draw the line on both sides of the paper. Folding across the diagonal is more difficult, but once she can manage these simple folds she is well on the way to making boats, planes and animals.

## Ripping and snipping

Children find "cutting out" with scissors tricky because it involves two separate skills. The first is learning how to use scissors, the second how to cut around a shape. Teach each skill separately. Make some long narrow strips of paper. Give your child some blunt-ended scissors and a bowl. The game is to snip little sections of paper into the bowl (she can use these in collages). Once she has mastered this, make the strips wider so they need two snips rather than one.

Ripping is more difficult than it looks: trying to tear around a picture can be frustrating, as she will invariably tear the image. Show her how to tear out shapes from newspaper first.

## Paper flowers

To make carnations, fold a paper handkerchief in half lengthwise and cut along the fold. Now fold each half back and forth making an accordian fold. There should be five or six folds. Bend this over in the middle and staple across above the bend. Fluff out the tissue to make a flower. Small children will like doing the fluffing; older ones may be able to do the folding too. Tape the flowers to small garden stakes and put into a vase.

If this is too difficult for your child and she is not content with fluffing, cut or rip petal shapes from tissue or crepe paper and tape these onto sticks.

### WHAT YOUR CHILD LEARNS

• **Folding paper**
This makes fingers more dexterous and lays foundations for shape recognition, division and geometry.

• **Ripping and snipping**
These activities teach your child how to use scissors, a key skill for most craft activities.

• **Paper flowers**
Making flowers gives your child an "end product," and teaches her patience: it takes time to make one well.

# Construction and other similar activities

*Twisting, turning and hammering all improve your child's manipulative skills*

Construction toys are intended, primarily, to improve and stimulate your child's skill at spatial thinking. Many of these toys also require fairly precise hand skills and offer plenty of practice for your child in using her hands.

## Screws and bolts

There are lots of toy versions of a simple tool kit, some designed so that a child can easily put a plastic screw in the correct place or insert plastic bolts. Screwdrivers are difficult to maneuver unless they fit accurately into the screw head. The same is true for wrenches and nuts. Cheap toy tools are frustrating. It is better to buy a short, stubby "real" screwdriver and some big screws that your child can place into pre-drilled holes. Kits to make model cars and trains are well made but usually too complex for a young child, unless you are prepared to help.

## Banging in nails

Plastic hammers do not work with real nails but they are ideal with pegs. Peg boards are classic toys: the child bangs a set of pegs flush, then turns the toy over and starts again. When he progresses to using nails, there is no real advantage in using toy tools. Instead, buy a small hammer, a piece of soft wood and some chunky nails. If your child lacks the skill or strength for these, he could hammer nails into plastic blocks.

## Simple twisting toys

The simplest sort of twisting toy that you can buy or make is a big wooden or plastic nut on a large bolt. There are plenty of variations on this theme on the market. Many – for instance, kits that can be built into cars – are too complex for the youngest children. It is better to take out a couple of parts of such kits and let your child play with them until he is older.

### WHAT YOUR CHILD LEARNS

All construction activities reinforce your child's spatial awareness and teach him about the nature of materials – what can be hammered together, what needs to be screwed. Fitting a nut on to a bolt requires precise finger movements. Hammering pegs onto a board is a great way to release any frustration.

## Simple sewing

Most preschool children cannot manage a needle and thread, but if your child is interested start him off with a simple sewing kit. Look for one that provides a series of holes to weave the needle and thread through; the simplest are made from stiff cardboard rather than cloth. Once he can manage these, progress to perforated cloth, a bodkin and wool. Sewing is rather like doing jigsaw puzzles in that a child who is interested can rapidly become highly skilled at it – some six-year-olds can follow a simple embroidery pattern using long stitches and coarse burlap.

## Play-shopping

A collection of packages and boxes makes an excellent basis for a game of play-shopping. All he needs is money (you could make your own bills from paper and collect together small coins and/or buttons). A cash register and some paper bags to put the shopping in add to the realism.

## Dressing up

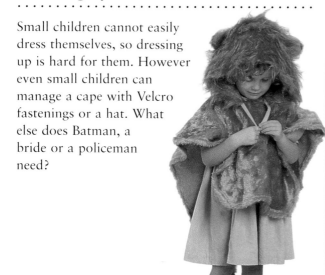

Small children cannot easily dress themselves, so dressing up is hard for them. However even small children can manage a cape with Velcro fastenings or a hat. What else does Batman, a bride or a policeman need?

### WHAT YOUR CHILD LEARNS

**• Sewing**
This gives your child the opportunity to make something and is a good way of coaxing an otherwise restless child to sit still for a while. The ability to decode a pattern helps prereading skills.

**• Play-shopping**
When he play-shops your child can mimic adult behavior, which he will love. This game also teaches pre-math skills.

**• Dressing up**
This improves imaginative play and coordination. Dressing up for fun also helps with the skills he needs to dress himself, which will be important when he starts school.

## A button whizz and cardboard whirr

You will need a length of strong wool or thin string and either a large button with four holes or a small circle of cardboard. The easiest way to shape the cardboard is to draw around a glass or mug then cut around the line. Your child can color in the cardboard if he wants. Pierce two holes either side of the center of the card. Now thread the string or wool through the holes in the cardboard, or through two diagonally opposite holes in the button. Leave a loop on one side and tie a knot on the other to make a second loop. Hold one loop in each hand and twist so that the string winds up. Pull to make it whirr and spin.

## Jelly jar snowshakers

You need a plastic model (a snowman is ideal), a screw-top jar and enough glycerine to fill it. (Glycerine can be bought at the pharmacy.) Stick the model to the inside of the lid with PVA glue. Fill the jar with the glycerine. Add some glitter and screw on the lid, then shake.

Remember that many of the creative activities suggested on pp. 88–93 help improve your child's hand skills too.

# 5

# *Learning to be creative*

When a child starts to draw, he usually keeps the crayon pressed to the page and moves his hand in a circular arc to produce curved scribbles. After a while he starts to take the crayon off the paper and his round scribbles are combined or replaced with lines and dots. His drawings have no meaning beyond the pleasure of making something happen, and even his first figure is probably not intentional. He sweeps his hand in a circle, makes his usual dots and lines and finds it looks like a person. This pleases him (and you), so next time he tries to do it again.

Over the next few years a child's drawings give a unique insight into how he sees the world. At first the most important aspect is that each figure he draws has what he considers the right parts; their number, size and position are much less important.

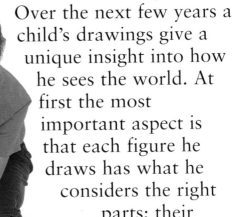

**Milestones in creative skills**

## YOUR CHILD'S DRAWINGS

**1½-2**
*years*

- His scribbles are not meant to be anything in particular, but they are not random. Squiggles on the left are balanced by something on the right.

**2-2½**
*years*

- He does not set out to draw anything in particular. If you ask him what he has drawn, he looks, then tells you what he thinks it is. If you ask him about the same picture tomorrow he may give a different answer.

**2½-3**
*years*

- He tells you what he is going to draw before he starts but if he thinks the drawing is starting to look like something else he abandons the original plan.

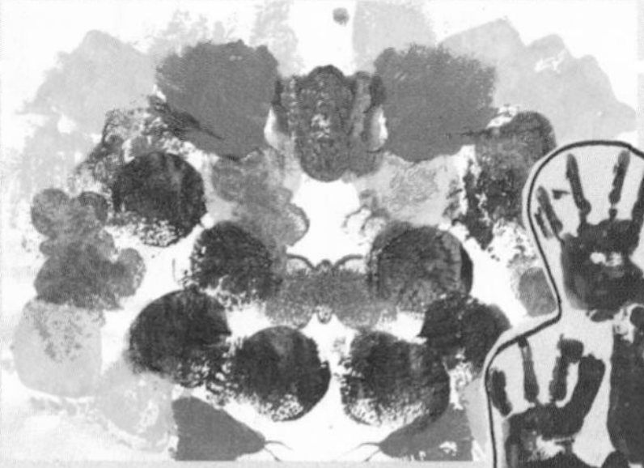

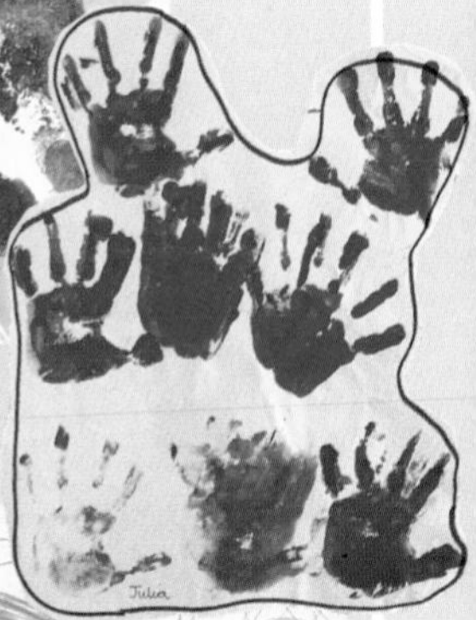

**3-3½**
*years*

- His drawings now have circles, squares, crosses, lines and dots combined in various ways.
- Dots and crosses are often enclosed in circles, and lines may radiate out from circles like a typical child's sun.
- Once he realizes that his drawings can look like faces or people he starts to fashion them intentionally. The lines come out at the bottom for legs, he makes two – or perhaps three – dots or tiny circles for eyes. He may still draw too many legs and place parts wrongly, such as eyes in one corner or legs coming out of the head.
- It is more important to include the parts in the picture than to put them in the right place.

**3½-4**
*years*

- Some parts may be missing but those that are included are in the right place: there may not be a body but the legs come out at the bottom and the arms at the side.

**4-5**
*years*

- His drawings become more elaborate. When he starts to add a new detail it is large and he does not count how many should be there, so that people may have three enormous fingers and houses are filled with windows.
- He may use circles rather than dots for eyes and include hair, necks, buttons and knees.

**5-6**
*years*

- Pictures become busier but they remain symbols of what he sees rather than pictures of reality. "My house" may have four windows and a door even if he lives in a flat.
- He may draw a baby in a woman's tummy and if a man is sitting on the stool he draws all of the stool with the man hovering above.

| WORKING IN OTHER MEDIA | HOW YOU CAN HELP |
|---|---|
| • He likes to feel rather than use clay and playdough and squeezes it in his hands. | • Provide a short stubby crayon and some paper or some blobs of paint on a tray for him to push around with his hands.<br>• Let him feel dough or pastry.<br>• Praise his efforts. |
| • He does not set out to make anything in particular and is quite happy rolling and cutting. | • He may still prefer to paint with his hands and fingers, but now enjoys using a chunky brush.<br>• He is happy to use one color for his paintings, drawings and playdough. |
| • He starts to make objects although his plans remain fluid: the doing rather than the making is central. | • He likes to have a choice of colors.<br>• He expects you to display his work: this is always the best reward. |
| • He can roll sections and break off bits of dough and push them back together.<br>• He can use a mold but remains fascinated with the material and often just rolls, stamps and cuts.<br>• If he encounters a new material – such as clay – he explores it by squeezing and cutting. | • He enjoys new materials and methods: messing with clay, using small paint brushes, making prints.<br> |
| • He makes balls and sausages and puts them together to make people.<br>• He flattens out balls and puts the sausages on the plate.<br>• He may now want to keep what he makes. | • He likes "silly" string sets that make hair or spaghetti.<br>• He draws more accurately with pens than paints but needs experience with both.<br>• He begins to shape his little squiggles into writing. |
| • His models become more elaborate.<br>• He may make a series of people and explore what happens when he rolls the colors together. | • A new technique can keep him engrossed for extended periods of time.<br>• His drawings become more elaborate.<br>• Display his works around the house, not only in his bedroom: bulletin boards help to "limit" the numbers.<br>• He may print his name on his paintings. |
| • He begins to use other modeling materials and increasingly wants to keep the models he makes.<br>• As he nears his seventh birthday, he can follow instructions to make simple jewelry, use elaborate molds and mix colors. | • A new technique can arouse the interest of a child who does not like drawing, but by now writing and school activities have superseded the need to develop the tool control used in drawing.<br>• If he does not like to express himself in this way it is his choice but, for a child who enjoys drawing, praise him to maintain and develop his skills. |

# How children learn to draw

*Young children do not draw what they see, but making marks on paper is a favorite activity in the preschool years*

It does not matter if you never manage the art of planing a piece of wood, but there are certain tools that everybody has to learn how to use. Eating utensils and writing implements head that list. While it takes relatively little skill to shovel food into the mouth with a fork or spoon, learning to control a pencil accurately demands a great deal of practice. Even if drawing provided a child with nothing but the skill of moving a pen on paper, it would still be an essential component of her education.

Children can begin to make marks on paper as soon as they are able to hold a crayon, but rarely draw anything recognizable until they are about three. Early drawing is excellent practice for twisting hand movements, and a good way of reinforcing a child's knowledge that she can make things happen. Putting her scribbles on the wall teaches her that what she achieves is important: so many of her games are simply put away in the toy box at the end of the day.

*Swirling lines, dots and squiggles characterize a child's first drawings. All you need to do is provide a few crayons and some paper, and sit not too far away, then your child can get on with it. Ask her to tell you about what she has drawn sometimes, but don't push her to answer always: she is not drawing anything in particular and may resent interruption.*

### Sweeps and little squiggles

Children make two sorts of marks when they first use crayons: big movements that evolve into more detailed drawings and smaller squiggles that may be included to "balance" the picture because children like each half of the paper to be equally busy. Adults often ignore these squiggles but with encouragement, they can be developed into handwriting (see pp. 226–227).

### Taking the crayon off the paper

The first change you will see in a young child's drawing is an increasing tendency to lift the crayon off the paper. At first this does not alter the drawings in any substantial way; a continuous looping line is replaced by two or three separate swirling systems that may overlap. Gradually, however, the crayon is taken off more often and you will see short lines, small loops, dots and crosses start to appear.

At this stage she does not set out to draw anything in particular. If you ask her what she has drawn, she looks, then tells you what she thinks it resembles. The answer may be arbitrary: if you ask her about the same picture tomorrow she may well give a different answer.

### Drawing with intention

By the time she approaches her third birthday a child who has been drawing from infancy can tell you what she is going to draw before she starts. However, although her intention may be clear, she is easily distracted. If a man starts to look more like a cat, she abandons her original plan. She tends to draw a section at a time with little regard for relative size or position. Her "face" may be no more than a few squiggles squashed in one corner of a large misshapen head. Sometimes there are two eyes; at other times there is one or maybe three. It is all a bit random.

By three and a half she is able to produce big and small circles, squarish shapes, crosses, lines and dots, which are combined in various ways. Dots and crosses are often enclosed in circles and she may call these people, animals or even houses. Lines radiate out from circles to form the sun or a man who looks a bit like a jellyfish with a number of legs coming from the bottom of the circle.

### Stick people

Once she realizes that these combinations look like faces or people she starts to fashion them intentionally. Lines come out at the bottom for legs, and she makes two – or maybe three – dots or tiny circles for eyes. At first she does not count parts of the body. If she is interested in making legs she could add four or five to the drawing. Nor does she bother much about the correct position or whether all the parts are there. Arms come out of heads and when she starts to add a body the arms stick out at waist level.

# Recognizable drawings

*By the age of four, most of the relevant elements are included in a drawing, and in the right place*

As your child passes his fourth birthday his drawings become much more recognizable. People may still lack details such as necks or feet but the basic elements are there and in roughly the right place. Hair is placed on the top of the head, eyes are above the mouth and legs always come out at the bottom of the body. Arms may still be missing and, if included, probably join the body at waist level but if they are there, there are now only two.

### Who is counting?
Your child draws what interests him. If he has new shoes, footwear features prominently in all his drawings. If he cuts his knee, his drawings may suddenly sprout knobbly knees. When he adds an interesting new element its importance is emphasized by its relative size. Fingers are huge, hair ribbons bigger than the head. He does not always count correctly, so his people may have three fingers on one hand and six on the other.

### Drawing what should be there
Children do not draw what they see, but what they think should be there. Sometimes this can cause problems. If a child draws a cat from the side, he still has to fit in four legs – even if this means lining two up under the belly or letting them grow out of the animal's back. Children drawing an elephant are never quite sure where to put the trunk. The face may look forward (as all faces tend to do, even if animals are drawn from the side), but that makes it difficult to attach the trunk. Sometimes a child compromises by twisting the animal's head to the side.

### What children draw
Because children always put in what should be there, drawings have a certain similarity. A cat has two pointed ears and lots of whiskers because that is what is important about cats. Dogs have four legs, a sun has rays of sunshine. Houses have four windows at the edge and a door in the middle. If you ask a child to draw a cup turned away from him, it will still have a handle.

### Houses on hills
Young children are completely distracted by the part of the drawing they are working on, so for example, if they are putting a chimney on a sloping roof they tend to line it up so that it is perpendicular to the slope and sits at an angle to the ground. Lines that are close together tend to be parallel, so if a child starts by making the fence of the house less than vertical, trees and window frames will line up with the fence rather than the edge of the paper. You can see this tendency most dramatically if you ask your child to draw a house on a steep hill.

## Boys and girls

Boys' pictures are often busier than girls', with more action and greater use of the edges of the page. Girls' drawings tend to have the subject placed slightly to the left of center (especially if it is a person) and the rest of the scene arranged around it. Boys are more likely to have two or three focal points – such as three planes or a car entering from the left and one leaving from the right. They add lots of little action details rather than "dressing" the stage as girls do.

## Drawing what he sees

Between the ages of five and seven, drawings become more scenic and often have more than one element. Houses are set within yards, cars

### Can you suggest any creative activities for a couple of boys who never sit still?

Could they fold paper to make planes? Or perhaps make glove puppets by sticking some eyes and hair onto an old sock, or paint faces onto paper plates and attach sticks to the back to make characters in a story? Other possibilities are making a car, train or boat out of some supermarket boxes. For a car add four wheels and a cushion seat; a toy steering wheel would provide the finishing touch. Paint the box with bright poster paint. For the wheels fix four silver pie plates using binder clips. Put in the cushion. Alternatively, cover the box with aluminum foil and make large wheels from cardboard. Use a bucket as a guide; draw around it and cut out the circles. Paint and fix as before. Stick two or more boxes together to make a train.

A large and a smaller cardboard box can be turned into a robot costume. You need to check that the smaller box fits over the head and the larger one over the body. Cut a face-sized hole in the smaller box, making sure this lines up so your child will be able to see out. Make holes for both arms and the head in the larger box. Cover with foil, folding it over the edges and fix with tape. Stick on bottle tops, corks and cardboard dials. They can then play space robots.

on streets, airplanes within a crowded sky. Yet they still remain symbols of what he sees rather than pictures of reality. Flowers may be as tall as the house; a baby is clearly visible in the woman's tummy; the stool is a circle placed above three legs and the man hovers above it. The age when a child begins to draw what he sees varies enormously (as does drawing ability), but by the time they are nine most children's drawings are more accurate copies of reality.

# Materials sourcebook
*What to make or buy to meet your child's needs for paper, and drawing and modeling equipment*

You can make some of the items your child needs to paint and model yourself to keep the costs down. Remember too that younger children are happy to paint with one or two colors, initially at least, so you can add to these a couple at a time. If you start with the primaries – blue, red, yellow – you can mix green, orange, purple and brown yourself. A small pack of crayons (8 or 10) is fine: if you buy an enormous set, the chances are many of them won't be used.

### Choosing crayons and pens
The easiest crayons for small hands are short and fat. Thin crayons tend to break because children press down on them much too hard. If your child wants to make fine lines felt-tip pens are probably easier to use, but make sure these are water soluble. Teach your child always to replace the lid when the pen is not in use. Some children are scrupulous about this but you will still need to check at the end of the drawing session.

### Paint
Poster paint is by far the easiest for young children to use. Older children can use little blocks of watercolor. You can also make paint. The easiest way to do this is to make a thin "sauce" of flour and water and color with powdered paint or food coloring. The finished paint should be no thicker

*You can buy tubs of poster paints as powder or ready mixed. Water-color blocks are too difficult for young children, who invariably make the paint too wet.*

*A wooden or plastic board, some rolling pins and cutters will satisfy your child's needs for playdough equipment. Since bits of playdough get trodden into carpets, it is worth making sure your child models at the table. If he has to be on the floor, putting everything on a large, lipped tray might help to contain the mess.*

than cream. Alternatively, dissolve a handful of soap flakes (not detergent) in water and add powdered paint or food coloring to it.

### Making paint pots
You will cut down on the general mess if you always put paint in a spill-resistant pot. You can buy these from craft stores or make them from old dishwashing-liquid containers or plastic water bottles. Cut off the top of the bottle just below the shoulder and remove the cap. Then cut a 4–6 inch (10–15 cm) section from the bottle base. Invert the neck and place it in the bottle base. Fix into place using a contact adhesive. These can be used for water or paint.

### Choosing brushes
It is always easier to have one brush for each paint color. The youngest children are happy to work with one color, but older ones need two or three, each with its own brush to avoid mixing colors. Thick brushes are probably the best ones for small children to use. Older children enjoy the challenge of a fine brush: the skill needed to manipulate it is quite different.

## Other applicators

Make-up sponges, crumpled paper, bundles of cloth, shapes cut from a bath sponge, cotton balls, fingers, hands and feet can all be used to apply paint. Use a package of small plastic plates or bowls (this saves on the cleaning up) to hold the paint, or squirt it directly onto a Formica tabletop or a large tray. Children can dip the applicators into the paint and transfer them to paper.

## Paper

Pads of different colored paper are good for art. For painting you can buy rolls of paper designed for use with easels. Easels need putting up and down and can be hard to store, but they do "contain" painting. If your child does not have an easel, cut sheets from a paper roll or use the backs of ends of wallpaper or computer printout (although this goes soggy if a child puts too much paint on it). For drawing, add the backs of large envelopes or junk mail.

*Making a papier-mâché model gives your child a real sense of pride and achievement. Leave the model to dry in a warm place and she can paint and decorate it once it is completely dry.*

## MODELING MATERIALS

Commercial doughs can be expensive and dry out easily unless you are careful with them. Children also go through vast amounts. It is more economical and easy to make your own.

### • Making salt dough

Mix equal amounts of salt and flour. Add a little cooking oil and enough water to make a dough. Knead this until it is soft and stretchy.

This dough can be hardened by baking in the bottom of a low oven, but will take several hours to harden completely. It can then be painted and varnished. The uncooked dough keeps for weeks in a plastic bag because the salt stops it going off.

### • Making playdough

Playdough has less salt than salt dough. Unlike salt dough it cannot be dried or painted. Use three parts flour to one part salt then add oil and water as for salt dough. Varying the amount of oil and warming the mixture in a pan before kneading it will give a slightly different texture.

If you want to color the dough, use food coloring or powdered paint; you could also add a few drops of flavouring to make it fragrant (mint, rosewater and vanilla work well). This will keep almost indefinitely in a plastic bag – again, the salt preserves.

### • Papier-mâché

Tear about 40 sheets of newspaper into tiny pieces. Collect these in a bucket, cover with water and let it stand for 24 hours. Pour off, then squeeze out any surplus water.

Make up a cupful of wallpaper paste following the instructions on the packet (check that it does not have added fungicide). Knead the paste and paper together until the mixture feels like soft clay.

### • Covering a mold

Make up a small bowl of wallpaper paste (without fungicide). Tear a newspaper into strips. Cover the mold – balloons and flowerpots are easiest to start with – with grease. Soak the strips of paper in the paste, then lay them on the mold so that they overlap slightly. Cover the mold completely and let this layer dry. Add a second layer, let this dry and add another layer. Most molds need about six or seven layers. Leave in a warm place for a few days to let it dry completely. Pop the balloon or remove the flowerpot. Your model can now be painted.

Papier-mâché models should not be immersed in, or used to contain, water.

# Drawing and painting

*You can broaden the scope of your child's painting and drawing sessions beyond making marks with a crayon or brush*

Children like painting and drawing and the opportunity to make up what they are working as they go along, but they also appreciate your help in mastering more imaginative techniques.

### Splatter painting

This is messy but fun. The child takes a brushful of runny paint, holds it over the paper and taps the brush. Putting cardboard shapes – such as Moon and stars or animal stencils – on the paper before splattering produces interesting effects. These can then be colored in separately or left blank. The result makes good wrapping paper.

### Leaf prints

Collect some leaves. Paint all over the surface of the leaf, taking care not to use too much paint. Press the leaf onto some paper paint-side down. Cover with another sheet of paper and smooth down, then peel away the leaf. If it's a bit smudgy, try again: the second print should be better.

### Potato printing

Cut a potato or turnip in half and dig out a simple design – star, heart, flower – on the cut end. Brush on paint and press the potato onto some paper. A print in thick paint on tissue paper makes good wrapping paper.

### Blow painting

Make a runny mixture of powdered paint and water, and thicken it slightly with soap flakes. Put this on a baking tray. Give your child a straw and let her blow the paint about. Two colors that blend to make a third (such as blue and yellow) give interesting results.

An alternative is to make a thinner paint and blow it across slightly shiny paper. If you want a permanent record, take a print by putting a blank sheet of paper over it and rubbing gently.

### Paste pictures

Start by making some thick flour paste (see p. 86). Add some food coloring and spread the paste over thick paper or cardboard (the shiny side of a cereal box would do). Comb this with a comb or fork.

### Scratch pad

Build up layers of wax crayon one on top of the other on a sheet of thick cardboard. Start with light tints, and work toward a dark color such as black or brown. The child can then scratch through the layers with a blunt pencil to reveal the different colors.

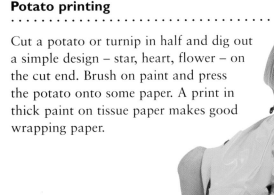

## Folding paintings

Make a crease down the middle of a piece of paper. Ask your child to paint a pattern on one side of this crease, then fold the paper over, pressing it down firmly. When the paper is opened out there is a symmetrical picture.

You can vary the technique by blobbing various colors of thickened paint on both sides of the crease. Fold and smooth out, pushing the thickened areas slightly. Unfold as before.

This technique also works well with glitter glue. Dot glitter glue all over the paper, fold it in two then open it out to reveal a shimmering butterfly.

## Hand and finger paint

The easiest way to "paint" is to put a few blobs of thick paint on to a Formica tabletop, large tray or baking sheet. Let your child move the paint with her hands and fingers to make interesting shapes. If you want a permanent record make a print. An older child will like "proper" fingerpaints.

## Rubbing

Put some coins under a sheet of paper and rub over them with a soft pencil or a wax crayon. It is possible to make rubbings from anything with a firm, rough surface, so you could also try tree bark, table mats, large-veined leaves, buttons and corduroy or any other kind of open-weave fabric.

## Sponging

Show your child how to dip the sponge in the paint, take the excess off by dabbing it on a piece of scrap paper, then dot the sponge over the paper. A light touch works best. You achieve better results if you stick to a single color for each sponge, rather than trying to use one for several shades.

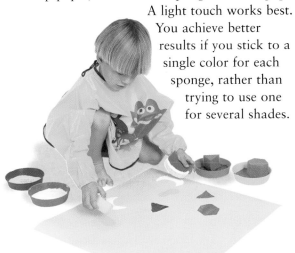

## WHAT YOUR CHILD LEARNS

**• Hand and finger painting**
This is completely different from holding a crayon or paintbrush and is a good tactile experience. It is also messy, which children love and need: it is important to be able to explore media as they choose.

**• Sponging, potato printing, leaf printing**
These are a good introduction to shapes.

**• Rubbing**
Taking a rubbing brings in the dimension of texture; it also requires fairly precise hand skills to reproduce a small object, such as a coin, in this way.

**• Spattering and blow painting**
These are fun, but also teach your child to control his movements: too heavy a splatter makes a mess; too strong a breath will send his line out of control. Using two or more colors introduces color mixing.

**• Folding paintings**
These teach your child about symmetry: that the image on one side of the fold is the mirror of that on the other. They also offer an element of surprise: it is impossible to know how your painting will look until you open it out.

# Dough and clay

*Your child's relationship with and enjoyment of dough and clay changes and develops in his early years*

For the youngest children all you need is playdough and even older ones go back to it time and again. Older children, however, also enjoy playing with a greater variety of modeling materials.

### Rolling and cutting

Two- and three-year-olds rarely want to make anything with dough; they are happy to squeeze, roll and cut it. You can buy small rolling pins in most toy shops. Alternatively, cut some short lengths from a broom handle or curtain pole, but be sure to sand the cut edge down so there are no wood splinters. Use ordinary pastry cutters or buy small versions and molds from a toy shop. You will also need a sturdy plastic knife and a board: toy boards tend to be rather small, so look out for a cheap kitchen chopping board.

A child who can use cutters on playdough can also use them on pastry or cookie dough. Add raisins or chocolate drops for eyes to an animal figure. A four-year-old can fill tart shells with pastry and jam and, after you have baked them, eat the results for dessert.

### Taking impressions

Clay is particularly good for taking impressions but you could also use salt dough. Roll the dough into smooth round balls – about the size of a golf ball. Press them against hard rough surfaces such as walls, trees, shoe treads or the patterned ends of cutlery. The patterns can then be dried. You could also roll out the dough and press various objects into it to make patterns.

### Making permanent objects

Although for a small child much of the pleasure of modeling comes from the feel of the material, an older child may want to make something he can keep. There are a number of different materials you can use for lasting models: plaster of Paris, Fimo, various types of easy-dry clay (some are ready mixed, others need mixing), salt dough and papier-mâché (see p. 87).

### Using salt dough

Salt dough is excellent for models like dolls' food; use small cutters to make little cakes, or roll out the dough and cut three small squares to push together in the middle to make a sandwich. You could add food coloring to the dough when you make it, but baking tends to dull the colors. Your child may prefer to paint the models after they are baked.

## Using plaster of Paris

You can buy pots of plaster of Paris, together with flexible molds, in toy shops. Although these are too difficult for preschoolers to manage without help, the activity is good for children and adults or older siblings to do together. Young children like the professional look of the finished figures.

## Using papier-mâché

Papier-mâché can be used like clay or salt dough to make figures, animals, dolls' furniture or food. Although it takes some time to dry it does not need baking, which means that an older child could make an enormous model. Start large models by molding the papier-mâché around a starter shape; if the starter needs to be removed use the technique described on page 87. Otherwise your child can simply use a cardboard box as a base. Models can be painted and varnished after they have completely dried out, but remember that a large model may take a week to dry.

## Using clay

Clay has a wonderful feel but is messy: little bits dry to a fine powder. If you have a suitable space – you could consider using it in the garden in summer – it is great to work with.

### WHAT YOUR CHILD LEARNS

**• Taking impressions**
This is a good introduction to opposites, mirror images and negatives: the impression he makes in his dough is the reverse of what he sees on whatever he has chosen to press his clay into, so that high points become valleys and low areas peaks. The original and its impression fit together like a lock and key. Taking impressions is also ideal for a child who doesn't know what he wants to make, or who gets frustrated when his model fails to live up to his expectations.

**• Making permanent objects**
These give a great sense of achievement and in future years your child will love looking back at his early creations. Modeling also improves his spatial thinking as he tries to recreate an object in three dimensions.

**• Clay, salt dough, papier-mâché**
All modeling materials behave slightly differently, so your child learns to adapt his techniques to suit his materials. Creating "things" enhances his imaginative skills – food for a tea party, a chair for the smallest doll. Modeling is also a wonderful tactile experience.

# Sticking, gluing and fixing

*Making a collage is a great way to introduce your child to a variety of materials, as well as giving him hours of fun*

You can use almost any material in a collage and, if you have the space, it's worth keeping a couple of boxes of scraps. There is nothing more frustrating than knowing that you have thrown away the perfect finishing touch for one of your child's masterpieces.

## WHAT TO KEEP FOR COLLAGE

- **Paper and card**
Paper towel and toilet paper rolls; egg cartons; scraps of tissue, crêpe or wrapping paper; ends of aluminum foil

- **Household objects**
Old buttons and shoelaces; scraps of fabric; cotton balls; scraps of wool

- **Out and about**
Feathers; pebbles; shells; leaves

- **From your pantry**
Lentils, chick peas and other dried legumes; pasta shapes; cocoa; flour

- **Worth buying**
Glitter; contact paper or shapes; a few sequins

- **Glue and paste**
The easiest glue to use is the sort that comes ready mixed in a pen or a jar with a built-in applicator. This makes it easy for the child to put it exactly where it is needed. An alternative is to make cold-water paste from a handful of flour dissolved in cold water. Just put the water in the bowl and slowly add the flour, stirring continuously until you have a thick paste. A medium-sized brush probably works best.

## Simple dropping

Let your child spread PVA or a cold-water paste with a small amount of coloring added over a sheet of paper. (Other types of glue are suitable but it is often difficult to see whether transparent glues are spread evenly.) Now she simply drops items on the sticky paper. Glitter, cocoa, sand, sugar, lentils, sequins, egg shells, rice or little snips of paper all work well. Heavier items such as lentils and beans need a stronger glue than cocoa or glitter.

## Fancy dropping

Draw around various shapes and carefully glue inside the shape. Drop the shapes onto the glue. Shake off any excess once the glue has dried. On the same principle, you can buy kits containing predrawn images to which glue can be applied, or stencils from which precut areas can be removed to leave sticky areas that make a picture, together with bags of different colored sand. These are less free than dropping, but help your child make a recognizable picture, which she may like.

Fancy dropping works in reverse too. Spread the paper with paste, and put a cup onto the paper. Drop glitter or cocoa all over the paper then remove the cup. The empty circle can be left as it is or filled with little snips of paper or cotton balls.

## Sticking

Sticking is more difficult than dropping because the glue has to be put in the right place – which is not obvious to a child. The problem is that a child likes to look at what she is gluing, so puts glue on the front rather than the back of the picture. You can help to alleviate this by suggesting she put the object face down on a piece of scrap paper to glue, but after a while the excess glue on the scrap paper will transfer itself to the front of the picture she is sticking.

## A big picture

Draw a simple picture on a big piece of paper. If you are not skilled you could put a newspaper on the table, cover this with your paper, put a poster over and draw around the image pressing hard. The imprint should be easy to see and can then be drawn in. Make it simple: a rabbit, Humpty Dumpty, a car or a train. Now collect your materials. Cotton balls are good for fur, washed egg shells broken into pieces make excellent skin and wool and packing material stand in for hair. The rest can be made from strips of cloth or paper. If your child is sticking she needs to work a small section at a time. If she is sprinkling she can do the whole section at once. Whichever is the case, paint the area with PVA, taking care not to go over the lines, then sprinkle or stick. Let this dry and start a new area.

## WHAT YOUR CHILD LEARNS

### • Dropping
This teaches your child about the nature of different materials: that some (the lighter ones) stick easily and others need more glue; that some stay where they are dropped while others might roll or bounce to another part of the picture. Gluing inside a shape requires precise wrist and finger movements.

### • Sticking
Although accurate placing of shapes is difficult, children enjoy practicing and find sticking fun. Sticking helps hand-eye coordination.

### • A big picture
Children like to have a finished picture, and the bigger the piece of art the better as far as your child is concerned. Making collage pictures also encourages your child to think about and investigate his materials: what makes the best hair or cat's whiskers?

## Using contact paper

Contact paper makes sticking easy, especially if you use ready-cut shapes. These can be used to make mosaics and pictures or in combination with other techniques. Sticking shapes onto predrawn pictures in a book is a real challenge for a preschool child. It is far easier for you to prepare various shapes and present your child with all the elements of a simple scene – such as a beach scene – and let him make the picture. This is especially easy if you draw a picture for her to copy so she knows where to put the boat, fishes and waves.

# 6 People and objects

At first a baby's attention is focused on people, although anyone who takes notice of her will do – it is only after about six months that she attaches herself to specific caregivers and is nervous with strangers. She is fascinated by other babies and children, and the more she sees of them the better. At a year old, she hates it when you leave; it takes a while to learn the confidence that you will return.

Objects are of less interest initially, but ones that move when she swipes them or rattle when shaken start to arouse her enthusiasm and make her squirm with excitement. By the age of three she definitely knows what is hers and what isn't. She starts to identify with characters in books and on TV, but still thinks that you know what goes on in her world even when you're not present.

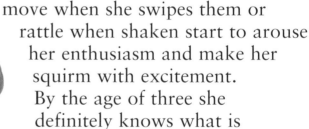

## Milestones in relating to people

| | **WHAT YOUR BABY DOES** |
|---|---|
| **At birth** | ● A baby settles better with familiar people.<br>● She watches intently when someone talks to her and imitates their facial expressions.<br>● She smiles directly at people and expects to be given her turn in "conversations" (by eight weeks).<br>● She directs her attachment behaviors to everyone (by eight weeks). |
| **16** *weeks* | ● She is interested in people and recognizes those who are familiar.<br>● She is bored if left alone.<br>● She squirms with excitement, squeals and laughs.<br>● She does not realize there is only one "Mommy"; she thinks there is a new Mommy every time she sees her. |
| **20** *weeks* | ● She smiles at other babies, especially the one in the mirror.<br>● She loves people and recognizes everyone who is familiar.<br>● She is more discriminating about who she directs her attachment behaviors to.<br>● Her moods change quickly.<br>● She smiles more at those she knows and is soothed by them. |
| **30** *weeks* | ● She starts to form specific attachments and may always want her primary caregiver.<br>● She changes from "come here signals" like smiling to "proximity seeking and keeping" signals like clinging.<br>● She starts to fear strangers.<br>● She looks for you when you hide and misses you when you are gone. |
| **1** *year* | ● Fear of strangers and strange places increases; she is disturbed when you leave (at 34–38 weeks).<br>● She is afraid to be left even in familiar places and is anxious until you return (at 34–38 weeks).<br>● She tries to please you and uses you as a safety-base when away from home (at 34–38 weeks).<br>● She stops if you tell her "no," waves and imitates expressions and action.<br>● She likes to make you laugh.<br>● She pulls at your clothes to attract attention.<br>● She reacts to your moods, and can express joy and frustration. She can be jealous.<br>● She likes other children but does not play with them.<br>● She anticipates your action: for example, having her arms ready for her jacket. |
| **2** *years* | ● She imitates those she knows and likes to do what they do (by 1½ years).<br>● She does not realize that hitting or biting hurts; she thinks it just makes others cry (by 1½ years).<br>● She starts to play with other children but cannot put herself in another's place and will snatch toys and may hit and bite; she may enjoy the reaction she gets. |
| **3** *years* | ● She can contrast herself with others.<br>● She is possessive about her belongings.<br>● She has fewer tantrums but may quarrel with her siblings.<br>● She pretends she is someone else. She begins to show sympathy and empathy for characters in stories.<br>● She still behaves as if you see the world through her eyes; she tells you about something that happened at nursery school as if you were there. |
| **4** *years* | ● She understands that other people have thoughts, experiences and feelings that are different from hers and begins to take this into account in her interactions with others. |

| **HOW YOU CAN TELL** | **WHAT YOU CAN DO** |
|---|---|
| • Watch her mouth move as you talk to her.<br>• Stick out your tongue and see if she copies – be patient, it takes time. | • Watch her mouth move as you talk to her.<br>• Make faces for her to copy: exaggerated gestures are best.<br><br> |
| • Sit in front of a pair of mirrors; she will love seeing you reflected many times.<br>• Pause and wait after you leave the room: she settles when her attention is attracted to something new. | • Talk to her often, pausing to let her reply. |
| • Sit her in the supermarket cart and watch her interact with strangers.<br>• If you sit in front of a pair of mirrors now she may be afraid to see so many reflections. | • Be warm and consistent with her: this is when it starts to become important. |
| • She suddenly becomes shy and will not go to Grandma if she has not seen her for a few weeks. | • Don't push her into the arms of strangers.<br>• Don't leave her if she is unhappy: this is the worst time for parents to start leaving a child with another caregiver for the first time. |
| • She will cling as you try to leave and be inconsolable after you have gone (at 34–38 weeks).<br>• She seems more a little person, less a baby, but you cannot quite put your finger on why (by 44 weeks).<br>• She is devoted to you. | • This is not a good time to go on vacation. If it is the only time you can go take plenty of familiar belongings with you.<br>• Encourage her to have a comfort object: a teddy or a blanket to hold and hug to boost confidence.<br>• Point objects out to her. |
| • She trots behind you with her vacuum cleaner (by 1½ years).<br>• She is good with her babysitter and saves her tantrums for you. | • Make sure she has the tools to imitate your action.<br>• Walk away from tantrums if you can; hug her tightly if you can't. Always kiss and make up afterward. |
| • She often plays at being someone else and dresses up frequently.<br>• She does not take your view into account and expects you to see what she sees. | • Get out the photograph album and look at the photos.<br>• Talk about her friends and relations: she likes to know that lots of people love her. |
| • She explains when she knows you were not present. | • Find time every day to sit down for a cuddle and a gossip.<br>• Let her dress up frequently. |

**Milestones in learning about objects**

| | WHAT BABIES CAN DO |
|---|---|
| **At birth** | ● She does not know where she ends and the world begins.<br>● She does not look for an object she drops. |
| **20** *weeks* | ● She watches an object go behind a screen and looks for it emerging on the far side, but she is not surprised if a different object comes out. |
| **40** *weeks* | ● She watches if she drops a toy but only for as long as she can see part of it. If it rolls completely out of view she does not look. |
| **14** *months* | ● She moves one object to reach another which was hidden from view.<br>● She looks for objects where she last saw them. |
| **18** *months* | ● She is more purposeful in the way she explores objects. |
| **2** *years* | ● She unwraps packages and takes the lid off boxes.<br>● She names objects and uses them uniquely.<br>● She understands the meaning of "inside," "under" and "on top." |
| **3** *years* | ● She begins to understand what "one" and "lots" mean.<br>● She makes comparisons.<br>● She knows some colors. |
| **4** *years* | ● She can count and begins to understand what numbers mean.<br>● She can put three or four items in order. |
| **6** *years* | ● She still thinks that when liquid is poured from a short fat glass into a tall thin one there is more liquid and that seven sweets stretched out in a long line is more than seven in a short line. |

| How you can tell | What you can do |
|---|---|
| • Hide something under a cloth, take it away then lift the cloth. At first she will not be surprised; later she is. | • Put objects into her hand.<br>• Put her in a high chair so she has a better view of the world. |
| • Cover a teddy with a cloth, then put your hand under and take out the teddy replacing it with a car. She will not be surprised. | • Play games of peek-a-boo.<br>• If she can crawl chase her around the sofa. |
| • She will not watch what happens to objects you drop.<br>• She looks for objects where they usually are even if she sees you moving them. Put a toy under a cloth and let her find it. Do this again a few times, now put the toy behind your back. She will still look under the cloth. | • Don't get too frustrated when she throws objects out of the high chair: she needs the practice.<br>• Look for toys with little doors and hiding places. |
| • She can look away from what she is doing and return to it.<br>• She puts two ideas together to make a plan: throwing the ball and then running after it, for instance. | • When you are looking for something ask her to help.<br>• Give her a pail to collect items in; she likes to look at them in one place, then take them out and study them in another. |
| • Her behavior seems to flow; she no longer seems to flit from one activity to another.<br>• She acts rather than simply reacting. | • Look for toys that do things: simple puzzles, crayons, board games.<br>• Give her books: she will enjoy turning the pages. |
| • She is much more purposeful and persistent in everything she does. | • Look for books with lots of familiar objects in them; point and name and let her turn the pages.<br>• Let her practice putting objects inside, under and on top. Stacking cups are ideal for this. |
| • She may ask for "Too many sweets" and tell you her sister has a bigger piece of cake. | • Look for puzzles that put items in sequences: small to big; one to ten. |
| • She makes constant comparisons between what she and others have. | • Play matching games. |
| • She spontaneously groups items into colors or insists on needing the green brick her brother is playing with.<br>• She insists that tall glasses are best. | • Play games with simple logic. |

# Learning about love

*Babies learn about love as they discover about everything else, from the words and actions of those who care for them*

*Before your baby can reach out to explore your face, she knows your smell and your voice. And by the time she is able to smile, she knows you as someone familiar. She will smile at you more readily than at others.*

The difference between your love for your newborn baby and hers for you is that who she is matters to you while who you are does not matter to her. If she was taken away and given to someone else (as babies who are adopted are) she would settle into her new home without a backward glance. As long as she has someone to love her, she does not care who that someone is. You, on the other hand, are precise. In a ward full of babies only one matters.

### How parents become attached

Falling in love with a baby is not that different from falling in love with anyone else, except perhaps that it is less cautious and usually happens faster. The main difference is that from the start you know that your baby will always have the capacity to break your heart. This is something that really does last forever. Whatever happens to you or to your child in the future, the relationship between you remains part of both your lives, part even of your daily thoughts. It is the permanence of this love that makes the word bonding seem right.

### What is bonding?

The word bonding gives the impression that love should be instant – like contact adhesive that is spread across the participants by the process of birth. For maybe a quarter of mothers and somewhat fewer fathers it is pretty much like that. However, for most parents love grows over the first few days. For some it takes weeks or even months. The time it takes to start love is not a measure of its ultimate depth. It is probably more a function of how familiar the child looks at birth. It is perhaps easier to fall in love with someone who already looks exactly as if she is part of the family. The act of giving birth is not vital to this process. Fathers, siblings and grandparents bond, as do parents who adopt children.

### How babies recognize parents

Babies come to recognize their parents rapidly. Within days of birth they show more interest in their mother's breast pads than those of other women. Within a week they know the voices of their primary caregivers, and turn to them most eagerly. Within a couple of weeks they know their faces, and when they begin to smile they do so readily.

This knowledge is a matter of familiarity. Your baby knows the smell of those bodies she often rests against, the voices she often hears close by, the faces she looks up to as she is cuddled. Familiarity makes her feel secure. If you leave her she misses that security but she does not miss you, initially at least. To miss someone you need to remember them when they have gone away and tiny babies do not. They simply recognize that some people are familiar. To them out of sight is out of mind. It is as if you disappear in a puff of smoke as you leave the room, like turning off the TV.

## What babies think about themselves

At first a baby does not know where she stops and the rest of the world begins. When she was in the womb there was no reason to suppose that the heartbeat and pumping blood she heard constantly did not belong to her, nor that those muffled voices she sometimes heard were not her voice. After birth some parts of her world disappear and reappear and some remain with her at all times. The things she sees when she turns her head to the right are not constant. The feeling in her neck when she turns her head is constant. A baby is about six weeks old before she can separate the variable stimuli from those that remain constant and comes to realize that the constant ones are part of where her body stops. It will, however, be some years before she knows where her mind stops and where other minds begin.

## What babies think about others

A newborn baby's span of attention is short. While she looks she sees but moments after she turns away she has forgotten what she was looking at. Until she can begin to stretch out her attention span she cannot put together the fact that sometimes she sees and hears you, and at other times she hears but does not see. She has to realize that if she turns to the sound of your voice she will see the same person, and if she looks at you and then you speak it is always the same voice. Only when she recognizes the constancy of these things does she realize there is only one you.

## Not always unique

Although every object and person is in fact unique, older children and adults do not treat them as such. The penny in your pocket is just another penny and you do not know or care whether you have owned that particular penny before. It is only when uniqueness matters that you start to care. The houses in a new development are just so many boxes until someone you know moves into one. The people in a crowd are just people unless they happen to be your friends.

To a baby in the first months you are like that penny – familiar and distinct from other people, but not unique. Your baby does not realize there is only one of you and is not in the least surprised to see you reflected many times in a pair of dressing table mirrors. By five months her view of you changes; she realizes your uniqueness and is perturbed by all those reflections.

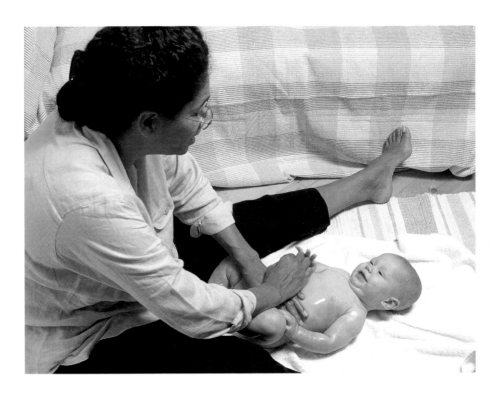

*Massage is a wonderful way to teach your baby about loving touch. Make sure the room is warm and use plenty of massage oil. Don't hurry a massage but work slowly and evenly, taking care not to apply too much pressure to delicate areas, such as the spine. You will feel your baby relax under your hands.*

# Sunny or difficult?

*How you influence your baby's behavior and disposition through your interaction with him*

Not all babies are alike. Some are sunny, some moody and difficult, others passive or shy. No baby is universally difficult or always sunny but certain characteristics do tend to go together. A vigorous baby is often less cuddly and more irritable and restless than a more passive one. A child who quickly settles into a sleeping routine also feeds and fills his diaper in a regular pattern. Such babies adjust easily to change. A difficult baby tends to be less regular in his habits. He is slow to develop regular feeding and sleeping patterns and a change in his routine makes him irritable and upset.

Slow-to-warm-up children are between these extremes, showing a cautious but positive resistance to change. Such babies neither resist violently nor rush headlong into the fray. They whimper, turn away or hold on a little tighter.

### Born or made?
Children are to some extent born easy or difficult, but the differences cannot all be laid at the door of the genes. Easy babies can be made difficult by pain, and pussyfooting around a difficult child can reinforce his despotic tendencies. The effects may be long-lasting. More bad-tempered people have had early childhood illnesses (such as eczema or ear infections) than chance would indicate.

### Difficult times
Studies carried out in Germany suggest that even the easiest babies have difficult periods, and the most tricky are sometimes sunnier. All children become more difficult as their bodies make the changes that catapult them forward into the next stage of their development. As the change is made, and the ability consolidated by practice, babies become easier. For most babies there is a difficult phase between five and twelve weeks, another at seven to nine months (often blamed on teething), and another at about two years.

### Beginning to miss you
By five months your baby knows that you are unique. Although he understands that there is only one of you, he still does not know you exist when he cannot see you. To learn this, his attention span has to stretch. He needs to be able to glance away and remember what he was seeing,

*Studies have revealed that circumcised boys were initially difficult and demanding, as might be expected if circumcision hurt. Three months later any pain had certainly gone but these boys remained demanding. Watching their mothers showed that they responded to their sons' cries more quickly and readily than the mothers of uncircumcised boys did. Being difficult gets results.*

*It is easy to encourage a sunny baby to stay sunny by responding to her smiles. She soon learns a smile brings you to applaud her successes. It is also easy to reinforce a difficult baby by rushing to her cries, tiptoeing around her difficulties and trying not to upset her. Despotic or benevolent, all small children want to be dictators. Democracy has to be learned.*

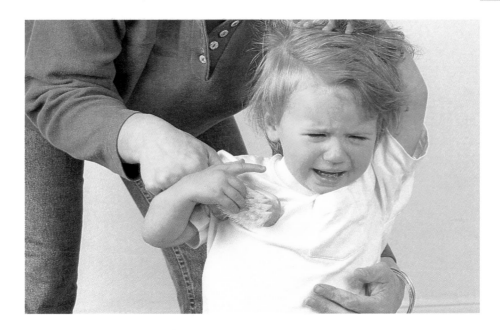

look back and check it has not changed. This ability develops between seven and nine months.

Once he knows you exist when you are not with him, he can begin to miss you and to worry when you prepare to leave. He starts to cling to you. As he begins to know that people do not appear and disappear, he also realizes he knows some people and not others. He becomes fearful of strangers. You can no longer play pass the baby. If he is in a stranger's arms he screams and, since he does not remember people for long, the "stranger" can be someone he has seen many times before.

### Being loved

The bond between a child, his family and his caregivers is usually called attachment. Most of the research has concentrated on the attachments formed between a child and her mother although your child also forms strong attachments to his father, siblings, regular caregivers and those relatives, neighbors and friends who show him love. The more loved a child feels the more secure he is.

### Meshing together

Over the first weeks and months a mutual pattern of attachment behaviors occurs. The baby signals his needs and his love by crying, snuggling, smiling and being responsive to his caregiver. He looks and gurgles when caregivers talk to him, he squirms when they tickle. His caregiver enters into

this "dance" by responding: returning his smiles, talking to his gurgles, reassuring his unease, giving cuddles when they are needed but not interfering when they are not ... in short by letting the child signal his needs and develop his independence.

As more research is carried out on children it becomes clear that the nature of early attachment pervades many aspects of life, and that securely attached children have a head start in life.

## TROUBLESHOOTING

**My son was always a cuddly baby and he is still a snuggly child, but my six-month-old daughter never seems to want a hug. Are boys and girls really so different?**

No, but children are different. Some early studies showed that baby boys were more demanding than baby girls, but these have not always been replicated. One consistent finding is that mothers are more likely to cuddle daughters who are upset, and try to distract their boys. Many parents agree with researchers that something of a child's temperament and character seems to be there in the earliest days, but a great deal is built on this base. Children learn by imitating their loved ones. In warm and physical families children tend to follow suit sooner or later, although it may be that your son will always be more cuddly than your daughter. Whether this is because he started out that way, or because his willingness to be hugged has meant he has clocked up more cuddles is impossible to say.

# Learning about objects

*The ability to realize where her body ends and the world begins is crucial to your baby's understanding of the nature of objects*

A baby's earliest experience is the womb, where there is little variety. Sounds may change, and the light may vary a little depending on how thick and concealing her mother's clothes are; she may note a pressure difference when her mother takes a bath. The main changes she experiences are when her mother shifts posture or starts to move. Nothing of this has any relevance to objects. Her world does not extend beyond the walls of her mother's womb, and nothing she does makes any difference to that world. She therefore has no reason to separate the world into me and them, here and there, or objects and living things. Birth changes all that.

### Learning what is important

Initially babies are not tuned into objects. The world is a buzzing pandemonium of stimuli – or would be if a newborn took much notice of it, but she does not. Her systems are focused on people, and they are her first concern. The sounds she tunes into are those of the human voice, the sights those of the human face. She is also aware of movement and on the whole it is people rather than objects that move. It is only after she has learned to recognize those who care for her and to uncurl and begin to smile at the world that she begins to concern herself with the objects around her. First

she learns where she stops and the rest of the world begins. Then she becomes interested in the outside world. By six to eight weeks she is raring to go.

### Learning about constancy

One of the first lessons a child has to learn about objects is that they look different depending on the angle, light and distance you see them from. The image formed on the back of the eye is like a photograph. Its size depends on how far away it is and its brightness on how much light it reflects. Its shape varies according to where it is viewed from and its color on the nature of the light falling on it.

What you "see" is not the image itself, but an interpretation of it. Colors do not change if you walk from the garden into yellow artificial light; objects do not seem bigger because you walk toward them, nor do they change shape as you stand up and alter the angle of view. On the whole the objects you see remain constant in spite of the huge changes in the retinal image. They do so because of the way the brain interprets that image.

It is not certain when a baby learns to interpret what she sees, or indeed how much is learned and how much preprogrammed into the brain. Babies are known to have

*Toys with hiding places, locks and keys help your child to investigate the constancy of objects. Although he has hidden something inside his box and turned the key, he peeps in to check it is still there.*

*It is only after her first birthday that a child knows that something she cannot see still exists and will actively look for it.*

Everything is like an old penny. Babies are about six months old before they start to realize they have only one crib, one buggy and one car seat.

### Learning about permanence

There is one more quality a baby has to learn about objects: that they exist even when she cannot see them. She learns this slowly. In the first phase – at about seven months – she learns that objects can slip from view and reappear. She watches as you "choo–choo" a train behind the chair and is ready and waiting for it to come out on the opposite side. Although this looks impressive, she does not yet realize that the train exists behind the chair. She just knows something should reappear. "Choo" the train from one side and choo a teddy out at the other and she does not look surprised; she is content. It is only in her second year that she expects the exact train she saw going behind the chair to come out from the opposite side. While she looks for belongings she drops at about nine months, she does not continue to look if they roll out of sight. Nor does she look at objects you drop. Even when she knows that the train that went behind the chair is the same as the one that should come out again, she still looks for it where it is usually kept, not behind the chair where she last saw it.

at least the rudiments in place by two to three months of age, but there is also evidence of improvement over the next few months.

### Learning about identity

Objects have an identity. Often, we ignore their "uniqueness," treating objects such as coins as if they were interchangeable. Adults do this from convenience, tiny babies do it from necessity. They have not yet learned that each person and object is unique, and so treat even their loved ones as if they were new, but familiar, each time they meet.

*Your baby's first clue that there is a world apart from her comes when she realizes that* *her body is finite. Her hands are on the ends of her arms and beyond that is "not her."*

### Learning more about objects

In her second year a child investigates further. She tests how objects go inside, underneath, on top and behind one another. She puts little toys into a bag and takes them out again. She puts them back then does it again. She puts something behind the door of her garage, opens the door to peep at it, then closes the door again. She tries to balance one plastic bottle on top of another, fails, so tries to balance tin cans. She may hide the car keys in the seat of her sit-and-ride, carry off your earrings in her little bag and try to wedge a large teddy into a small space. It is the failures, as well as the successes, that help her to understand.

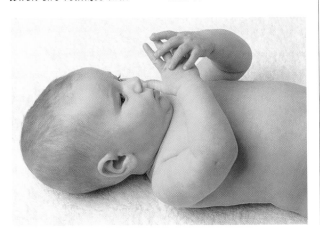

# Hide-and-seek

*Simple variations on a time-honored theme are still the best way to reinforce what your child learns about objects*

Making people and objects appear and disappear is an activity that children love for several years. The younger the child the more she will enjoy doing the same thing over and over again. All you need to do is match the activity to your child's age and current interests.

## Peekaboo

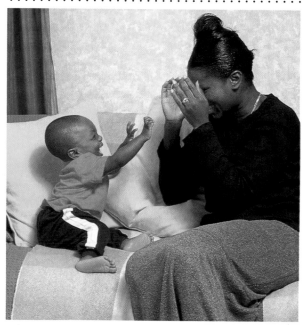

This game needs no explanation! You duck out of sight and pop up again into view. You can say whatever you like when you pop up, but say something as this is all part of the game. The only drawback with this game is that your child will not want to stop.

## A drawer to play in

Babies love to empty cabinets and drawers. They also like to play underfoot. One way to combine these two needs is to give the child a drawer of her own to empty and fill at will. A low drawer in a part of the kitchen away from the stove, and/or one in the family room will keep your child amused while you carry on with the chores.

## A den behind the sofa

The easiest way to make a den for a small child is to pull the sofa out from the wall leaving a child-sized space for her to play in. She will love you to peek into her den. Sit a few teddies in the den for her to visit. Alternatively, throw a large tablecloth, flat sheet or blanket over the kitchen table.

## Ping-Pong bath time

Ping-Pong balls make great bath-time toys. Throw two or three into the bath and show your child how to pull them underwater and then let them go. They pop up to the surface. This is even better if you put bubbles in the bath first.

## Books

Books are excellent hide and seek toys. Everything that is not on the page in view is hidden. A child familiar with a book can hurry forward to her favorite picture. Turn the page and you find it, turn back and it's lost. Little flaps with things hidden behind them simply repeat the excitement of turning the page.

Flaps in books amuse younger children, but older preschoolers prefer to find a figure hidden in

---

### WHAT YOUR CHILD LEARNS

**• Peekaboo**
This is a wonderful social game which babies are always ready to play. A sociable baby can elicit a game of peekaboo from anyone in a line who is willing to play!

**• A drawer to play in**
Filling, emptying and sorting are premath skills.

**• A den behind the sofa**
Dens help your child's imaginative play: a den is never simply itself, but a boat, tent or castle. Likewise, the toys in it are not teddies and dolls but your child's companions in her adventure.

## WHAT YOUR CHILD LEARNS

### • Jack-in-the-box
This is a good "anticipation" game that will have your child roaring with laughter. She will laugh even more if you pretend to be surprised to see the rabbit.

### • Ping-Pong bath time
Floating and sinking – and working out which objects do what – is an early science skill. Water play, in general, enhances a child's understanding of the nature of materials and is great fun (see pp. 140–141).

### • Books
Looking for objects on the page is the first step in recognizing the shapes of letters, a prereading skill.

a landscape. At the simplest level the child looks for a small creature that appears somewhere in the picture. In more complex books the child looks for an individual among a sea of faces (see p. 47).

### Jack-in-the-box

You can still find traditional jack-in-the-boxes, which children love. But you can also make your own variation. You will need a small furry rabbit, a stick and a piece of stiff cardboard. Cut a circle of cardboard using a dinner plate. Make a cut in the center and remove a pie-sized piece. Roll the circle into a cone and fix with glue and staples. Now attach the rabbit to the stick, then pass the rabbit-free end of the stick through the base of the cone. You now have a rabbit that can be hidden from view in the cone. Pop it up above the cone for your child to see, then pull it down to hide. Remember that this is a toy you show your child. It is not safe for her to play with it alone. You could elaborate on the

design by covering the cardboard with cloth and attaching a "skirt" to the rabbit with the hem stuck to the rim of the cone.

### Getting warmer
When the child is out of the room hide a small treat to find. When she is getting near the treat she is warm. When she moves away she is cold, but when she comes really close she is hot! Give a running commentary until the treat is found.

### Making rainbows
This is a simple "Now you see it, now you don't" game to play with an older child on a sunny day in the backyard. You need bright sunshine and a fine spray from a garden hose. Spray the water high into the air and look for the rainbow. (It is always on the opposite side from the sun.)

### Matchboxes
Matchboxes make excellent collecting and storage boxes for an older child's small treasures. They can be used to store briefly a few ladybugs, some tiny shells or a secret supply of small sweets. You can give older children the task of finding five interesting items to put in the matchbox, use it to make a bed for a tiny doll, or stick two together to make a chest for the doll's house. If you attach a handle, this can be a suitcase for a small teddy who is going on vacation.

## WHAT YOUR CHILD LEARNS

### • Making rainbows
People and most objects are constant, and exist if you can't see them. But a rainbow is transitory: it shimmers for a few seconds, then fades. If you manage to create another, it is different. This teaches your child that there is yet another truth about some objects. It also introduces the subject of light and how it behaves.

### • Matchboxes
Children love "treasures" and collecting, sorting and storing become increasingly important to them (see pp. 110–111). This activity also improves their imaginative skills.

# Loving and learning

*You can reinforce your child's attachments to objects and people through the activities you share*

Soft toys and comfort objects can teach a child a great deal about love and blur the line between people and objects: to your child her beloved teddy bear is as real as her brother or sister. It is not, however, necessary to spend a fortune on soft toys; many can be made or improvised.

## A comfort object

Not all children have a comfort object, but those that do seem to learn how to cope with strange situations better than those who do not. It is possible that long practice with a "cuddle for courage" teaches the child how to put himself into a state of mind where he can overcome his fears and get on with the task in hand. Children first become attached to comfort objects at about seven to nine months. For some that object is a thumb or pacifier, for others their mother's breast or a bottle. The remainder form an attachment to something from their bed, such as a blanket, sheet or teddy. You can direct your child toward a teddy by always tucking one in beside him at night, but remember that not all children form such attachments.

## Cuddle cuddle

A room full of soft toys is likely to be largely ignored until the child's second and third year, but it is never too early to use one to play cuddle. Find a soft animal that is not too big and give it a big cuddle, saying "Ah cuddle, cuddle" as you do. A 10-month-old will soon copy what you do.

### WHAT YOUR CHILD LEARNS

• **Cuddle cuddle**
Mimicking teaches your child how to express emotion, and reinforces ways to channel that feeling. The action is also like an early word: a sign that says "This teddy." A cuddly toy can be a comforter into her school years.

• **Streamers, egg carton animals, rag doll**
Crafts improve your child's creative and imaginative skills and give her the chance to make something to keep. Because each child produces something different from the same template, these toys are highly personal.

## Paper doll streamers

Cut a sheet of writing paper in half lengthwise and make a series of accordion folds each about 1 inch (3 cm) apart. Now carefully draw half a person on one side of the fold. There should be half a head and body, one arm and a leg. The arm should stretch out to the other fold. You could also stretch out the leg to the fold if you wanted to. Now cut around the line, remembering not to snip the ends of the arm (or leg if you want these to join). Pull out and you have a row of dolls who can dance and play.

## Egg carton animals

Divide the egg carton into individual sections. A 12-egg carton would make 24 animals, a 6-egg carton 12. Add pipe cleaner legs and antennae, cardboard ears, felt feet, woolly hair. The creatures can be as basic or as fabulous as your child's imagination. By threading a string through a number of sections you can make a dinosaur and by piling them up you can make a funny figure. Everything can, of course, be painted.

## A rag doll

Rag dolls are beautiful gifts and, if someone has taken the time to make one for your baby, she is likely to treasure it as she gets older. But you can make an easy – and versatile – doll in a few minutes on a rainy day. All you need is a small square of cotton – 4 x 4 inches (10 x 10 cm) is fine but you could use a bigger or smaller piece if you wish – and some wool. Fold the cloth down the center. Roll each edge into the center. You should now have two rolls sitting next to each other. Make a fold about a third of the way down, and bring the two sets of rolls to meet each other. The top of this fold is the head. Tie the wool two or three times around the double section – about a third of the way down – to form a neck. You now have a head with two short and two long rolls of fabric hanging from it.

Wrap another piece of wool around the neck and cross it before taking the wool under the shorter rolls and around the longer rolls to form a waist. Pull out the short rolls to form arms. Tie off the hands and tie the ends of the longer rolls to make feet. Turn the doll over and draw the face.

## Pets as friends

Pets play many different roles in children's lives. A child who is well-loved has plenty of love to give to a pet. A child who is often lonely may need to feel there is someone extra loving her. Learning to love and care for a pet is an important part of childhood for many children, especially those who do not have siblings. However, preschool children are too young to take sole responsibility for a pet. A four-year-old can feed and water a hamster, but may often need reminding to do so. She also needs to be supervised when she cleans out the cage. If you are not prepared to take over care when necessary it is easier to settle for a kitten, which is more able to look after itself, or to wait until the child is about six or seven years old.

### WHAT YOUR CHILD LEARNS

Children gain an enormous amount from having a pet.
• They learn that there are animals which are smaller and more vulnerable than them that need their love, care and protection.
• The knowledge that a creature may depend on her for survival enhances a child's sense of responsibility.
• Her self-esteem can be greatly enhanced by the trust you have invested in her to look after a pet.
• Learning how animals behave – when they sleep, what they like to eat, how to keep them clean – broadens a child's experience.

# Collecting, gathering and finding

*Sorting different objects from those that are the same is a good way to make sense of the world*

From toddlerhood up, children love collecting, arranging and storing, and there are plenty of activities you could try.

## A nature table

Toddlers love to collect items in a little bag. An older child may enjoy displaying a collection, so set up a place on a shelf or table in her bedroom. She can display leaves, flowers (fresh, dried or pressed: but remember that in some areas picking wildflowers imay not be permitted), dough casts of tree bark (see pp. 90–91), pine cones, acorns and seashells. She could also include pictures she has drawn. Label everything. She may like to decorate the labels or even to write them herself.

## Worm watch

Earthworms burrow in the soil, creating airways that bring vital air to the roots of plants.

If you have an old fish tank you could try farming some earthworms. (Earthworms can be obtained early morning or evening by turning over soil with a garden fork, or purchased at a fishing tackle supply store.)

Procedure:
1. Put some small pieces of Fun tak on the base of the worm farm tank and secure it in position with Fun tak.
2. Fill the cup or jug with peat and pour into the worm farm tank until the peat is about ¾ inch deep.
3. Spray the peat, using the plant sprayer, until it is moist. Do not waterlog the peat.
4. Repeat steps 2 and 3 with sand, then with garden soil, and then with chalky soil.
5. Repeat steps 2 to 4 (with peat, then sand, then garden soil, then chalky soil). You should now have a worm farm with eight zones made up of different soil types.
6. Put the worms on the soil surface. DO NOT PUSH the worms into the soil. They will make their own way through the layers.

7. GENTLY add some cut grass and leaves on top of the worms.
8. Cover the worm farm with the black plastic sheet or other lightproof covering (AVOID DIRECT SUNLIGHT). Leave it in a cool (not cold) place.

## WHAT YOUR CHILD LEARNS

### • A nature table
This is a good way to bring the natural world indoors and introduces nature and early science to your child – something city children often miss out on.

### • Picking berries
This raises the notion of how plants grow and improves your child's ability to classify objects. Older children may enjoy weighing what they have picked, which introduces the concept of weights and measures.

### • Worm watch
This may awaken your child's interest in the natural world, and introduces the idea of food from nature.

## Picking berries

Being careful to avoid poisonous varieties, give your child a small bag or box to hold the berries and show her how to pick them from a bush or patch. If you do not have wild fruit growing nearby, a trip to a "pick your own" fruit farm is an easy alternative.

## Supermarket search

The easiest way to liven up a shopping trip is to make a list for your child. Drawing is easiest, but you can cut out pictures from advertisements and stick these onto an index card. The child has to look for the products on the card. Have a few stars to place against the pictures as she finds what you need.

## Watching the builders

Large machinery can be alarming close up, but from a distance most children are fascinated. Take a series of photographs of the building site as it is cleared and the building progresses. Put these on cards and show her how to arrange them in order or stick them in a scrapbook comic-book fashion.

## Letters

Pick a letter then search for objects that begin with it. B is for baby, Bertie, Bethany; M for Mommy, Meg and Matt. But what else? Can she find her initial on shop signs, road names and cans in the supermarket? Can she find her age on road signs?

## Collectibles

Most six- to seven-year-olds have a collection. In the past it might have consisted of stamps, seashells or coins. These days it is more likely to be collectible toys: action figures, stuffed animals, monsters. It is hard to resist pressure from peers and television advertisements. The packs of cards available at the corner store may not always be to adult taste, but they are a cheap option and have the advantage that most children can collect enough to sort and classify them in different ways. This is what children need and like to do with the cards.

## WHAT YOUR CHILD LEARNS

### • Supermarket search
As well as making the shopping more fun, this improves your child's observational skills as she searches for the items on her list. It also helps her ability to sort and group: the apples will be in the fruit and vegetable section, cornflakes with the cereals and ice cream with the frozen foods.

### • Watching the builders
Sequencing is one of the principles a child has to grasp to understand mathematics; placing things comic-book fashion will help her learn how words are placed on the page, which is a vital skill for new readers.

### • Letters, number plates
These activities improve your child's observational skills and her ability to sort and classify.

### • Collectibles
Sorting and classifying is an important mathematical skill. The technique of thinking about things in more than one way (which is what a child does when she sees a card as being both a swop and a member of a certain group) is the basis for logical thought.

# 7 *Developing intellectual skills*

Intellectual skills include learning, memory, thinking and reasoning and underlie your intelligent interaction with the world. Schoolwork stretches intellectual skills but it is not the basis of them, nor does it always engage them fully. A child who cannot remember any dates from history lessons may be able to reel off all the scores and statistics of his favorite baseball team. The difference is that he is bored by history and aroused and interested by baseball. Children like to learn and do so naturally if adults provide the correct environment, but they tune out without the right stimulation. A lively

game naming different makes of cars running around the yard or singing his favorite songs may be far better preparations for school than learning to count or saying his ABC's.

## HOW MEMORY DEVELOPS

### 6 weeks

- He recognizes individuals by smell (by the first day), voice (in the first few days) and sight (by the end of the first week).
- He cannot remember people when they are not there.
- The only world that exists is the one he perceives at that moment.

### 20 weeks

- He begins to realize certain things are unique.
- If he drops something he forgets all about it and does not miss you when you leave him.
- He darts from one activity to the next.

### 42 weeks

- He begins to anticipate and seems to remember events.
- He knows that you exist when you leave the room.
- He may look for objects he drops.
- He peeps around corners and loves peekaboo.
- He understands "no."

### 1 year

- He remembers how to play pat-a-cake, where his favorite picture in the book is and what simple requests mean.
- He points to show you objects and may name one or two.
- He can look away and return to what he was doing.
- He can put two ideas together to make a plan and his behavior begins to flow.

### 1½ years

- He expects certain objects to be in specific places, and particular events to occur at set times.
- He can say some words and understand many more.
- He does not forget immediately and persists in wanting something you have taken away.
- He protests when he does not get his own way.
- He unwraps packages.

### 2 years

- He explores, watches and investigates. He can plan quite complex activities in advance.
- His behavior flows; he clearly puts ideas together.
- He puts words together to make simple sentences and can follow simple instructions; he can recall what to do.
- He mimics what you do.

### 4 years

- His memory span expands and he acts as if he has a continuous plan and a train of thought.
- He no longer breaks sentences down into two words.
- He gives reasons and solves problems. He understands rules.
- He communicates what he is thinking.

### 5 years

- He gives and discusses reasons.
- His memory span expands further and he begins to make comparisons.
- He understands that everyone's experience and thoughts are unique.
- He can talk about what happened in the past and does not rely on external cues to remember them.

| ABILITY TO LEARN | WAY OF THINKING |
|---|---|
| • He learns to ignore what remains constant so that he can attend to those aspects that change.<br>• He can learn that one event follows another.<br>• He learns to make things happen.<br>• He imitates facial expressions. | • He has no continuity of thought or feeling of continuing existence.<br>• He does not know that objects exist when he cannot see them: he thinks everything he sees is new – even people. |
| • He strings activities together: he reaches for the toy and then takes it to his mouth.<br>• He is beginning to be able to do two activities of his choosing at the same time, like shouting and reaching. | • He realizes that he has only one mother.<br>• He can bang his rattle and shout at the same time (by 26 weeks). Soon he can simultaneously have an intention and perform an act. |
| • He has learned to use objects in different ways.<br>• He puts longer sequences of behavior together.<br>• He begins to imitate other people's behavior. | • He begins to understand that people and objects still exist when he cannot see them.<br>• He coordinates and plans.<br>• He quickly looks up if something seems interesting and can return to what he was doing afterward. |
| • He imitates more, watching and copying actions.<br>• Behavior seems much more organized. He will take longer breaks in an activity before returning.<br>• He uses objects uniquely. He does not hammer with a cup and no longer puts most items in his mouth. | • He is no longer limited to two thoughts and can integrate several behaviors, so he may remember that his truck is in the hall, go to find it and bring it into the family room. |
| • He is much more aware that he can take action.<br>• He is constantly trying and practicing.<br>• He can follow simple directions.<br>• He acts to please or annoy you. | • He seems to know what went before and predicts what is next.<br>• He knows if you skip a page in a book.<br>• He watches people and imitates. |
| • He begins to imitate the intention of others, rather than mimicking their action.<br>• He plans activities but still learns mostly by trial and error. | • Language is much more important.<br>• He begins to understand concepts such as "one" or "more."<br>• He begins to give reasons.<br>• He makes comparisons and understands rules. |
| • He gives reasons and solves problems, understands and respects rules. | • He talks fluently, asks questions, understands answers.<br>• He can learn by being told.<br>• He may understand what simple numbers mean; he gives and discusses reasons.<br>• He makes frequent comparisons. |
| • He uses language to work things out.<br>• He gives reasons and solves problems.<br>• He can order some objects.<br>• He begins to reason (after sixth birthday). | • He listens carefully and understands more complex rules.<br>• He explains and likes to please.<br>• He can reason (after seventh birthday).<br>• He realizes that objects remain the same even if they are in different packages (after seventh birthday). |

**Milestones in relating to the world**

## WHAT YOUR BABY CAN DO

**At birth**
- He responds to the world with a set of reflexes.
- He can hold a thought for only a moment at a time and does not have a sense of time continuing.

**16 weeks**
- Your baby investigates himself. Until he knows what is "me" and what is not he cannot make much sense of his environment; by 16 weeks he understands the distinction.

**32 weeks**
- He starts to investigate the world.
- He can hold a thought in mind for a little longer but does not look for objects he drops.
- He has no sense of time continuing.
- He is beginning to string two behaviors together.

**1 year**
- He can now hold thoughts in mind for long enough to make a simple plan of what he intends to do.
- Object permanence (the idea that things always exist even if not seen) begins to emerge.

**1½ years**
- He starts to experiment, treating objects in different ways and checking out how he can manipulate both objects and people.
- His schemes of how the world works are more abstract; if something works in one situation he tries it in another.

**2 years**
- He begins to string ideas together.
- He can leave one idea or activity "hanging" while he does or thinks about something else.
- Language begins to play a more central role.

**4 years**
- There is clear evidence that the child can think. He must be able to think about what he cannot see. Language gives him the ability to do this.
- He pretends, talks and give reasons.
- He can imitate what he saw yesterday and is still primarily influenced by what he can see.
- He thinks he is the center of the world and inanimate objects are alive.

**6 years**
- He knows that other people have minds, and that his mind is not privy to anyone else's.
- He believes what he senses to be true, and his perceptions are not logical: he still thinks the amount of juice in a cup depends on its shape, and that he has a brother but his brother does not.
- He can divide items into simple categories, but these are often odd.

| **HOW YOU CAN TELL** | **WHAT YOU CAN DO** |
|---|---|
| • Your baby is curled up; he does not actively investigate. | • Lay him on his back so that he can see his hands.<br>• Make faces for him to copy. |
| • He looks at his hands. | • Give him a wrist rattle, or tie a little bell around his wrist so that he can find his hands more easily.<br>• Give him objects to swipe. |
| • He reaches out to touch, then grab.<br>• He uses his mouth to explore.<br>• He moves things to one side to reach for something else (at seven to eight months). | • Give him objects to explore.<br>  • Play peekaboo.<br>  • Stretch his memory when you play knee-bouncing games by making him wait.<br>  • Give certain toys certain functions. |
| • He starts to treat objects in appropriate ways: he cuddles teddies and presses the button on his jack-in-the-box.<br>• He knows a hammer makes a better noise than a foam covered stick. | • Wait for him to communicate before you respond.<br>  • Play games in which he has to find objects that are hidden.<br>  • Show him books. |
| • He is constantly busy. He imitates.<br>• He cries to get attention and says or indicates "No!".<br>• He constantly hides and finds objects, for example, hiding candy under a cushion. | • Give him toys he can use for imitation.<br>• Talk to him often. |
| • He goes to the cupboard to fetch a toy he needs.<br>• He gives a doll a spoonful of pretend food.<br>• He looks up as you talk to him, then returns to his game.<br>• He communicates with words and signs. | • Chat as you work and he plays. |
| • He talks about things in the past and future.<br>• He groups objects but the divisions may have no formal logic.<br>• He pretends, enjoys stories, asks for and gives reasons.<br>• He thinks the Moon follows him down the street and that the chair he bumped into is "naughty." | • Look for books and puzzles that help him categorize.<br>• Make a toy chest and give him the tools for pretend play.<br>• Play simple board games.<br>• Talk about what he does.<br>• Take excursions. |
| • He fills in enough background information for adults to understand him; he knows that you no longer share his thoughts.<br>• He fights with his brother to use the tall glass.<br>• He can sort items into simple categories.<br>• He does not use strategy when playing games. | • Look for opportunities to match and sort items, such as setting the table, sorting the wash or putting socks into pairs. |

# How children learn
*The basic principles that underpin your child's intellectual development*

The ability to learn is based on many factors. Some are present before birth; others are acquired in the first few months and years of life. The interaction between them is at the heart of everything that an adult has learned.

### Habituation
The ability to "switch off" when something persists is known as habituation. Habituation stops you hearing the ticking clock or the sounds of traffic. Babies seem to habituate even before they are born. If you play a sound through a loudspeaker on the mother's stomach wall a baby is startled. If the sound is then played at regular intervals the baby stops responding. If the sound changes he responds again. This shows he can learn to ignore a regular, predictable event. When the loudspeaker is removed the baby responds to the absence of sound. The vital things in the world change. Habituation to what is constant makes it easier to notice when something changes.

### Learning to predict
A second type of learning is predicting that something is about to happen. When you hear footsteps approaching, you expect to see someone coming into view. A baby in his stroller comes to predict that a face will appear from a stimulus – hearing footsteps – which originally has nothing to do with a head. The sound of a can opening brings the cat running because it has learned that this sound predicts food. It is not certain how old babies are when they begin to predict; some evidence suggests they can do this in the womb.

Being able to predict does not mean the baby is aware that footsteps are followed by a face. He just responds in much the same way that adults start to salivate when they smell food, although they are probably not aware of doing so.

### Discovering the consequences of action
Learning to predict that something is going to happen is called classical or Pavlovian conditioning, after the Russian physiologist Ivan Petrovich Pavlov

*Your automatic response when your baby cries is to go to him and pick him up. From this he learns that he is* *important and that if he is upset he will be comforted. But he also learns that a sure way to be picked up is to cry.*

who discovered it. Learning the consequences of an action is called operant conditioning, and much of the best-known work in this area was by American psychologist B. F. Skinner. Tests have shown that a tiny baby can learn to turn his head to switch on a slide projector, or wave his arm to make a mobile move. He also learns to cry so you pick him up and smile so you smile back. A baby can learn to make things happen without necessarily realizing he is doing so, just as an adult can.

### Learning he can learn
The important factor is not so much learning itself as realizing that you can learn, less bringing about events and more intending to make them happen. A baby may be able to knock a teddy and make it move without knowing he is making the movement or having any intention of doing so. He just knocks, gets excited and knocks again. Once he knows he can make things happen, and

starts to act with intention, he can begin to control his world. When he sees something that interests him he can reach out to touch it. When he wants to explore he can bring the object in his hand to his lips and tongue. Although babies can probably learn to make things happen at about six weeks they are closer to 12 weeks old before they start to do this intentionally.

### Imitating

People learn many actions by trial and error. As you grow older you probably learn most by imitating other people or through formal training. Small children can imitate facial expressions in the earliest days after birth. After the first year they begin to copy adult movements (and may, for example, follow you around with a toy vacuum cleaner), by the third year they are able to copy your intentions. So, for instance, your child offers pretend food to a doll as he has seen you offer food to his baby brother.

### Practice makes perfect

Whether he is trying out ways to grab your attention or jumping off the stairs, a child tests and tries everything he learns. The younger he is the less he can rely on what you say and the more he needs to do things for himself. This is one reason why children do everything over and over again. Variety may be the spice of adult life, but it is repetition and constancy that motivate small children. All play is learning, pitched by a child at exactly the right level.

*The knowledge that waving his arm in a particular way makes the bells on his rattle sound marks the start of your baby's realization that he can exert some control over his world.*

*A child who has watched you tuck a sleeping baby into his crib and pull up the covers will repeat your actions when she puts her doll to bed (above). You may even hear her repeat the words you usually say, probably even in the tone of voice you use.*

# Attention span and memory

*How your child reacts to events and actions, and starts to learn to remember them*

If you throw a handful of candy on the table an adult sees there are six or seven, but cannot tell if there are 18 or 19 without counting. Adults can remember a seven-digit telephone number, but not the longer number on a credit card. Adults have a span of attention of about seven items and manage more if they are grouped in some way: 76 89 33 21 65 is possible but 10 single numbers is not.

Children have shorter spans. Tiny babies have a span of one, toddlers three, and even at seven the span is only about five.

## WHY BABIES HATE HOLIDAYS

Babies cannot remember without cues. They need to go back into the situation before they remember what happened there. This is why 6–12-month-old babies hate going on vacation. They rely on the cues of a familiar room and a routine to summon up the memory of what happened before. Take them away and they flounder. When everything is new they have to busy themselves with making sense of it all and there simply is not enough time to assimilate the information they have taken on board.

If you take a baby of under a year on vacation try to keep as many familiar elements as possible. Take his favorite blanket, a few known toys and an old faithful teddy. Play the games you always do. Against the background of old familiar routines she may be able to grab the odd reminder that there was life yesterday.

## How a small span limits thought

One of the main functions of the span of attention is to hold onto a thought long enough to turn it over in your mind and relate it to other ideas. With a span of seven it is possible to use it like a scratch pad and think things through without the help of props. With a typical child's span of five these props become more important. With a typical toddler span it is impossible to sort thoughts out logically or to relate current ideas to others that she may have stored away. Toddlers cannot use logic to solve problems because their scratch pad memory is just not big enough. They tend to believe what they see even if it does not make sense.

## How a small span limits language

Toddlers talk in short sentences because they have to. They do not have a scratch pad big enough to organize a long sentence. To say something complicated they break it down into short utterances they can handle (see pp. 158–159).

## Expanding the span

Your child's span of attention expands as she grows, but in the meantime you can help by reading her familiar stories and nursery rhymes. When something is familiar she can "group" information into bigger sections and so hold more in her span than usual.

## Remembering events

Certain events stick in the mind: those who we alive at the time still remember what they wer doing when President Kennedy was shot; ma people will always remember where they w and what they were doing when they hea Princess Diana was dead. When events are adults remember them specifically, so you ca recall what you had for breakfast this mornin Most of these "events" slip into a general "havi breakfast" memory although certain special breakfasts will remain as event memories.

*If a familiar toy is always on the second shelf of the cabinet, your child will associate that toy with the cabinet. If it is not there one day, he may become confused.*

Tiny babies do not remember events. They only recognize that they have seen something before. Although by the time they are 10 months old they may remember that something happened in a particular place, they still recall this only when they are put back into that place.

### Helping babies remember events

Babies need cues to memory to be big and bold and repeated often. She likes her games to be exactly the same as yesterday. She likes to look at the same book and to pause longest at the same picture every time.

Help her to remember by playing certain games with certain toys and doing things in the same place and the same way. Words you use over and over become associated with certain actions and events: "Up you come," "In you go," "Yumyum banana," "All gone juice, all gone dinner." This

familiarity helps her to remember the last time she heard the words and therefore to understand what the words mean.

### Knowing that…

You know that 2+2 equals 4 and that Spain is in Europe. You probably know lots of other facts too, but couldn't say where you learned them. Words are the cues you need to recall these facts. If you were asked to name the capital of Bulgaria, you might not get it. But if you were told it began with an S, you might recall it. An adult's knowledge of facts depends so much on language, which babies do not have, that it seems unlikely that babies have such memories or that children rely on them as much as adults do.

### Remembering action

You may forget the name of a TV host but you never forget how to ride a bicycle. You cannot say how you do something, but when you have to you can do it. Memories of action are enduring, probably because the action is repeated over and over again so that it is easy to remember what to do.

## TROUBLESHOOTING

**I have tried hard to help her but my daughter just does not seem able to learn the names of her colors. Do you think she could be color blind?**

It is possible, but unlikely. Color blindness is caused by a sex linked recessive gene. The gene is located on the X chromosome. Girls have two X chromosomes so in order for a girl to be color blind she must inherit the gene from both her parents – you would have to have a male relative who is color blind, and her father would have to be color blind too since any man carrying the gene is color blind (men have only one X chromosome). About 1 in 10 boys is color blind but only 1 in 100 girls. I suggest you forget about teaching her all the colors and concentrate instead on teaching her one at a time. If you show her something red can she go and find some thing else the same color? Can she collect all the red bricks to build a house? Go out and pick flowers that are all one color. Add the name when you are sure that she can pick out red.

# How children think
*The differences in a child's and an adult's way of organizing the world*

Children are not simply adults who know less. Small children and adults process information in quite different ways. From the information a child gathers he develops a "best guess" or scheme of the world as he currently knows it. As he gathers more information he finds that his guess has to change, so he makes a more sophisticated stab at how things are and reorganizes the information he has already gathered along those lines.

When your baby first reaches out for a toy, he may develop a simple concept of it: it belongs to the category "things I can touch." Initially such objects are distinct from "things that go in my mouth." However, once he starts reaching out for his bottle, and takes toys into his mouth, his division of the world no longer holds. Some objects can be both touched and put into his mouth, so he has to make a new scheme of things. This might be that there are items he can hold and put in his mouth, and objects that he can touch but neither hold nor put in his mouth. A child always classifies objects by his actions. That is the

way he thinks. In time this classification also proves too simple, so he makes his scheme more complicated still. These "best guesses" are ways of understanding the world and also of organizing it.

### Sensory-motor understanding
A baby gathers almost all his information by looking and touching. An experience results from an action, and he tries to make sense of it by replicating that experience. He carries out the same movement again. Initially his movements center on his body, but by about three months he starts to reach out to investigate the world. By eight months he begins to abstract techniques from their context. If something has worked in one situation he tries it in another. Underlying this new skill is the ability to separate the rule of how things are from the context in which it was learned.

### Concepts
This separating of a scheme from a background is how the idea of a concept develops. What do two socks and two spoons have in common? The concept two. A red light and a red flower? Red. The ability to form concepts underlies both language and mathematics.

### Under, over, in and out
In the months after their first birthday children spend a great deal of time investigating objects and how they share space. Part of this involves the development of the concepts of under, over, in, out, up and down. By putting lots of small toys inside many bigger ones and then taking them out, a child comes to realize what it is that different objects that are "in" have in common.

### Learning colors
Children learn colors later. Color is a more difficult concept because there are more than two colors and, while an object is either in or out, colors merge. It is not clear – even to adults – where blue stops and green begins, or yellow stops and orange begins.

*Objects that nestle inside one another give your child practice at sequencing and ordering, and also introduce the concept of classes and subclasses.*

### Numeration

Although preschool children can relate numbers to objects, most have a poor understanding of the relationship between numbers above three. They may not understand that if there are eight buses and nine candies, there are more sweets than buses. Nor does a child understand that a number such as six is made up of three groups of two or two groups of three. This understanding – in place by the age of about seven – makes it possible to see what mathematics is about.

### Classes and subclasses

If you ask a five-year-old whether there are more daisy flowers or roses in a bunch of six roses and three daisies, he cannot tell you, but, by the time he is eight years old, he can. By the age of eight, but not before, a child understands that certain classes (such as flowers and vegetables) sit above smaller subclasses, such as daisy, rose, carrot or leek. More important, he understands that an overriding class can never be smaller than one of its subclasses – that there must always be more plants than there are fruits or vegetables.

*Number games help your child to sort concepts – matching the two on the die to the two on the board means that he or she has to recognize what "two" is.*

### Understanding relative values

Some concepts are more difficult to understand than others. A red coat and a red flower are both red, but a big flower is smaller than a small coat, and a tall flower is shorter than a short tree. Big and little, short and tall, fat and thin are often judged in relation to a norm. Given the complexity, preschoolers are good at such tasks, although this does not mean that they can put a series of objects of different sizes into an ascending order. They may be able to make judgments about pairs but sequences take longer to master.

### Sequencing

Preschoolers tend to classify by using the extremes of the scale. So, for example, a boy at playgroup is good or bad, and your child loves or hates him. Nothing is neutral. A child sometimes adds a middle value, but can rarely cope with a longer sequence. Matching one sequence to another your child does understand may help him to sort this out. If Daddy equals big, Tom middle-size and baby small, he may be able to put the Daddy, Tom and baby in order of size. But he is unlikely to be able to cope with a longer sequence. Most children are about seven before they can infallibly order items.

*Children can often count before they go to school, giving parents the false idea that they can understand numbers. But they rarely go above about three.*

# Games to help memory
*Many everyday activities can help your child's memory*

Bear in mind when playing games to help your child's memory that it is easier to remember actions than words and to recall one-time events than everyday activities.

## Action books

For the under twos, action is memory. If he "eats" the sandwich in his book and "drinks" the picture of juice, he will remember it next time. If he wiggles his foot when he sees the show, pets the kitten and kisses the baby, he has a series of different acts for each page. These actions are like words – signs that he knows what is on the page. In time he will be able to replace each action with an appropriate word.

## Wait for it

As memory span expands in the second half of your child's first year, make him bridge a memory gap by playing games in which he has to "ask"

### USING TOYS AS PROPS

**• Animals**
In their first year children learn by their actions. Toys which have a specific function – a penguin that pecks his tummy, a teddy that strokes his cheek – cause them to make specific responses and, thereby, to remember the game more clearly. It really does not matter what you choose to do or which toy you select. But you must make sure that whatever the toy does one day he always does the next; the point is that the game must remain the same.

**• A few toys**
Children habituate to their surroundings, so a toy that comes out once a week is more interesting than one that appears every day. Try to balance old and new, so that there is a familiar toy for when your child is tired but something new for when he wants to investigate. Keep the rest of the toys in the toy box.
It is much easier for your child to remember what he played with yesterday if he only used a few toys (it makes it easier to clear up too).

for the next part. Jiggle him in the crook of your foot and then stop and wait until he "asks" for more. Offer him a toy and wait until he reaches for it before you give it to him. Distract him while he plays by calling his name, then let him return to whatever he is doing.

## Outings to remember

If a unique event is shared, it is easier for two people to talk about the experience. A visit to the fire station, a drink of juice in a café or a trip to the zoo all give fuel for pretend play and gossip. Stretch your child's capacities by asking him to tell you the story or by drawing a picture. Perhaps he can take the teddies on a similar outing.

## Dominoes

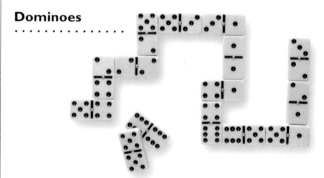

You can play with adult dominoes, although those designed for children to play with are often coded by color as well as by number, which makes the game easier for smaller children. Divide the dominoes between the players. Each player in turn puts down a domino, matching a number on one of the dominoes already on the table. If a player can't go, he loses a turn. The winner is the first player to get rid of all his dominoes.

### Milk-and-cookie klatch

As children begin to remember words rather than action, have a daily session when you talk about your day. What did you do this morning? What did you see at the park? Who did he play with? Have a snack and sit and chat.

### Pairs

All you need is a number of cards that have the same picture. A pack might have 48 cards, or 24 pairs (use fewer pairs for the smallest child). You can buy packs of cards for playing pairs, or stick your own pictures on the face of an old pack of playing cards. At the start of the game all the cards are face down, then each player in turn turns over two cards. If they are a pair, the player removes them and has another turn. If they are not a pair, the next player has a turn. At the end of the game the player with the most pairs wins.

## WHAT YOUR CHILD LEARNS

**• Outings to remember**
Unique events are easier to isolate and recall than routine ones; a shared outing gives a talking point.

**• Milk-and-cookie klatch**
This regular routine encourages your child to plan what he is going to say, as well as encouraging him to put actions into words.

**• Pairs**
As well as training your child's memory, this also helps his spatial thinking.

**• Dominoes**
This helps your child to learn numbers and to match like with like.

Four-year-olds are often better than adults at remembering a card's location, which makes this one of the few games you and your child can play on an equal footing. But younger children have no strategy and often give the game away by turning over the card they know how to locate first.

# Action rhymes

*A child's memory is based on action so action rhymes, played with you or an older child, are great memory joggers*

Children remember best when sentences are repeated and there are actions to accompany the words. Arousal also helps learning, so excitement and laughter increase the probability that your child will remember tomorrow what you did today. Add rhyme and rhythm and action songs and you have all the ingredients to help fragile memories remember.

## Pat-a-cake

*Pat-a-cake patty-cake baker's man*
*Bake me a cake as fast as you can*
*Prick it and pat it and mark it with B*
*And put it in the oven for baby and me.*

Clap your hands in time to the rhythm of the rhyme and encourage your baby to clap along too.

## This little piggy

*This little piggy went to market*
*This little piggy stayed at home*
*This little piggy had roast beef*
*This little piggy had none*
*And this little piggy*
*Went wee wee wee all the way home*

Count the first five lines on your baby's toes, then on the "wee wee wee" race your hand up his leg to tickle his tummy.

## Simon says

*Simon says put your hands on your head*
*Simon says tickle your tummy*
*Simon says jump in the air*
*Simon says touch your toes*
*Hop around*

When Simon says to do something the child follows suit, but if Simon doesn't say, he should not perform the action.

## The wheels on the bus

*The wheels on the bus go round and round*
*Round and round, round and round*
*The wheels on the bus go round and round*
*All day long*
Your child makes circles with his arms

*The wipers on the bus go swish swish swish*
He moves his arms back and forth like wipers

*The horn on the bus goes honk honk honk*
He squeezes an imaginary horn

## Here we go 'round the mulberry bush

*Here we go 'round the mulberry bush*
*The mulberry bush*
*The mulberry bush*
*Here we go 'round the mulberry bush*
*So early in the morning.*

Trace a circle on your child's palm as you go round and round the bush, one step, two steps, move up his arm. The tickle is under the arm. It's a good game for an older sibling to play with the baby.

## One, two, buckle my shoe

*One, two, buckle my shoe*
*Three, four, shut the door*
*Five, six, pick up sticks*
*Seven, eight, lay them straight*
*Nine, ten, a big fat hen.*

Count one to five on the fingers of one hand and six to ten on the other. Point your finger when you ask why it was let go, and make a biting movement on the answer. Hold up the bitten finger at the end.

## WHAT YOUR CHILD LEARNS

**• Listening**
Some action games demand that your child listen carefully: if he misses Simon says, for example, he will be out.

**• Vocabulary**
Many action rhymes use words that may be unfamiliar, or are intoned in a different way. Rhyme is an important component of later reading skills because it encourages children to hear the little sounds that make up words.

**• Action**
When a memory includes action it is rarely forgotten. Despite the years that elapse between playing it themselves and with their children, most parents can instantly recall the words of "The wheels on the bus".

**• Anticipation**
After a few games, your child remembers when he is going to be tickled and will laugh even before you start to tickle him.

## I'm a little teapot

*I'm a little teapot small and stout*
*Here's my handle and here's my spout*
*When it's teatime hear me shout*
*Pick me up and pour me out*

Your child puts one hand on his hip to make the handle and holds the other outstretched to make the spout. When it's time to pour, he bends sideways from the waist.

# Helping children learn

*Children can learn what you teach them, but they also take on some lessons that you don't want them to*

There are many ways in which children learn. The earliest is by making something happen, but later methods include imitation, working it out for themselves and by being told. They also learn, however, from your attitudes and from what you say and do.

### Making it happen

A tiny baby can initiate an event, even if she does not realize at first that she can. As soon as she is uncurled and kicking, her kicks can be used to make something happen. Hang pom-poms where you know her flailing arms will knock them or attach a ribbon to her foot so that she can move a mobile as she kicks. Attach a small bell to her sock so that when she starts to kick the bell tinkles and when she is still the tinkling stops. She will soon learn what is making the sound.

### Mirrors under the table

Your baby likes to see herself (see pp. 96–97). A mirror fixed to the underside of a table does more, however, because it reflects movement. If you don't want to do this, open out a cardboard box and attach kitchen foil to one face. Lay the box on its side with the shiny surface at the top so that the baby can see her movement. It does not matter if the picture is not clear: you are reflecting movement, not trying to give a mirror image.

### Songs and sleep

Everyone wakes during the night but in a familiar place people turn over and go back to sleep. If things are different when children wake they may check their surroundings and by this time are much more likely to be wide awake. If you always sing your child to sleep in the evening she will miss your song when she stirs in the night and wake up more fully. If singing predicts sleep she will learn to feel sleepy when you sing. How does she feel when she wakes in the middle of the night and does not know how to make herself sleepy again? She certainly won't feel able to turn over and go to sleep again, so she cries for you to come and put her to sleep.

### Learning to sleep by himself

Start with a warm bath, then a gentle wind down with a cuddle and a song. Move to the bedroom, tuck your baby in and say goodnight. If going to

*A bedtime routine with plenty of cues that it is now time to sleep may help your child to settle, but you will find you have fewer interrupted nights if you do not stay until your child is fast asleep.*

*You can buy toy household tools, but lightweight or slightly smaller versions of the* *real thing are just as good and will make your child feel even more helpful.*

sleep depends on him rather than you he will learn to make himself sleepy. If he cries go and check that all is well, say goodnight and leave. If he is still crying, harden your heart and let him cry it out. If you always run back when he cries, he knows what he must do to get you back. If he reaches hysterical proportions, go back in, calm him down, then start again. It may take two or three nights for him to learn how to go to sleep without your help, but he will. Once he can do this in the evening he can do it at night too. If he wakes in the night he will be able to rollover and get back to sleep.

### It's better to be bad

If a certain sort of behavior gets you what you need, you do it again (the basic principle of operant conditioning, see pp. 118–19). If your child screams because his socks are twisted and you run and straighten them, he will scream for you every time his socks are twisted. If he sits at the table drawing while you prepare supper, he receives no reward for being good. If he is frustrated by his puzzle and starts to cry until you come to sort it out, he learns that getting upset brings help. Should a child be good or bad if he wants you to take notice? Should he play quietly or make a fuss when you are busy?

### What you don't mean to teach

Sally believes in healthy eating and freshly prepares all Nancy's food. Ruth likes everything in its place so Claire was taught to put her toys away as soon as she had finished playing with them. Why is Nancy a fussy eater and Claire untidy? Because nobody notices when Nancy leaves her socks on the floor or Claire does not eat her vegetables.

Children want to be the center of their parents' world. In busy households nagging and shouting are better than no attention. A child can always find your weak spot, the one area where she knows she'll trigger a response to bad behavior.

### Have duster, will copy

Preschoolers want to be "just like Daddy" and learn a great deal from watching grown-ups and copying what they do. Dusting may seem like a dull activity for a child but that is because adults dislike it. Small children like to mimic a loved one's movements; later they wish to imitate intention too, so may make the dinner "just like Mommy." They may even plan how best to clean a floor.

*Imitation does not have to be dull. If your child grows bored with imitating you, he can copy animals:* *can he crawl like a snake? walk like a duck? hop like a frog? The possibilities are endless.*

# Forming concepts

*Games and activities to help your child sort out the nature of things*

The fact that concepts are difficult to grasp and most children are of school age before they do so is no reason not to help your child to understand.

### A teddy bears' picnic

There is nothing like a few finishing touches to turn a teddy bears' picnic or a dolls' tea party into a treat. Make some tiny sandwiches (cream cheese or peanut butter ones do not fall apart), or roll out a slice from a sandwich loaf until it is thin and elongated, cut off the crusts and spread with cream cheese or mashed banana. Starting at one of the long edges, roll up the bread; there should be two or three turns. Cut small pinwheel sections from the bread. (You can make bigger wheels by starting to roll at a short side; if you spread them with something sticky you can cut them in half.) A cupcake is realistic, if you tie a ribbon around it. Alternatively cut small cakes from a larger one using a pastry cutter. Add tiny sweets, raisins and segments of tangerine and you have a feast. Put a cloth on the ground and let your child lay out the tea set. Can he give each doll a sandwich?

### Finding a match

This leaf is from one of the bushes in the garden. Can you find which? Here is an S for snake. Should we look out for it on road signs? Can we find a can of tuna like the ones we have for lunch? Here is a black cat. Can we find another? This is where we bought your coat. Can we find another like it? Can we find a car like Grandma's?

### Odd one out

Give your child the task of sorting the odd one out, a game that can be as easy or difficult as you like. There are five cups in the dishwasher but only one glass; six apples in the fruit bowl with one banana; a carrot in the breadbox; four animals and one farmer; four pigs and one cow; six cards with letters and one card with a number.

## Sorting

When you pack the food at the supermarket fill one bag with items that your child can put away: make sure they usually go into cupboards that he can reach. Where do the vegetables go? What about the fruit? Can he sort the cans from the packages?

When you have a load of wash, ask your child to sort sweaters from pants, his T-shirts from yours, the red socks from the blue.

There are many categories you can talk about here, and if you don't want to discuss them he will still enjoy sorting.

## A yellow day

Today is a yellow day. Wear your yellow sweater, have scrambled eggs for breakfast, do a yellow painting and play with yellow dough. Pick some yellow flowers from the garden. Have a cheese pizza, followed by peaches and custard, count the yellow cars on the way to playgroup, and stop for a banana milk shake on the way home.

What would you eat on a blue day?

## Who lives where?

Which animals live in the air and which in water? Which live up in the air and which climb trees then come down again? Draw a picture of some trees, grass, sky and water large enough to cover a metal tray. Stick it on the tray. Now cut out some animal shapes – birds, cats, fish – and attach a magnet to each (you can buy these in craft or toy stores). Should the fish go in the trees today?

## In and out

A little bag can be filled and emptied; stacking cups can be put one inside the other; a few candies will make a can rattle. A pocket and a matchbox can be filled with small treasures, and a teddy can keep charge of the toys in the cabinet.

## Under, over, up and down

If your child has a nook under the table, she can be setting tea for the teddies while you are setting tea for the people. Is your child going to eat in teddy world or people world?

## WHAT YOUR CHILD LEARNS

### • Sorting
This helps your child to categorize and to begin to understand that some things can belong to more than one category: a sock can be his and red; a carrot can be a vegetable and something that goes in the fridge. Children love to help. Giving you a hand with grown-up chores enhances their sense of responsibility.

### • In and out
These activities – and countless more opportunities – give your child practice at considering how two items can share the same space one minute and not the next. It also gives him a chance to think about opposites.

### • A yellow day
This reinforces your child's ability to learn colors.

### • Who lives where?
This activity teaches your child a little about the natural world, but it also helps him to categorize and sort groups.

# 8 Learning about space

With a little practice most adults can park a car, and those who live in cities have to learn how to squeeze into spaces of little more than a car's length. And they do. If you stand at your front door, you can probably point in the direction of the nearest shop. You may also be able to point toward more distant places, the nearest town, the capital city or even a distant country. You can take shortcuts, remember the way home, and use a diagram to put together self-assembly furniture. You can design a flower bed, pack the luggage into the trunk of the car and put together an outfit with flair. The basis of such skills is your understanding of space. Engineering and design are also spatial skills, less obviously so is mathematics (or so many believe). Some classify music as well in this way.

## Milestones in spatial skills

### WHAT YOUR CHILD CAN DO

**6 weeks**
- She does not know where she stops and the rest of the world begins.
- She can locate a sound in front of her, but not one behind; she turns to the correct side if she hears a sound, but cannot locate it.
- She probably does not build up a picture of the world; she certainly does not look systematically.

**20 weeks**
- She looks around her more systematically, scanning the entire picture.
- She can locate sounds.
- She does not look for objects she drops.
- She may perceive depth but does not always act as if she can.

**26 weeks**
- She begins to look for things she drops.

**18 months**
- She can use a sit-and-ride, changing direction as she goes; she can push a truck through a gap.
- She orients her hand correctly before grabbing.
- She can find where something is hidden and is able to take account of her own position and movement when searching.

**2 years**
- She can pull a toy behind her.

**3 years**
- Her drawings may be recognizable, but vital elements are often missing and nothing is to scale.
- She describes things as if she is always at the center; she doesn't realize your view may be different.
- She does not search systematically for objects she loses.
- She cannot point to a place which is out of sight.

**4 years**
- Her drawings have few diagonal lines; chimneys tend to sit at an angle to the edge of the page.
- She takes your perspective into account when describing events.

**5 years**
- Children dart and dodge, wrestle and cut across corners when chasing friends.
- Chimneys may still be at an angle to the roof, but there are more diagonal lines in the picture.

**6-7 years**
- Boys start to use more space in play than girls.
- More children, especially boys, now line up their drawings with the edge of the page.
- She can point to places she cannot see, but only adjoining rooms; she may not, for example, be able to point from the family room to an upstairs room.

| **HOW YOU CAN TELL** | **HOW YOU CAN HELP** |
|---|---|
| ● Babies tend to look at their own body rather than distant objects. | ● Lay your baby on her back so that she can see her hands. |
| ● She begins to look at and investigate objects. | ● Interact frequently: show her toys, talk to her often as you move about the room. |
| ● Her eyes follow objects she drops to the floor. | ● Pick objects up when she drops them.<br>● Offer her items to play with. |
| ● Children become mobile.<br>● They hide objects and find them again. | ● Give her a toddler truck and later a sit-and-ride.<br>● Give her simple construction toys and large soft blocks.<br>● Play hide and seek games. |
| ● A child often drags a large teddy behind her. | ● Buy pullalong toys.<br>● Help her to play with bricks and construction toys.<br>● Give her crayons and paper. |
| ● She may draw a head and add a few lines for legs.<br>● She talks about what she is looking at through the window as if you can see out too, even if you are in the next room. | ● Encourage spatial play: drawing, playdough, jigsaws and blocks.<br>● Chase her around the furniture. |
| ● She can give details which tell you where to look. | ● Encourage sand and water play, chasing and other social games as well as model making and building.<br>● Let her push a doll carriage to the park or ride her bike in a larger space.<br>● Encourage her to walk. |
| ● When she is with other children she runs around. | ● Let her play with other children.<br>● Encourage wild play.<br>● Put her drawings on display. |
| ● Her drawings begin to look more grown-up.<br>● If you ask her to, she can point to an adjoining room, the front door and the backyard. | ● Encourage children to do more complex puzzles and construct with smaller blocks.<br>● Allow children to play some distance from you where this is safe. |

# The play of boys and girls

*Gender differences certainly exist in the way children play, but these are not usually apparent in the preschool years*

If you walk into a playground of eight- to ten-year-olds the difference between how boys and girls play is obvious. Girls congregate around the edges, talking and playing traditional games that involve jumping up and down on the spot, like skipping or hopscotch. Balls are bounced or thrown against the wall, rarely kicked or thrown any distance. Girls juggle balls, clap each other's hands in elaborate patterns and accompany all these games with songs. Boys take up the center ground, and even when standing next to each other they shout short instructions and comments: "Over here!," "That's dumb!," "Yes!" Their games use large areas and they race from one end of the playground to the other. Ball games involve kicking and throwing the ball to each other or kicking and running with it over long distances without losing it to an opponent. Games may have chants, but there are no songs.

### When do these differences start?

Although it often seems at nursery school that girls are the first to sit at the activity tables, while the boys head for the bikes and climbing frames, there are in fact no reliable differences between boys' and girls' play in school until they are about seven years old. Those parents who have both sons and daughters might dispute this but, until young children come under the influence of their older peers, boys are less likely to act as boys "should" and girls like girls "should."

### Are the differences marked?

In public, the differences in boys' and girls' play are often great. But the differences in private play are much smaller, suggesting that peer pressure has a role. Nonetheless, the average girl uses less space and talks more as she plays by herself than the typical boy does. There are exceptions, however.

### The drawings of boys and girls

Boys' and girls' drawings differ in both subject matter and composition. Girls put the main subject center stage and arrange the detail symmetrically around it. So, for example, there is a house in the middle, flowers on either side, a sun in the top right and birds on the left.

*Elaborate clapping games, in which hands move in predetermined patterns, accompanied by nonsense rhymes are an activity in which groups of girls engage publicly. In private, a boy may be as willing as a girl to play, but only when his peers can't see.*

*Although once boys are older it can be difficult to persuade them to sit still, a preschooler often has the patience to sit and work out a mechanism or solve a problem for himself. He may take up only as much space as a girl would and chat to himself as he works.*

Boys' drawings, like their games, are widely spread and they use the whole page. There are planes flying, people in all corners and the subject of the painting may come from a combination of elements: a street scene, a battlefield, a railway line or road winding all over the page.

## Playing with dolls

These days the toy stores abound with dolls intended for boys. They are not called dolls, but are sold under brand names or labeled "models" or "figures." The difference in name reflects the mode of play. Dolls intended for girls are designed to be dressed, cared for and put into buggies and cars to be driven about. They sit and play roles in games of house or school, they get married, go to discos but above all they are talked to. Talk is the main feature of doll-play in girls. A story is told, an experience recreated.

Dolls intended for boys are designed for action. They fight, fly in planes, shoot. They rarely talk but, like the boys themselves, they shout, make shooting noises and other sounds appropriate to the battlefield.

## Playing with little worlds

Traditionally girls had dolls' houses; boys forts with soldiers. Train sets and garages edged out the soldiers for boys and animals replaced the human family in the dolls' houses. The houses themselves may have become schools, malls or playgrounds but the major distinction remains. In boys' games the figures go out. In girls' they stay in.

## Construction kits and jigsaws

Market research suggests that construction kits are primarily bought for boys, and jigsaw puzzles for girls. There is a large overlap, especially in the early years. But as children approach school age, in general, girls enjoy toys that require them to fit things into predefined places, while boys build freely. Boys are not more skilled with their hands than girls; it is in seeing how pieces fit together that boys tend to excel.

## What do the differences mean?

There are few differences between men and women that have been found again and again, and most have declined over the years. Higher levels of physical aggression in men (and young boys) is one that remains constant, differences in spatial abilities is another, although this too may be diminishing. Girls' superiority in some tests of verbal skill, like the earlier development of language, and the lower occurrence of language problems such as stuttering and dyslexia remain. This does not mean that such differences are built-in or "in the genes." They may be, but they could also be "in the culture." Although men's and women's lives are now more similar than in the past, children's culture is still distinct, as is the way parents treat sons and daughters. If spatial differences developed through play, they would be immune to society's changing values.

# Rough-and-tumble
*Why messy and physical play are important for young children*

Many young animals play rough-and-tumble games. Put two kittens together and they chase, wrestle, roll around together, stalk, pounce, dodge and dart. Puppies go down on their front paws and bark an invitation to each other, then rush off together, tails wagging. Kittens open their mouths wide when they invite play, as do young monkeys and small babies. Young rats even play "king of the castle," jumping up onto a mound then being knocked off by a partner. If you prevent rats, kittens or puppies from engaging in rough-and-tumble they burst into activity at the first possible opportunity. Stop them playing altogether and they grow up to be inflexible individuals, unable to deal with their peers.

## Letting off steam

Children need to let off steam, not least because they learn so much as they run around. They rarely walk if they can run, or sit still if they can squirm about. A group of normal healthy children who are confined to the car for a few hours explode into exuberant activity when they are set free. The longer you confine them to the car the more surely they "burst." The bigger the "burst" the sillier they become. Bursting is highly contagious. If two or three start racing, others often join in. They push, they scream, they race, they giggle and shout until you are forced to intervene and calm them down. Without intervention it may well end in tears, but it is such fun until it does.

## What are they learning?

Looking at the other members of the animal kingdom who rough and tumble gives a clue as to what children's exuberance is all about. All those animals who live in complex social groups or hunt and eat meat play like this; animals who are solitary and vegetarian (like mice and hamsters) hardly play at all. Those that are both social and hunt – such as dogs – are particularly playful. What have hunting and social living got in common? They have to take note of how someone else moves and predict where and what they do next.

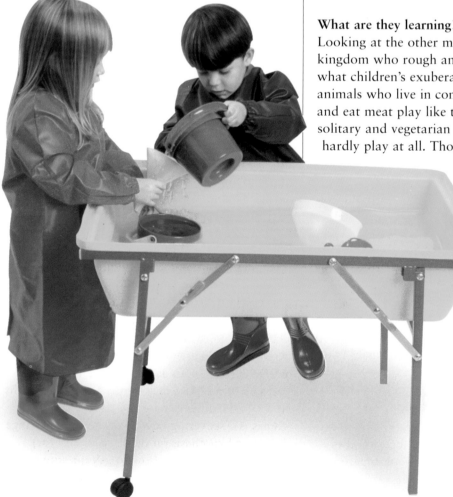

*If you have space or a portable bath, water play is more contained. But the bath or a bowl of water on the table is enough to allow your child to experiment with what floats and sinks.*

*Sand is one of the most versatile materials for your child to experiment with. Buy silver sand from an educational supplier.*

### From large to small scale

Psychologists looking at how human beings understand how to connect objects have found that it is often easier to translate from big to small than to do it the other way around. This suggests that boys and girls may learn more about space from running around with other children than from sitting and constructing buildings from blocks.

### Experimenting

Whether they are running around, climbing or jumping, small children find out "how to" by doing things over and over again. Many of these discovery games involve getting dirty and wet. There is a lot to learn from such games and it would be a pity to stop them.

By stamping in puddles and pouring water from one cup to another, children play through their ideas about the nature of water. Why do some things float and others sink? Are things that float bigger? Does the shape matter? Why does water sometimes soak into objects and at other times stay on the surface? How does water reflect light? When does water flow and which way does it go? The answers are obvious to adults because they have already found them out. None is apparent to a small child.

This does not mean that children solve all the problems that their play poses, or get the right answers; they don't. The answers they come up with tend to be more animistic than an adult's. Water "wants" to flow downhill because it "wants" to return to the other water. Water does not wet her feet because she is wearing her rain boots. These are not adequate answers, but they are good enough for your child for now.

### The nature of solids and liquids

Sand is an interesting material because it can both flow like a fluid and be molded like a solid. Children can pour it from jugs or shape it with buckets. They can build roads through it or watch it flow down hills. Preschool children believe what their eyes tell them, and often sight is fooled. To suggest that children are working out the principles of physics and math as they play is to misunderstand how they think. They learn truths as they experiment, but the main value in such games is discovering how to find out and change a current hypothesis on the basis of contrary evidence. If you know how to ask questions, sooner or later you find the right answer.

# Water play

*Examining how water behaves in a variety of situations is great fun*

A portable plastic tub is a good investment if you have the budget and the space, but most parents don't and this is, in any case, standard nursery and playgroup equipment. Bathtubs are also among the easiest toys to improvise.

## Playing at the sink

Pulling a chair up to the sink must be one of the easiest and surest ways of amusing a preschool child. A sink full of water, a chair to stand on and a few plastic cups is all that you need. Make sure there are no sharp knives or other objects within reach. If the floor is not easy to mop, a drop cloth and newspaper help keep the water from doing damage. The newspaper is useful even if the floor can be mopped because it prevents it from becoming slippery underfoot. A waterproof apron helps protect your child's clothes. Don't give the child too many play objects. Reaching out along the work surface to grab a distant cup is a recipe for an accident. A pitcher or bowl, a couple of cups and a sponge are enough.

## Taps!

Playing with a dripping tap encourages a different approach from playing with a bowl of water. A cup dipped into water is filled in one go, one placed under a dripping tap fills gradually and if left begins to overflow. Part of the delight of such games is filling and emptying, hence the popularity of playing in the kitchen drain or at the outdoor faucet. The kitchen faucet is a poor substitute because often it does not provide the child with the purpose of filling anything. A double sink is better, but nothing quite matches the magic of filling a bucket under the outdoor faucet and lugging it across to the wading pool or a muddy section of the garden.

## In the bath

There is no reason why your child should not have a bath during the day just for playing. There is a huge variety of bath toys. Children need something that floats, something that can be made to sink, something to pour and something to push through the water. Don't forget the washcloth and sponge which can be filled and squeezed out. Check that any dolls that go into the bath will come out unscathed – dolls' hair does not always stand up to being immersed in water.

### TOYS FOR WATER PLAY

- Pitcher with a spout to pour water out and to watch it entering through a small hole
- Cup to catch liquid, scoop it up and tip it out in one fell swoop
- Duck to float, to push about in the water and to ride the waves and currents she makes
- Boat to float and perhaps to sink
- Ping-Pong ball to push underwater and let it leap to the surface
- Sponge to soak up water, drip and squeeze
- Waterwheel to watch it turn like magic as she pours water into the top
- Toy to make her laugh
- Sieve to see the water disappear

## Washing the table

Children do not understand the difference between work and play. As far as they are concerned if it's fun it can't be work. Since water is always fun, water work is seen as a treat not a chore. If children regularly "play" at washing the kitchen table or the bathroom floor they become surprisingly good at it. Show them how to wring out the cloth and sponge and how to wash the area systematically. If they find this hard you can always introduce a drying phase, wiping the table with a kitchen towel after the washing.

## A bowlfull of bubbles

Pour bubble bath or dishwashing liquid into a bowl. Use a whisk to make a good head of bubbles. Give your child a sieve to scoop up the bubbles, take them away then whisk up the water to make some more. Drop pebbles into the bowl and let her fish for them. Show her how to push the bubbles to one side and gather them behind a barrier. Then add some soap or oil and watch them all disappear forever.

## Early swimming

Babies rarely have any fear of the water in their first year, and happily swim underwater if you have the courage to let them go for a moment. But unless you keep up the lessons this early confidence does not always last. Many children

who happily splashed about as babies are nervous of the water as toddlers. Often the problem is getting their face wet. Hair washing may lie at the root of this problem. It is unwise to force a nervous child to put her face in the water of the pool. The noise and bustle of the baths is frightening enough for a small child. Instead let her come to terms with a wet face gradually by encouraging her to take showers and to "swim" in a shallow bath. Just fill the tub with a few inches of water and let her lie on her tummy and splash with her legs. She can even wear her water wings. Once she is confident about the occasional drip on her face, encourage her to dip her head briefly into the water. You can now gradually progress to the swimming pool. Hold her firmly, and let her play on the steps until she feels more confident and the pool has become more familiar to her. Introduced gradually, most children gain confidence, although some will always like the water more than others.

## WHAT YOUR CHILD LEARNS

Water play, above all, is fun, but it has many other useful points to teach your child.

### • Filling and emptying
How fast or slowly a container fills and empties; what makes it overflow; what objects can be poured from most easily; which don't pour at all.

### • How water changes
What makes a bubble; why do bubbles disappear; why do bubbles "fly"; how fast does water spread on a table?

### • Ease with water
The ability to swim gives a child enormous confidence.

# Let's build!

*Making sure that your child has all the materials she needs to realize her building projects*

You don't need a large amount of building materials to satisfy your child's creative and spatial endeavors, but what you do buy or borrow should be chosen with care.

### Big buildings

Nursery schools often have large blocks that children can use to construct dens and walls. Few families can afford to buy enough of these to make realistic structures. You could use large boxes, cereal cartons or some chunks of foam (the kind used for cushions) instead. Ask the store where you buy the foam if they can cut it into blocks about 12 inches (30 cm) square. A dozen blocks and a blanket make a fine den.

### Wooden and cloth blocks

Cheap plastic blocks cause children endless frustration, because unless a block is well shaped it is impossible to build with it. It is difficult for a toddler to place one block on top of another even when the stack is fairly stable and impossible if it is not. Soft cloth-covered blocks stack well because they are much bigger than their wooden counterparts. The fact that they can be squeezed in the hand as the child lifts them into place

*If you have the space, you could build a permanent sandbox in the yard. Just enclose a small area with a low wall – one brick high should be tall enough. You could make a lid from plastic sheeting or wood.*

## THE RIGHT SYSTEM

• **Toddlers**
Young children cannot place accurately so they need a system that is forgiving and/or one in which the pieces are large and can be shunted rather than placed in position.

• **2–3 year olds**
At this stage children can cope with more pieces but still need them to be chunky. They like building systems that grow quickly.

• **4–5 year olds**
A child with building experience can deal with much smaller pieces and more intricate building systems.

• **5–7 year olds**
At this age children may well have a favorite system. They can now use little pieces, but only the most dexterous will be able to deal alone with motors, pulleys and technical construction kits.

makes it easier for the smallest child to deal with something big. Older children may think of them as too babyish, but they are excellent for the youngest builders.

### Making a sandbox

There are only two requirements for a child's sandbox: the sand should be soft and there must be a cover. Soft sand is much smaller grained and smoother to the touch than sharp sand. The cover is necessary to keep out cats. You can buy plastic sandboxes with covers, but check that the lid stays put. A cheap solution is to buy a small trash can to hold the sand, and a large plastic drop cloth. Lay the sheet on the floor and empty the bucket of sand onto it. At the end of the game return the sand and the plastic sheeting to the trash can.

### A shoebox house

Ask your local shoestore for spare shoeboxes; you will need at least four, and preferably six. These can be put into two piles of three to make a double-fronted six-roomed house. Clip between floors with a couple of paper clips. Do the same along the edges of the box that make adjoining walls. If you have enough space you could make a permanent structure by gluing and/or stapling the boxes together.

You can use contact paper to make colorful flooring for each room and paint the interior walls or use ends of rolls of wallpaper or dolls' house paper (this is fairly cheap to buy from model shops). Make furniture and "kitchen units" from matchboxes or the packages used for single portions of raisins or breakfast cereal. Create circular tables from the "spacers" that come with takeout pizzas, and cover them with

## TOYS FOR SANDBOXES

- Small spade for moving sand into buckets and patting it into a mold.
- Spare spade for when friends come to play.
- Large spade for big earth-moving jobs.
- Miniature yard broom to brush the sand back into the sandbox and smooth the surface.
- Rake to make roads.
- Bucket or two to carry sand and make castles.
- Some molds or cutters to make patterns.
- Some plastic cars to play roads.
- Dumper truck to move sand around.
- Water wheel: dry sand will turn the wheel just as water would.
- Coarse sieve: make sure the sand will pass through.
- Funnel to draw patterns in the sand.

small circular cloths. Use pinking shears to cut the material out to avoid the cloth fraying. Make rugs from carpet samples and beds from boxes covered in fabric.

*Dolls' houses are expensive items, and often children do not use them enough to warrant the expense. Give a play one a good "trial run" before buying the real thing.*

# Play me a tune
*Musical activities to enrich your child's early years*

To make music your child first has to learn how to listen (see pp. 50–53 and 168–169 for ideas on improving your child's listening skills). The easiest way to teach her to listen to the rhythm of a song is to bounce her on your knee in time to the beat.

### A toy piano

A toy piano or xylophone is the most common first "instrument" and these are fine for a child to mess about with, but don't expect a tune. Few children ever achieve this. These instruments do, nonetheless, help your child to learn about tones.

## REAL MUSIC LESSONS

Many music teachers believe that the surest way to turn a child off music is to start formal lessons too early. Unless you are willing to put in a huge amount of time and effort there is no point starting your two-year-old on a small violin. Even if you are, the impetus must come from your child. Most children cannot cope with formal lessons before they are about eight years old; in any case, instruments that are blown are best left until your child's second front teeth have firmly grown.

### Join me!

To listen and make music a child has to understand both rhythm and tone. It takes a lot of skill to play the tune, but much less to keep the rhythm. Playing in the rhythm section for a communal sing song, accompanying you as you play the piano, or even shaking a can of rice in time to a tape recording teaches the child the essential pleasure of music making: a joint activity.

### Sand dancing

Lay down a piece of brown paper, and cover it with dry, sharp sand. The child slides on the sand making rhythmic noises. If you put on a record with a good beat she may be able to "play" along.

### Sing a song

Children love to sing. Children under three rarely realize that songs have to have words and tunes. If they enjoy making their own "music" let them do so. There is plenty of time later to fit it into a proper musical mold.

### A shaker

The simplest shakers are just boxes, cans and jars containing rice, small stones, sand or dried beans. By varying the combinations you can alter the sound. Remember to screw the lid on firmly, especially if there is a child under three around. Don't overfill the jar. The best sounds are made when there is enough space for the "music" to resonate.

## Clap along

Children like all sorts of music; the major proviso is that it has to have a beat clear enough to clap along to. Many classical pieces have a very clear rhythm: Ravel's Bolero and Beethoven's Fifth are obvious examples.

## Tambourine, triangle and whistle

If you often play together as a family, you might like to buy some real percussion instruments. Shakers, tambourines, triangles, bells or a simple toy drum are fairly cheap and easy to find. A referee's whistle is another simple instrument which can be played on the beat.

## High low

This is a difficult game that is suitable only for children who have good listening abilities. Sit on the stairs with your child. Sing two notes. If the second note goes up she moves up a step. If it goes down she moves down. Make it as simple as possible at first. Remember young children have a limited range. It is best to use only a few notes. (If you cannot sing two notes in this way, play them on the xylophone.)

## Tap me a tune

Once your child is enjoying "shaking" along with various songs, see if he is able to tap out a tune. Can he tap out "Baa, Baa Black Sheep?" Can he recognize "Three blind mice"?

## Move to the rhythm

Dancing is an excellent way to feel not only the rhythm but also the emotional tone of the music. Let your child dance as informally as she pleases. There is plenty of time to learn how to do it more formally later.

### WHAT YOUR CHILD LEARNS

- The ability to listen is a key skill, on which many later accomplishments – such as reading – depend.
- An appreciation of music is a life-enriching skill.
- Keeping to a rhythm is a prerequisite for gymnastics and dancing.
- Children like to make music; it gives them the opportunity to bang and shake objects and generally make a noise.
- Songs that rhyme help expand your child's vocabulary, and contribute to her prereading skills.

# Playing out

*Games and activities for the most boisterous children to play outdoors*

The best toy a child can find in the yard is another child. Yards just call out for exuberant play. On a bright sunny day ask a friend to bring around his or her children or take yours to the park. It is so much easier to let off steam if there is a playmate to encourage you.

## Wading pools

There is an enormous range of wading pools, from the basic inflatable type to a luxury hard-sided pool with a built-in slide. Whatever you spend on the pool remember that a child should never be left alone in water. It takes very little to drown in. If it is too cold to go into the water the child can have plenty of fun sailing boats and ducks or fishing for leaves.

## Bikes for the yard

Since riding in the yard is usually part of an imaginary game, speed is unimportant – a sit-and-ride is ideal. Look for versions which will fire her imagination. Sit-in cars, tractors, fire engines or bulldozers are ideal. If you often have children over to play it helps if there is more than one vehicle, if you can afford it.

## Follow the line

Draw a chalk line along the driveway and around the patio. Place a piece of string across the lawn. You child's task is to follow it exactly, placing each foot on the line as she goes.

## Walking on flowerpots

Line up a series of strong plastic or terracotta flowerpots. Your child's task is to walk across them – like stepping-stones. This is not as easy as it looks so don't make the pots too high.

## Horse riding

Many children like broomstick horses, riding them around the house and yard and even taking them to the park where they can be tied to the fence. You can buy hobby horses with real heads and a wheel at the back, but these are expensive and not worth it until you are sure your child is interested. In the meantime use a broom. You could tie a cloth over the bristles to make a head and add reins, or simply leave it all to your child's imagination. The child sits astride the broom shank and rides with the brush in the air and the handle trailing on the floor.

## Fishing for leaves

Fill the wading pool with a few inches of water. Add a few leaves or make some fish out of paper or lollipop sticks. Then take out the fishing nets and let her catch the fish then throw them back.

If you live near a stream, you could play this game for real.

### FISHING IN THE POOL

You need only a few props to make plenty of items to float in your wading pool
- Cocktail sticks: you can use these on their own as floats, or fix little sails to corks with them
- Corks – if you fix a sail to the top remember to weight the opposite side or it will overturn
- Popsicle sticks or bits of twigs
- Folded paper: fold squares to make little boats.
- Big leaves
- Coasters
- Individual cupcake foils

## A muddy game

Children love mud. Sand pies are a pleasure and a bucket of water delightful but neither give quite the same pleasure of real mud pies. This is not an everyday game, but more of a once in a while treat. Mud pies work best if you have sticky mud, so sandy or chalky soil are no good at all. A heavy clay soil is ideal.

### WHAT YOUR CHILD LEARNS

**• Wading pools**
These are fun and give an area in which to contain water outdoors. They help increase your child's confidence around water.

**• Walking on flowerpots**
This game improves your child's balance and ability to plan and coordinate action.

**• Fishing for leaves**
This gives your child's play a purpose and increases her ability to aline a net and a leaf. It also reinforces the differences between the objects that float and those that sink.

**• A muddy game**
Mud is versatile and messy; few games offer the tactile satisfaction of making a mud pie.

**• Watering the garden**
This is a grown-up task that children love to imitate, but it also helps them learn about living creatures and start to appreciate that without water flowers die.

## Watering the garden

A little watering can, a dripping faucet and a garden in need of water – or plenty of containers, which require frequent watering in summer: put them together and you keep a child happy for a long stretch. Toddlers tend to water the same plants over and over again, so they need a little watching and directing. Older children can be instructed how to water systematically. You will still need to check, but children are usually more than willing to give a little more water to the plants.

## Garden toys

Follow the advice given on pp. 216–17 when choosing garden toys and remember to provide a soft landing in case a child falls. Bark chippings can be bought at most garden centers and are in keeping with most outdoor styles. A thick pile will not stop a child hurting herself but will prevent serious injury.

# Playing in
*Being boisterous in a small space is not as difficult as it sounds*

Children need to let off steam. Busy parents need peace and relaxation. Unfortunately, the two are incompatible. It would be good if children could confine their noisy play to the backyard or their bedrooms or shout and scream without an audience, but they cannot. There are ways you can both be satisfied, however.

## Making cakes

Even if you rarely bake, it is worth making a tray of muffins or a chocolate cake just to keep children amused on a rainy afternoon (it is easier if you have a mixer). Your child can help you to measure out the ingredients; you put them into the mixer bowl and whisk while he greases the cake pans. You put on the oven while he fills the pans. He licks the bowl while they cook. Then he can wash his hands and face ready to sit down for milk, cake and a chat.

Most cake recipes are quite forgiving: as long as the quantities are in the ballpark of those required they work well. If in doubt just beat them for an extra minute or two. The additional air makes all the difference.

## Setting a time

Set aside a time each day for messy play, say between 11 and 12 in the morning. This is the time when your child can play at the sink, use the Playdough on a drop cloth on the floor, paint or even use an indoor sandbox. Play starts on the stroke of 11 and stops on the stroke of 12. Regimented? Of course. But children love their days to be predictable. The advantage of the precise stop and start is that you do not have cries of "Just another minute, Mommy" when you are wanting to clean up before you go out.

## Jumping off the stairs

What could be easier than heaping a pile of cushions at the bottom of the stairs? Arranging a pile in front of the sofa, perhaps, but that is a little harder on the furniture.

## Sugar!

If you cannot bear the idea of a sandbox in the house – and in a small house it may not be practical to let the children take over all of the available living space – a bowl of sugar or rice acts as a good substitute for dry sand. Just letting it run through the fingers may seem a bit dull to you, but it won't to a two-year-old. Add a jug to pour with, a wooden spoon to stir with and a few cups to fill and it will keep a three-year-old amused too.

## A messy place

There is no point in trying to confine a mess to the bedroom or nursery while you sit in the tidy living room or the immaculate kitchen. Children like to be with adults. On days when a child can't play outside, the answer is to contain the mess to one area. This means not only putting down a large drop cloth, but also enclosing this with some sort of barrier. A large wading pool works well as an indoor sand play area. The bath is a self-contained water play area. Playdough – like real dough – is best confined to the kitchen and if the bathroom is tiled your child can always paint while you take a bath.

## Polishing the floor

This is ideal if you have a wooden, tiled or cork floor. Pour some polish on the floor, then put some old socks on the children (and on yourself if you want to play too). You glide on buffers until the floor is glossy and glowing. You then have to buff up only the edges and corners, but since these receive little wear and tear they rarely need waxing anyway.

## Waltzing on your feet

You may remember this from your childhood. The child puts his feet on top of yours and as the music plays you waltz around the floor. A chair or cushions to fall onto adds to the fun.

## Throwing paper planes

You need a few sheets of paper for this game: the junk mail will provide enough for a squadron of colorful planes. Fold each sheet in half lengthwise. Then fold down the top corners to make the nose. Bend out the wings at an angle to the nose. A little Blu-tack to weight the nose may improve the flight. Whose plane will go the farthest? Try flying them from an upstairs window while the children wait in the yard to catch them.

### WHAT YOUR CHILD LEARNS

**• Setting a time; a messy place**
These make life easier for you without short-changing your child's natural enthusiasm. Children also like routine; it makes them feel secure.

**• Sugar**
Rice or sugar can be poured, sifted and patted into shapes, just as sand can, and is easier to contain.

**• Making cakes**
Baking helps children to understand that ingredients can change when they are cooked. It also gives them the opportunity to make something. The fact that you can all eat the cake together is a bonus.

**• Waltzing on your feet**
This is great fun and helps your child respond to music: should you go faster or slower? Can you both lift your feet at the same time?

**• Throwing paper planes**
This improves your child's hand skills and gives you a chance to play guessing games.

# 9 Learning to use language

Human beings do not have to talk in order to communicate, but words certainly make conveying information and thoughts much clearer. In early life, body language plays a larger part. It is not just faces that show emotions – gestures do, too. You may throw your arms wide in happiness or slump in sadness. You may not even notice that you read many of these signs. But everyone can read the more deliberate signs, such as facial expressions, pointing, touching, shoulder shrugs and hugs and kisses. Children begin to make these signs in the first weeks of life, although they are probably not aware that they do. They start to use signs to communicate intentions at about seven to eight months.

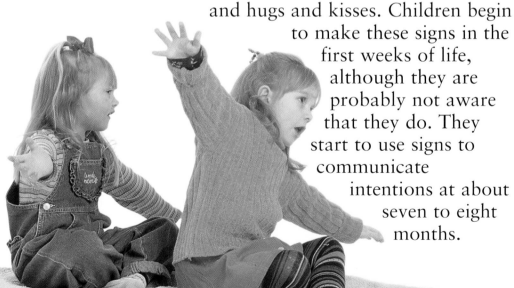

**Milestones in communication**

## WHAT YOUR CHILD CAN DO

### 4 weeks

- A baby smiles or half smiles in his sleep. This is not wind; it reflects the fact that he is moving from a light to deeper sleep or vice versa.
- He shows distress by crying.

### 12 weeks

- If you make a face he will copy it. If you talk he makes lip movements. If you do not let him have his turn he cries.
- He is beginning to smile, but this is not yet a full-faced grin, just a pulling back of the lips (by seven weeks).
- He begins to express rage by angry crying (by seven weeks).
- His smile becomes more frequent and clearly expresses pleasure. At eight weeks a high-pitched voice and a nodding head make a baby smile; by 12 weeks a stationary face does.
- The smile is now a broad-faced grin.

### 6 months

- Your baby watches you, interacts frequently, and kicks, waves his arms, babbles and coos in response to your questions.
- He shows his delight in your company but persists in taking his turn; he soon grows bored if you do not pause to let him have a turn.
- He expresses wariness.
- He laughs out loud, blows raspberries, whispers, growls and yells.
- He begins to look at you to see if you are responding.

### 9 months

- He shows anger and joy (by seven months) and also expresses fear.
- He begins to make signs – lifting his arms to be picked up and banging a spoon to summon dinner.
- He may follow your gaze, looking where you look.

### 12 months

- He has more signs and may begin to point.
- He may lead you to the objects he needs.
- He may tug at a skirt to be picked up.

### 18 months

- He shows elation, anxiety, anger and petulance.

### 2 years

- He expresses shame, defiance and hurt.
- He assembles sentences by combining hand signs with words, flinging out an arm which is equal to saying "Look" and pointing and saying "Cat."

### 3 years

- He expresses pride, love and guilt.
- He understands the emotions of others and responds to the sadness of those he loves.

### 5 years

- He may stand mimicking your pose, and copy your tone of voice.

| HOW YOU CAN TELL | HOW YOU CAN HELP |
|---|---|
| ● By watching how he responds to you: return his smile; talk but wait for a reply. | ● Always respond to your baby's signals. |
| ● By watching what your baby does when you ask him questions or make faces.<br>● By testing out what makes him smile most – is it talking and moving your head or keeping it still? | ● Go in close and talk; let him have his turn.<br>● Exchange facial expressions.<br>● Interact frequently; make him laugh.<br>● Respond whenever he tries to respond to you. |
| ● By watching his interactions with you.<br>● By being sensitive to the emotions he expresses. | ● Be sensitive to his needs.<br>● Laugh when he blows a raspberry; let him know that you think communicating is clever. |
| ● By looking for signs that he is telling you what he wants. | ● Follow his gaze and look at whatever you talk about to him. |
| ● By watching the signs he makes. | ● Expect him to make signs. |
| ● By watching how he uses his face and body when he interacts. | ● Express in words what he shows in signs and facial expressions. |
| ● By watching him in different situations. | ● Continue to be responsive. |
| ● By recognizing what he expresses. | ● Talk about feelings and emotions. |
| ● By noticing that he is using your words and gestures. | ● Play games that help to encourage imitation. |

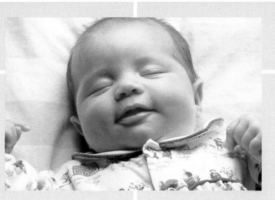

**Milestones in learning to talk**

| | | **WHAT YOUR BABY CAN DO** |
|---|---|---|
| **16** *weeks* | | <ul><li>He moves in time to your voice. He turns to you as you speak and recognizes your voice (by the end of the first week).</li><li>He has no language, but he is learning the basics.</li><li>He makes little mouth movements in answer to your questions (by four weeks).</li><li>He makes "goo" sounds (by eight weeks).</li><li>He can distinguish one language sound from another.</li></ul> |
| **32** *weeks* | | <ul><li>Your baby's skull has developed enough for him to begin to articulate sounds. He starts with vowels and moves on to all the other sounds made in every language.</li></ul> |
| **40** *weeks* | | <ul><li>Your baby begins to show a preference for the sounds he hears in the language(s) spoken around him.</li><li>His babbling begins to have the intonation of language.</li><li>He may say "words" like "Dada" or "Mumum." Although he may occasionally be looking at you when he says it, he will say it in other contexts too. It is not a real word – he is not conveying the information "I'm looking at Daddy."</li></ul> |
| **14** *months* | | <ul><li>He now makes only the sounds found in the languages he hears.</li><li>His babbling has all the rhythm of language.</li><li>He says his first word (any time after eight months). First words generally relate to objects: cats, dogs and buses are popular, as are sounds associated with food such as "Yummm."</li></ul> |
| **21** *months* | | <ul><li>Children add words to their vocabulary; some weeks there are lots of new words, others none at all.</li><li>Most children now have 50 to 200 words.</li></ul> |
| **2** *years* | | <ul><li>He begins to put words together into simple two-word sentences.</li><li>He starts to use "I," "Me" and "You."</li><li>He can follow verbal instructions and listen to simple stories.</li></ul> |
| **3** *years* | | <ul><li>The average child knows 800 words, but still talks in short sentences. If he has something complex to communicate he says it in two or three sentences.</li><li>He uses word order to convey meaning.</li><li>He starts to incorporate the endings and alterations to words which change the grammar and meaning, starting with "ing" (the present progressive) and the plural.</li></ul> |
| **5** *years* | | <ul><li>Most children have acquired all the main grammatical rules of the language(s) they hear by age four and one-half.</li></ul> |

| HOW YOU CAN TELL | HOW YOU CAN HELP |
|---|---|
| ● By recognizing that he responds to what you say. | ● Interact.<br>● Talk. It does not matter that he cannot understand – he needs to hear language. |
| ● By listening to the sounds he makes. | ● Encourage him to babble by talking back. |
| ● By listening: it begins to sound as if he is trying to tell you something. | ● Talk back; encourage him to make sounds and respond when he does, as in "Ughugh"; "You want to be picked up, do you?" |
| ● By listening: it now definitely sounds as if he is trying to tell you something. Parents always hear those first words! | ● Treat his babbles as if he is talking to you. Answer him. Reinforce those first words with translations – "Pst"; "Yes it's a PUSSYCAT." |
| ● By listening, talking and encouraging him to talk. | ● Show him picture books.<br>● Point out items to him and name them.<br>● Always let him know you understand what he means. |
| ● By listening, asking and answering questions. | ● Expand sentences for him so he knows you understand. |
| ● By talking together, and asking questions and using the different parts of speech. | ● Talk to him often and read to him. |
| ● By talking together about the past, present and future.<br>● By expecting your child to be verbally skilled. | ● Encourage him to use different parts of speech by discussing activities you have done in the past and will do in the future. |

# Taking turns

*Conversations are important when you talk to a baby: one who does not receive the chance to participate soon becomes bored*

Talking to a baby – even a newborn one – comes naturally, even though you know that he cannot possibly understand what you are saying to him. Psychologists who have watched parents with small babies report that they move in close to the child when they talk, look him in the eye and nod their head up and down as they talk. They therefore provide just the right image for a child who sees movement better than stationary things, and can focus only on objects 10–12 inches (25–30 cm) from their eyes. Parents also raise their voice an octave or two. "Hello" they say in a high pitch, trying to catch the baby's eye. They wait just long enough for the baby to say "Hello" in reply, then carry on with the conversation – "How are you this morning?"; pause for reply; "Did you have a nice sleep?"; pause for reply; "You did have a nice sleep."

### It is nothing the baby says

At first a baby has no control over what you say to him. He does not "tell" you what to say or how to say it; that seems to come naturally. At some point in the first few weeks, however, babies start to respond, showing an interest in what adults say. They act as if they understand. They do not. What they understand is that you are their friend.

### Talking and answering

It does not matter what you say to a small baby. It just matters that you say something. Within a week or two a baby not only starts to respond to your talk, but he also demands his turn. At first his responses are little movements of the mouth. Later they incorporate all his developing skills. Later still words will take the place of hand signs, facial expressions and noises. At the moment the meaning does not count: all that matters is that you and he have a conversation.

### It works both ways

A conversation is a two-way interaction. If your baby does not have his turn it is a monologue and babies – like adults – quickly grow bored with someone who drones on and on. Conversations have all sorts of rules. People who are listening are supposed to look at the speaker and meet his or her eye from time to time. They should indicate when they want their turn (by glancing away and meeting the eye again), and speakers are meant to signal when they are prepared to hand over (if they want to hog the stage they don't meet the listener's eye). Conversations are carried out at certain distances apart, with each culture having its own rules. Close friends

*Although your baby cannot talk, she can make her wishes known in gestures. At first she turns her head away when she dislikes something; later she may push the spoon to one side.*

*Talk about the weather, the price of shares, the political news. Chat about the plants in the garden or ask for advice on what to have for lunch.*

*The important point is not what you say – he does not understand – but that you say it, and within an actual two-way interaction.*

and family huddle together. Parents and tiny children go closest of all. When people talk with faces close, they also touch more as they converse.

### My turn now

A baby who never had a turn in a conversation would take no notice of anyone else. If you talk to a baby without pausing, he looks away and loses interest. If you talk without a single pause he starts to cry. The same goes for smiling and laughing. A smile followed by a pause is reassuring, a laugh that stops gives a good feeling. But a smile that goes on and on becomes sinister, as does a laugh. Babies react in similar ways. If you keep on smiling they will start to scream.

### Putting the parts in place

By the time they are six or seven months old children know that dialogues use sounds and usually add noises to their interactions with adults. By seven to nine months they realize that the interactions convey information, and when this happens they begin making signs (see pp. 158–59).

### Words and action

Words that are just said are not really language, but noises that sound like the words you know. When a six-month-old says "Dada" you are delighted. But the child does not know what Dada means, he just knows that you are pleased when he says it. Real words are put into the context of conversations. They are intended to convey a precise meaning. "Psst" is always said when the cat is near, "Dodo" when he sees the dog. When he says these things he expects you to respond and to understand what he is referring too.

He will often point as he talks. He will always look at what he and you are talking about. Children as young as six or seven months follow the direction you are pointing in and look at what you are indicating. Some children bury words in strings of babble, but always wait for you to acknowledge that you understand. Others simply point at the object they want to talk about then say their new word. It is the context that makes it clear they are really talking. The art of conversation tells them when and how to say it.

*Your baby may stick out his tongue, smile, wave his arms, coo, gurgle and blow*

*raspberries. These gestures are the basis of conversation.*

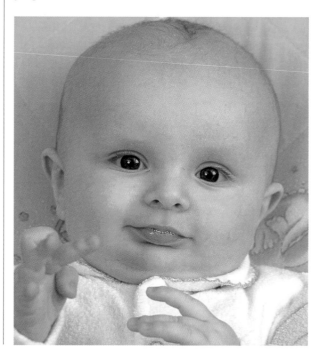

# Early language

*Even before a baby can talk, he communicates with his parents and siblings through signs, looks and gestures*

Communication is not simply about using words with meaning; to a baby who does not have the skills to talk, communication is about signs.

### The first sign

Few parents miss their child's first word, but many don't register their first sign. You may suddenly realize that his little bottom is bouncing up and down before you start to jog him on your knee or that he has raised his arms as you begin to pick him up. By about eight months most children have one or two signs; by eleven months they may have many more.

### The first word

Babies usually start with names. Among the most common are a name for caregivers and a word he uses for cats, dogs, cup or bottle and food. Sometimes these are close to real words; other times they are indistinct. Many children use the sounds animals make to name them, or the noise of eating for food. So whatever language he hears around him a dog will be something like "Ohoh" and food something like "Yummm." Do not try to correct him. This is perfectly all right and he will learn the correct word in time. At the moment what he needs most is encouragement and feedback. He needs to know you understand. So say "Yummm

*By his first birthday your baby is likely to have a repertoire of signs. The most common early signs are "Pick me up," "Bye bye," "Look," "More" and "No."*

dinner!" or "Ohoh – yes, it's a dog." This carries on the conversation, rewards him by telling him you understand and gives him the right word. Such a response is perfect and gives your baby every incentive to build on his newfound skills.

### Adding words

At 14 months the average child has only four or five words, but by the age of two this has increased to more than 200. Once children start to use words in quantity they add 30 to 50 a month. However, few of them learn at a steady pace. They may say 10 new words in a morning and then add nothing for a week or more. This is followed by a further period of rapid progress, then another pause.

## WHEN TO START WORRYING

If you are worried that your child is somewhat slow starting to talk, it is always worth asking for a hearing test whatever his age, and especially if he has a history of ear infections. Because hearing loss can be specific – your child may not be able to hear certain ranges of sounds while clearly picking up others – it is often difficult to identify problems. Children who develop dyslexia are often late starting to speak. If there is dyslexia in the family – and it does tend to run in families – late articulation but good understanding of word meanings may be an early sign of dyslexia. It was in my daughter's case.

## Picking out words

Children pick out their first words by listening for the emphasis, which is why many children call an elephant an "e-phant" and a giraffe a "raf." But although he says "e-phant" he may still expect you to pronounce it correctly. He may even emphatically say "e-phant" back to you if you talk about e-phants to him. Only when you say elephant properly is he happy about your speech.

## Understanding and saying words

Most children understand many more words than they can say and may be able to obey precise instructions while still saying few words. Others can say a word almost as soon as they know what it means. Quite a lot of the variation in the speed that children learn new words, and the clarity of their early speech, comes down to their ability to articulate words clearly. Researchers investigating how many words children understand before they can speak have found that 13-month-olds look at the objects their parents name. Adults tend to look at whatever they are talking about, too. So children start by looking at what you are focusing on and assume that the sounds you make refer to what they see.

## The three bears rule

The first words a child learns always follow the three bears rule. The word he learns is not too small and precise (poodle) nor too big and general (animal) but just right – dog. Basic words like "dog" and "chair" are easy to understand. You can point to plenty of examples and call them all by the same name. They are not exactly alike, but similar enough to fall easily into a class.

Words that refer to what he perceives as one class of objects are always easiest to learn. Learning what "three" or "yellow" means is much harder because the concepts of number and color are more abstract (see pp. 234–35).

## Learning about poodles

Once your child has learned the word dog you can teach him that some dogs are poodles. If he has a concept and you use a new name he assumes it refers to a subgroup. He will test out just what the group "poodles" includes by calling all curly-haired dogs by this name and seeing if he is right.

## Daddy is the mail carrier

Children often over-extend the meaning of words when they first start to use them. Learning a language from scratch is, after all, a difficult task. It has been calculated that the average child learns something like 13 new words a day between 18 months and two and a half years, so it is not surprising to find that they sometimes confuse meanings. Children do not stop to understand a word before they use it. They grab it, use it and then work out the precise meaning. So at first all men are "Daddy" and only later are they mail carriers, bus drivers and the real "Daddy."

He does this by taking note of what he hears. If he calls the mail carrier "Daddy" and you say "That's the mail carrier" he makes a note that "daddy" is wrong although he may not remember the word "mail carrier." He now has an empty concept ("The man who brings letters") waiting for a name. After a few more occasions of matching the word to the man he will get it right.

*The subtle differences between a truck, semi, car, tractor and fire engine are beyond a child who is just learning to talk. At this stage, most children have one or two generic words for all wheeled vehicles.*

# From words to sentences

*Most children can say many single words before they start to put them together to make sentences*

The early vocabularies of most children consist of many single words, most of them nouns. But not all children learn in this way. For a minority of children, first words consist of phrases such as "Stop it," "Want it," which are said quickly, as if they were a single word. Such children tend not to name the objects around them, but use their earliest words in social interactions to gain attention or describe their action.

### Word and sign combinations

Just as the earliest "words" are really signs, so the earliest sentences are combinations of signs and words. Pointing to the dog he says "Dodo." His meaning is clear: "Look, there's a dog." If he puts his hands out and says the word "cookie," he means "give me a cookie." He may also use words like sentences, even though he says them one at a time. For example, he might say "car" and, after you have repeated the word, "go."

### Two-word sentences

Most children have mastered about 200 words before they begin to speak in sentences, which happens at about 21 months old. The word count rather than the age is important. Once under way they progress rapidly. It is not unusual for a child to use 100 new two-word sentences in a month. The combinations they use express ownership ("Mommy coat"), action ("Car go"), location ("There chair"), demands ("Give cookie"), name and emphasis ("That house") and ask questions ("What this?").

### Telegraphic speech

Whatever language children learn to speak, their earliest sentences miss out the grammatical morphemes that modulate meaning, such as the "s" that marks the plural and the "-ed" that changes the tense of a verb, as well as prepositions such as in or on, possessives ('s) and articles (a, an, the). These omissions are what give their language a telegraphic quality.

### Using the grammar they hear

In English, word order is often used to denote the subject and object of a sentence, and children learning to speak English use a rigid word order to express meaning. So they say, for example, "Mommy kick" emphasizing that Mommy is the subject, and "kick ball" when stressing that the ball is the object that is to be kicked. Japanese does not use word order to denote subject and object (it uses particles instead), so children learning Japanese do not use a rigid word order at this telegraphic stage. They concentrate instead on putting the particle in the right place.

Research suggests that children all over the world learn the grammar of their languages in the same order. First they learn the present progressive, which is used to denote ongoing process. In English this is the "-ing" as in "sitting." This is followed by the prepositions in and on, then the plural and irregular past tense words such as "went." They then learn the possessive (in English 's), articles (a, the) and the regular past tense ("-ed"); any other grammatical rules follow.

*Familiar objects provide most of a child's early words – book, teddy, cup, crib – because most children use words to name the items around them, rather than to describe their actions or as a means of interacting with others.*

## Making mistakes

When children are learning these rules they often learn the irregular parts of speech first. So, for example, they learn "went" before they learn "walked." But once they have learned the rule "add -ed to express that something has already happened" they apply it even when they should not. So they tend to say goed and runned. Likewise they talk of sheeps and foots. When you hear these mistakes you can be sure that your child has learned the rule.

## The growth of vocabulary

Throughout the preschool years a child's vocabulary continues to grow. By 30 months he has about 450 words. By three that has doubled and by five it has more than doubled again. By six most children have a vocabulary of about 2,500 words. If you add names to that vocabulary the total would be even larger.

At three and a half years old, your child will now be able to use auxiliary verbs – "I am walking" – and express complex negatives such as "This isn't ice cream" and ask questions beginning with "what," "why" and "which." By the time he is five he will be able to tackle such complex statements such as "I will go although I don't want to" and "It was this one, wasn't it?" He is not confused by such complex statements as "James knew that John was going to win the race" and "The man showed the boy the cat."

*An adult who finds he has to talk, work and interact in a foreign milieu often has difficulty coping. But children immersed in another linguistic world manage well; more adept at making themselves understood without words, they also rapidly acquire the language that complements their skill.*

## A SECOND LANGUAGE

If children move to a new country they learn the language they hear spoken around them almost effortlessly. Not only do they learn quickly, they speak it as a native would. Adults find learning a new language hard work, and few ever talk like a native speaker. There is always a hint of an accent, just as many adults carry the trace of a childhood regional accent even though they have not lived in that area for many years. Languages are particularly easy to learn before children reach puberty, and much harder afterward.

Children who grow up hearing more than one language spoken around them learn to speak both. They don't seem to find this in the least confusing and can rapidly switch between the two. Studies suggest there may be a small delay in the first year, but that by the time they start school they are speaking both languages as well as children who have learned only one. If a child is learning to speak his mother's native language and his father's – different – mother tongue, confusion can be reduced in the early stages if each parent addresses him in his or her own language. Once the child is competent he will rapidly switch between the two languages.

# Speaking to you; speaking to his peers

*A child's way of speaking to his parents and other grown ups is different from the way he addresses his friends*

A child expects an adult to understand what he says, and when the two know each other well that child can usually convey his meaning. You fill in and expand your child's sentences because you can take the context into account. Often the words a child uses have a range of meanings. The phrase "Tom yard" may mean:

*Tom is going out to play in the yard*
*Tom wants to go out to play in the yard.*
*Tom was playing in the yard.*
*Tom has drawn a picture of his yard.*
*This is Tom's yard.*

Not only do you manage to pick out the right meaning but you also let him know that you understand what it is he is trying to say. Children know what they want to say and look surprised if you repeat back their words instead of expanding their telegraphic speech into the sentences they mean to say. So, for example, your child will expect you to say "Yes! Tom was playing in the yard."

*It is always easier for children to talk about topics that are part of their common experience, such as TV and videos. If they all watch the same stories they all know the rules and no one has to explain the story line to the other. They just need to play it through.*

### Knowing what to say but not saying it

Small children also expect you to pronounce what they want to say correctly – even if they do not. So, for example, a child who says "fevvy" rather than "ferry" will expect you to get the pronunciation correct. If a child says "Go fevvy," you answer "Yes, we are going on the ferry."

Sometimes it can be difficult to work out what a child intends, and this can be frustrating. He might say "Fis." Puzzled, you might answer "Fis." At this point the child is likely to correct you: "Fis." However, if you then realize he is trying to say fish and say so, he will smile because you have pronounced it correctly. But he will still say "Fis."

### Why can't he say it?

Children cannot speak in long sentences because they do not have the memory to organize them. So if they want to convey a complex idea they have to break it down into chunks small enough for them to organize. Instead of "Tom and Daddy are going to town in the car," your child says: "Tom town. Daddy car. Going town."

When a child listens he does not need to organize any of this, so he can take it in in one sentence. This does not mean he always gets it right. He is dependent on word order to understand the subject and the object of the sentence. So he is fine with "The puppy followed Tom home," but if you say to him "Tom was followed home by the puppy" he will ignore all the little words like "was" and "by" and think that Tom followed the puppy home.

*By the time they are two and a half children are good at interacting as they play together. They confine most of their conversation to times when they are engaged in joint activities, or are at least physically close to each other, although they do not always check that the listener is looking at them.*

## How parents speak to children

Motherese is the name given to the language mothers (and fathers) speak to their toddlers. Motherese is characterized by short, well-formed and very simple sentences that are spoken slowly and clearly. Words are selected so that each refers to something concrete, and are often repeated. You might say "Look at the car. That is a big car." Parents look toward the objects they mention, and rarely talk about things that are totally absent. Even four-year-old children adjust their speech in this way when talking to siblings. As adults do when talking to pets and lovers!

## Baby talk

Children often find it easier to repeat two sounds than to say one. So at first they say doubles, such as "Dodo" for dog. A little later they may change that second "Do" for another sound, making something like "Dogee." Children know what the right word is and when they are ready they use it. As children can cope with a second language they are seldom floored by different words.

## THE LANGUAGE OF DEAF CHILDREN

All children start to communicate using signs. Hearing children then switch over to words, letting signs play a lesser role. Deaf children who are taught sign language learn at a similar rate to speaking ones. Indeed, some studies have shown that they tend to learn faster. Most deaf children sign their first words by nine months and are putting signs together to make sentences by about 17 months.

Vocabulary can increase rapidly. In one study a child who had 384 signs one month had 604 four months later. The advantage does not last, and by two the difference between talking and signing children has disappeared.

## Language between children

It is not surprising, given the limitations of children's understanding and production of language, that the under twos find it difficult to converse. What they say is only really clear to those who know what they intend to say. However, since they are often delighted by each other's company, none of this much matters.

To be effective communicators children need to engage the attention of their listener, to be sensitive to whether they understand and to adapt what they say to make this possible. Much can be helped by gesture, looks and activity. Most of the words that one child says elicit a response from the other and, as children become competent, they adjust their speech to make sure that the listener understands. If the listener does not respond they repeat the message and may simplify it. These skills increase with age; by four years old a child who does not understand asks for clarification.

# Interactive games for babies or toddlers

*Expand your child's ability to conduct conversations by taking part in them*

Children learn the patterns and intonations of a language by listening to it. Listening to the radio will not teach them the meaning of words they do not yet know – or show them how to talk to someone – but it will teach them this pattern and rhythm. Later, when they have grasped the basic elements of language, radio programs and tapes can be used to increase their vocabulary and encourage them to love the sound of words.

## Party piece

All babies on the brink of language need a party piece, an action they can carry out in response to a question, something to show off to the neighbors. A party piece is good to feel clever and competent.

*How tall are you?* Stretch arms above the head.
*Wave bye bye.* Wave the hand.
*Blow me a kiss.* Blow on the palm of the hand.
*Give Grandma a big kiss.* Give a kiss.
*How does Gabby dance?*

## WHAT YOUR CHILD LEARNS

**• Where is?**
Asking them to find objects gives a way of "saying" they understand – and checking that they do – without having to voice words they cannot yet articulate.

**• Tickle my tummy**
Tickling is always interactive; it is impossible to tickle oneself. Asking questions is how children learn.

**• Incy wincy spider**
The actions make the rhyme memorable and everyone can join in. Rhyme helps a child distinguish small sounds: good for listening, speaking and, later, reading.

## Where is?

*Where is Tom's tummy?*
*Where is Tom's arm?*
*Where is your knee?*
*Can you touch your nose?*
*Where is Mommy's elbow?*
*Let's go and look for your shoes.*
*Which one is the baby pig?*
*Can you spot the cow?*

Match the question to your child's level of skill and remember that most children can understand many more words than they can say.

## Incy wincy spider

*The incy wincy spider climbed up the water spout,*
Put alternate fingers and thumbs together and climb the hands up into the air.
*Down comes the rain and washes spider out.*
Mime the rain falling.
*Out comes the sunshine, dries up all the rain,*
Mime the sunshine.
*So incy wincy spider climbs up the spout again.*
Mime the climbing action.

See pp. 126–27 for more action rhymes.

## Tickle my tummy

Because babies between six and 18 months adore being tickled this is an especially good game for encouraging them to "ask" for more or to show their anticipation with a small sign. Look out for these little signs and indicate to the child that you have seen them.
*"Are you ready for that tickle?"* Wait.
*"Yes I can see you are."* Wait.
*"Here comes the airplane to get that tummy."* Wait.
*"Here it comes."*

## Eat that peach

Small babies may not be able to say "Dog" when they see the picture – or peach, stairs or drink. But they may show you what the picture says by miming the appropriate action.
Stroke the rabbit.
Eat the peach.
Pat the dog.
Drink the juice.

## Looking at books

First books should have good clear pictures of familiar objects. Animals are always favorites, but at this age so are household objects like beds and cups and objects he sees on his walks such as cranes, trucks and cars. Point to each picture and say the name clearly. If you put the name in a sentence emphasize it. "Look here is the CAT." Ask questions to coax him to point: "Tom, can you see the CAT?"

## Dropsey

The old game of dropping the toys from the high chair rapidly develops into a flirtatious game of willpower and social exchange. He drops, he looks at you. You look back. He stretches out his hand. You say "You want me to pick it up?" He stretches out his hand again. He makes a noise. You give in, pick it up and give it back. He grins. He looks at you. He drops, and so on and so on.

### WHAT YOUR CHILD LEARNS

**• Eat that peach**
This reinforces word recognition and improves your child's vocabulary and comprehension. These actions are "sign" words.

**• Looking at books**
Books are invaluable in teaching your baby about many aspects of the world, and skills in almost all areas of development are enhanced by access to a variety of books. See p. 172 and pp. 228–231.

**• Dropsey**
Babies love repetition; this game provides wonderful social interaction.

# Dolls and teddies

*There are never enough friends to play all the games your child enjoys; dolls and teddies can fill many of the gaps*

Stuffed toys and dolls are more than simply friends and props for games; despite the fact that they cannot talk back, they are an excellent way for your child to practice talking, and they offer a ready audience as he tries out his verbal skills.

### Going for a drink

You will need a few small farm animals, some grass (a piece of green felt is fine) and a pond. The pond is easy to make by wrapping foil around a small piece of cardboard, or use a makeup mirror. Show him how each of the farm animals go down to the pond for a drink.

### Friends

Dolls and teddies are for talking to. Even before a child can speak many words he can put a spoon to a teddy's mouth and say "Eat up." Some children do not need the stimulus of a doll to practice talking. They go through the routines and patterns of speech in bed at night, happily taking both sides of a conversation or simply trying out the variety of sounds that might be said. Others

never do this. For them a doll or teddy who can act as their friend provides someone to talk to when everyone else is busy.

### Toys that do tricks

In the first year actions speak much louder than words. Here are a few examples of characteristics you can give toys; there are many more.
A teddy who will eat up his vegetables.
A doll who always says no to ice cream.
A frog who jumps.
Cars that go "vroom."
A donkey who says "Eeyore" and kicks.
A dog who licks his bowl clean.
Squirrels who steal crackers.
A teddy who looks at books and listens to stories.

The more actions he is shown the more "action words" your child learns, but do not crowd him. Introduce just a few and if he shows interest repeat them. Be consistent. Teddy and dolly always sit at the table for certain meals. Teddy is

---

## WHAT YOUR CHILD LEARNS

**• Toys that do tricks**
These help your child to understand what actions mean. In time, copying these actions will give him something to "say."

**• Going for a drink**
This helps your child to sort animals that at first glance are quite similar, such as cows, sheep and horses. As he begins to know the animals by name, introduce the sounds they make too.

given his vegetables every time. Dolly is always offered ice cream but politely turns it down. Dog always has his dinner in a bowl.

## Props for friends

Toddlers and preschoolers like imitation. They chatter if they copy activities in which you talk. So fetch teddy a dish and spoon and he can be fed. Bring out the baby bath so he can bath dolly. Make him a bed to tuck them in at night. You can buy all these props but since size and scale are irrelevant to most young preschoolers it is not necessary. A plastic dish and spoon, an old baby bottle and the chair he used before he could sit can all be recycled for a family of dolls. You can make a bed for a doll from a shoebox, and one for a teddy from a supermarket box.

## Dolls' hospital

The main prop for a hospital is plenty of beds – ask at the shoestore. Make bandages from scraps of cotton (or buy the real thing). Red dye on the bandage that you wrap around a doll's head makes the patient look more convincing. Bandage up a few legs and arms. Give each patient a chart made from stiff cardboard and paper clips. A doctor's kit would be a good addition. If your child does not have one, make a thermometer from a pencil (just wrap it in contact paper). Buy a toy watch and show him how to take the patient's pulse.

## Boys' dolls

Most boys speak little to their dolls; their games with their dolls are about movement and action, not words. But boys do talk as they play. They chatter as they build various structures, dress up, climb, jump and listen to stories. They also talk to their teddies and soft toys.

## Baby dolls

Baby dolls elicit lots of conversation, because children copy parenting activities in doll play – and these always include conversation! Whether the doll is in her buggy/cart, her shopping trolley or at school, the child is probably talking to her.

## Fashion dolls

There are more fashion dolls sold each year than there are girls under seven. Most girls have one at some stage and many have two or three. Parents do not always approve, but these dolls usually stimulate both social and verbal play.

## WHAT YOUR CHILD LEARNS

Dolls and teddies enhance skills in many areas.

### • Conversation
A child practices what he hears and repeats conversations with his stuffed toys and dolls.

### • Action
Parenting actions, in particular, are usually played out with stuffed toys – feeding, dressing, bathing, putting to bed. At the same time as he is imitating your actions, your child is mimicking your words, increasing his vocabulary and learning how to take part in the to and fro of conversation.

### • Hand skills
Bandaging a doll's arm and putting shoes, shorts, a dress or a jacket on a boy's or fashion doll require precise hand movements.

### • Spatial skills
Your child is almost certainly talking to the doll being wheeled to the park. Pushing the doll there is also improving your child's spatial awareness, as he steers the buggy down the road.

# Words, words, words

*Your child does not understand the meaning of every word you say, but using unfamiliar words in context will help her to do so*

Bombarding your child with words she does not understand does not enhance her vocabulary. But if you can repeat words in everyday situations, she will start to copy your speech.

## A running commentary

When you sit together sharing an activity or a space describe to her what you are doing in simple terms.
*I'm going to get the egg out of its shell to put in the cake mix.*
*I'm looking for a bigger brick to put here.*
*I'll draw mine with the green pen.*
*I'm going to wash the dishes.*
*I'm looking for my shoes.*

## Talking about playing

Sometimes you need to comment on what your child is doing, either by asking a question directly or by making a comment to elicit a reply.
*That is a great house you're drawing.*
*Why are you painting that green?*
*The man on the tractor looks ready to drive off.*
But don't overdo it! Sometimes children like to do their own thing without having to explain them to you or think about why. So, sometimes say nothing at all.

## Asking questions

Some questions have an obvious yes or no answer. But if you ask in a more open-ended way, your child has to think about the answer – and say more to you.
*How did you make that tower?*
*I wonder if that little man could ride in the boat?*
*Can you think of another way to do that?*
*Do you remember another story a bit like that?*
*Now where can we find that…*
*What do you think will happen if…*
*I can't get mine right… .How did you do it?*

## Poems, rhymes and fairy tales

Children love the rhythm and rhyme of poetry, even if they do not always understand the meaning. It is the verbal equivalent of watching TV, relaxing the child in a pleasing – but important – way. Poems introduce the pleasures of words to children, and also prime them in rhyme. The often-repeated fairy tales – as long as you tell them in exactly the same way each time – have a similar effect.

## Encouragement

Everyone likes praise, but toddlers are especially pleased if caregivers tell them they have done something well. Encouraged by your comments, your child will often delight in telling you how she did it. Don't always use the same words.
*I like that. Show me how you did it.*
*That's amazing. What did you do next?*
*Is that for me? Thank you, it's beautiful.*
*Wow, that's enormous. Do you think you can fit an elephant in there?*
*That's smart. I thought that was too difficult for you. I was wrong!*

## TROUBLESHOOTING

**My son is now three, but he is still not talking clearly. Do you think I should consider speech therapy?**

Many children have difficulty pronouncing certain sounds and they do not pronounce words in a mature way until they are six or seven. One problem is that the mouth, palate and vocal apparatus mature slowly and are not like those of an adult until the child is six years old. The other is that the brain processes that control articulation are also immature. It is difficult to judge whether your son has a serious problem without hearing him speak. If you are worried, it is worth having your child examined by an expert.

### Telephone

Four or more people sit in a circle. The first person whispers a short story to the second. The second person whispers it to the third and so on until the story comes back to the originator. The bigger the circle the more the story changes.

### Something to talk about

Outings are a focus for later conversation. Here are a few suggestions which make talking points. A trip on the bus (if you usually use the car). Going up the escalator in a department store. A walk in town at night, or walking down the street when the Moon is behind the houses. A visit to town to see the Christmas lights. Splashing in the puddles after rain.

### Pull the cloth

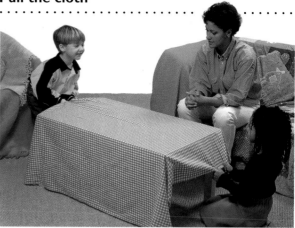

This is a game for at least two people (it's more fun with three or four). Everyone sits around a table covered with a cloth or an old blanket. Each person takes turns to saying "Pull" or "Let go." The next player has to do the opposite. It is surprisingly hard to do right. You can tell who makes a mistake because they either gain or lose the cloth.

## WHAT YOUR CHILD LEARNS

**•Talking about playing**
This shows you are interested in what your child is doing and it tells her that language should be used to describe what she is doing.

**• Poems, rhymes and fairy tales**
In time listening to poems and rhymes helps your child to break down the sounds that make up words, a vital skill for correct pronunciation and later reading.

**• Something to talk about**
Special outings – or at least those that are not often repeated – usually have their own vocabulary. In addition, preschoolers tend to remember these more readily than routines they go through every day.

**• Pull the cloth**
This teaches your child the importance of listening; it is also a great social, interactive game.

**• Telephone**
The differences each time the message is passed on are small, perhaps only one or two syllables. This game helps your child to isolate these different noises in a string of sounds, an important prereading skill.

# Talking games

*Playing games in which talking is the point improves your child's verbal skills*

Although most children talk about what they are doing a great deal of the time, you can still introduce games in which the object is to talk – describing actions, remembering events and encouraging listening.

## Stories without books

Small children always like a story in which they are the hero. Here are a few ideas you might use.
His adventures with a frog who saves the world and then always eats his fly sandwiches.
The terrible things he did when he was two.
How you both went into town to buy the coffee.
The day he found a lion in the yard.
How he lost – and found – his teddy.
The carpet that could fly him to magic places.

## History

Even tiny children have a history, and since they can rarely remember it they love to be told. Pick out some highlights to tell.
How he used to kick in your tummy when you had a bath.
How he screwed up his eyes and cried when he was born.
How he used to spit out his carrots.
How he used to crawl and hide behind the sofa, and once you thought he was lost.

## And the consequence was...

This game is usually played on scraps of paper, but smaller children will enjoy just saying something silly to continue the story. Take it in turns.

| | |
|---|---|
| *A man* | Daddy |
| *Met a woman* | Snow White |
| *He said to her* | Do you eat worms? |
| *She said to him* | Is it time for breakfast? |
| *And the consequence was* | They made a big pot of soup |

## The yes, no game

The task here is to avoid saying either yes or no. It is surprisingly difficult.
*Are you three?*
*Do you have a brother?*
*Is this your shoe?*
*Is Daddy home yet?*
*Did you remember to clean your teeth?*
It may be necessary to let him make a couple of mistakes – and strike out on three.

## Making choices

If you make a choice you are involved. A child who selects which bread to buy is part of the shopping trip. Of course you cannot let him choose everything; most parents do not have time for such leisurely shopping. But a few choices make him feel this is his activity too. He could:
Pick the apples in the self-serve section.
Decide which can of tuna to buy.
Decide which flavor jam to get.
Look for the toothpaste you always buy.
Look for the aisle that has the cat food.

## A plane in the family room

When adults look back on the vacations they took as children, it is often the memory of the journey that is most clear, perhaps because of the high pitch of excitement generated before departure. When today's adults were young, most vacation journeys were made by car; although children now are more likely to travel by plane, it is still a novelty for most. The vital ingredients for a pretend plane journey are:

Seats with passengers (stuffed toys sitting on cushions will do).
Dinner on a tray (save the trays from prepacked fruit or vegetables).
Ear phones (use some dark wool if you don't have any headsets; if you know a frequent traveler ask him or her to save those often given free).
A ticket.
A passport.
A hat for the air steward.

## Plans

Planning is difficult, especially when it is hard to hold information in your mind for long. Language helps, but preschoolers are still not good at it. Help your child to realize that everything has a plan by discussing:
The plan for the day?
The plan for getting dressed?
What you are having for lunch?
Where you are going shopping?
How you will travel to the park?

## WHAT YOUR CHILD LEARNS

**• Stories without books**
These improve your child's imaginative skills as well as encouraging verbal communication. Because there are no pictures to remind him he has to concentrate hard.

**• Making a choice**
You can use this as an opportunity to expand your child's vocabulary – is he buying red apples or green, sliced bread or uncut, bagels or muffins? It also improves his observational skills (this is the type of toothpaste we have) and helps his memory – the aisle after the cereals has the cat food.

**• The yes, no game**
This encourages listening, as well as expanding your child's vocabulary by making him search for alternatives to "Yes" and "No."

**•  A plane in the family room**
This helps your child's memory and encourages role play: one day he is the passenger, the next the steward.

**• A hotel under the stairs**
This also improves your child's memory and stimulates role play, as well as reminding him of some words he may not have known before and may not often use – reception; welcome; receipt; porter.

## A hotel under the stairs

Small children cannot always find the language skills to talk through experiences, so they play them through instead. This is a more sophisticated version of an action standing in for a word. Vacations are always packed with new experiences, and without going over some of them they will probably slip from your child's memory. Make a hotel in a quiet corner. The most important ingredients for a hotel are:

A reception desk with a phone.
A receipt book to make bills.
A small stapler to keep the papers together.
Something to stamp the receipt (you could buy an ink pad and make a stamp from a small carrot).
Lots of old keys, or credit cards if the hotel had locks that opened this way.
A welcome sign.
Signs pointing to the lounge and restaurant.
Pictograms for the restrooms.

# Activity books, videos and talking toys
*The role of technology and traditional methods in helping a child to talk*

There is now a vast array of books designed to expand your child's vocabulary. Round-the-clock television usually offers something for children and videos tailored for them have proliferated. There are also electronic and computer games marketed as "educational" and targeted at the parents of preschoolers.

### Picture books
These are an ideal way of expanding a child's vocabulary. The youngest children enjoy those that show familiar objects and situations; older children prefer those that extend their vocabulary. Don't be afraid to stretch children! Catalogs act as excellent picture books – and are free.

### Storybooks and tapes
At first children cannot follow a story without pictures to guide them through the plot. The under threes need something very simple, a few lines per picture is about right. The story should be straightforward and based on their own experience – even if it does have a fantasy element. As children's language and memory improve they can manage more elaborate stories and need less visual support to carry the tale. By the age of four or five most children can manage a story from a book without pictures, which means that they can also enjoy listening to a story on tape.

### Action books
Words and action interweave for small children and doing something is like saying "I know that word." Because action books are delicate, adults tend to look at them with a child, which is a plus, and the nature of an interactive book means that you discuss it as you both look at it. Since you will be looking at these books together check out the "talking value" of the action.

### Frightening stories
Fairy tales are often horrific: children cooked in ovens, wicked stepmothers, big bad wolves. Yet children love them. There was a movement in the 1960s to clean them up and make happy endings.

*Talking about your day, telling stories, reliving worries and anxieties is a wonderful way to be close to your child. Try to spend some time each day when all you need to do is relax and chat.*

*Recounting gruesome fairy tales to your child helps her to cope with all the harrowing elements in the outside world by confronting fears when there is nothing to be afraid of.*

This misses the point. Such stories are meant to deal with frightening issues. These are not tales for tapes, but stories to read on your knee.

### Videos

When everyone is tired or busy, videos provide a child with relaxation and his caregiver with the space for a coffee break. Few preschoolers can cope with a conversation about the video while watching it. They find dividing and switching attention much too hard at this stage – vision takes precedence and they are unlikely to listen. The mere fact that she watches the video over and over again ensures that she can both talk about it to you and play through the storyline with friends.

### Talking dolls and toys

Dolls that talk say things randomly. If a child needs a toy to answer questions she has to be able to make it say the right answer at the right time, which a doll can't do. These toys are appealing, but they do not encourage the child to talk.

Likewise, few talking toys do as well as, or more, than a book. Many do not provide information in a meaningful context. Computer programs can provide the child with sophisticated interactive learning. But cutting out the social context of learning is a disadvantage for the young.

## TELEVISION

Too much TV is bad for a small child. Even though there are pictures to go with the words tiny children probably do not listen. The visual dominates. They watch and do not hear. Television is therefore often a language-free environment for the smallest children. Even for older children the way people talk can make it difficult for them to follow a story line. They may watch programs designed for adults and older children but they do not understand them. Access to what children watch – and how much they watch – should be controlled, but with these provisos television can play many important roles in a child's life.

• Television allows children to flop and relax. Everyone needs a time to opt out, and this is not a bad thing when a child is tired. Leaving them for hours in front of a flickering screen is another matter.

• It can provide a shared experience and common ground for conversation. Families tend to be both small and isolated and most of children's social life centers around nursery and school. The problem with this is that children do not know each other's families. TV, therefore, is the common ground, something the verbally unskilled can talk about because the listener knows what is being discussed.

• It provides information about the world, broadening a child's horizons, and letting him see and experience things that would otherwise be unknown.

• If you watch together it's a good excuse for a cuddle and a chat.

• It is a source of activities and play ideas.

# 10 Acquiring a sense of self

$S$elf is the name given to the belief shared with others of our individuality, that a person has and always will be the same unique being. Alongside this personal view of who we are is also a view of others. The sense of self is so obvious to adults that most never stop to consider how complicated it must be for a baby to learn. A child who understands self and sees it as central to his interaction with the world needs to have self-worth. This is the basis of confidence, discipline and a belief in his own ability. As children develop a sense of self, parents need to boost self-esteem. Always make sure the good things you say to your baby outweigh the bad. If he does something particularly good – or naughty – praise or blame the behavior not the child. Up to the age of about seven months you can actually see your baby learning, and follow the process. After this age it becomes more complex and what a baby has learned is more obvious from his abilities.

**Milestones in self awareness**

| | **WHAT YOUR CHILD CAN DO** |
|---|---|
| **20** *weeks* | • Young babies do not understand that there is only one of each person. Your baby thinks that you are a new person each time she sees you. |
| **8** *months* | • At some time after seven months, your baby is able to think "I am the same person today that I was yesterday." <br> • She turns to you consistently if you call her name. <br> • She looks at herself in the mirror but does not realize that it is her; she is simply attracted by the baby.  |
| **22** *months* | • She consistently recognizes herself in the mirror and in current photographs but does not understand that she was the little baby in older snapshots. |
| **3** *years* | • She starts to describe herself in terms of what she possesses, such as "I am the little girl with the blue dress." <br> • She can tell you her gender and understands that there is a class of people called "Girls" who share certain characteristics; she cannot, however, say what these characteristics are. |
| **3½** *years* | • She suddenly realizes that other people have thoughts and feelings that are separate from hers. <br> • She understands that you cannot see what she has seen or know about things that happened when you were not there. |
| **5** *years* | • She realizes that there is a continuity about her life: that she was, is and will be the same person forever. |

| HOW YOU CAN TELL | HOW YOU CAN HELP |
|---|---|
| • Sit in front of a mirror and adjust it to show a number of views of you. If your baby smiles happily at the multiple reflections, she still thinks that you are a new person each time she sees you; if she looks perturbed it is because she has learned that you are unique and there should only be one of you. | • Play games like peekaboo to help the baby realize that people around her come and go.<br>• Call her from across the room, and smile as you walk past her. Seeing you both "here" and "there" helps her to understand and accept your continuity. |
| • If your baby cries when you leave her, she has realized that you continue to exist even when she cannot see you.<br>• She anticipates the next stage of a knee-bouncing game.<br>• She uses recognizable signs to communicate; after her first birthday she starts to use words. | • Any form of communication helps at this stage – play bouncing games or peekaboo.<br>• Use physical and verbal stimuli mixed – tickle your baby, point and ask questions.<br>• Most of all, respond to noises and actions. |
| • Sit your baby in front of a mirror and put a dab of cream on her nose. As she begins to understand her individuality she touches her nose, rather than her reflection. | • Play mirror games.<br>• Talk about your child's things, using her name.<br>• Remind your child of her abilities and skills: "Sarah can talk, can't you Sarah?"<br>• Play simple games of "Let's pretend."<br>• Show her photograph albums. |
| • She says "Me do it," "My coat," "Sarah go bed now."<br>• She does not like to share and may be upset if you give away outgrown clothes and toys. | • Be sensitive about possessive problems.<br>• Refer often to your child by her name, gender and abilities. |
| • She comes home from playgroup and rather than saying "You know that boy I was playing with" says "You know that boy whose Mom has a red car?"<br>• She may tell lies. Now that she realizes you can't see everything she does, she knows she can get away with them. | • Playing at being someone else, switching between the roles of self and other; or using objects to stand in for other things all help your child to practice the basic underlying skill: understanding that things can be looked at from separate points of view. |
| • She stops saying "When I grow up I am going to be a daddy."<br>• She recognizes her own baby pictures. | • Talk about the past and future.<br>• Play games that involve talking about the distant past. |

# Learning about me

*Language and memory are intrinsically linked, which makes it difficult for a baby to remember what has happened*

Without language it is hard to remember what has gone before. For the most part language allows us to dredge back through our memories and see ourselves in different contexts. Prelinguistic children depend on cues from their environment to remember events. A child remembers the park only when she visits tomorrow. If she is sitting in the kitchen, she remembers what happens there. But even these "kitchen memories" are fleeting. Until she is eight or nine months she forgets that the world exists when she is not looking at it, and if an object reminds her of something, she forgets the memory when she looks away. Adults also need cues to remember, but they can use words, hold memories for much longer and retain more than one thought at any time.

### What was I doing before?
Some time shortly before a child's first birthday you will become aware that she is able to look up at you and then go back to whatever activity she had under way before you came into the room. She is able to hold events in mind for a little longer than before. Her window of conscious experience has widened. While the window was fleeting she did not realize that her experience was continuous. She forgot from one moment to the next what had been happening to her. Everything depended on where she looked or the sounds that she heard.

Once she starts to communicate, the window opens further. She has a way to bridge experiences and string them together. She begins to understand more and more of what you say to her and to communicate more with you. By the time she can put words together to express intention and describe action, she realizes that this window of experience is not passive. Her experiences always have the same person in them. A small person. A person with a particular name who often wears a certain coat. That person is "me." Me who played, me in her coat and me drinking.

*The idea that a child continues to exist across time – that she played with a toy this morning, has her coat on to go to the park now and will have a drink when she returns – depends on having a broad enough span of conscious experience to put more than one idea together. The child understands "me" only when she can think back and remember an earlier event or look forward and predict another.*

### Recognizing photographs

At about the same time, a child begins to recognize photographs of herself as being "me" and to know herself in the mirror. Up to now she has been interested in the little girl in the mirror without any knowledge that it is her. If you put a dab of lipstick on a baby's forehead and sit her in front of a mirror, she will rub the glass. At about 21–23 months she rubs her forehead.

### Knowing that you feel

Although she knows about herself before she is two, she does not yet realize that self is private. She thinks you see, feel and want what she does. This partly explains her frustration when you do not jump up and give it to her! Two-year-olds still pull your hair, knock the baby over and steal a toy. They may know that this makes people cry or say "Ouch!," but cannot predict that it hurts. If she cannot feel it, why should you?

### You know that girl?

A three-year-old often talks as if you share her experience. If she can see it so should you. She tells you about playschool as if you had been there with her and expects you to remember the dog she saw on the way home, even though it was Grandma, not you, who collected her.

### That girl whose Mom has a yellow car

Sometime between about four and a half and five years of age, a child's view changes. She begins to realize that she has to explain her feelings and intentions. Other people do not necessarily know what she is thinking and experiencing. If she moves objects when you are not looking, she expects you to search for them where you last saw them, not in the new place she has put them. She realizes that others can be hurt and she may cry at sad stories. In short she knows that she has a window on the world which is hers and hers alone. And she knows you have one too. She has what psychologists call a theory of mind.

### Deception

Once a child develops the idea that everyone has a mind of their own, all sorts of possibilities open up. Not only must she explain scenes to those who do not see them, she can also tell them tales that are not true. Who took the last chocolate? No one saw her so it is safe to say "Not me." What did she do in school today? Nothing particularly interesting, but that isn't a riveting story so she can make one up. Her brother has finished his candies but she has some left. Where should she hide them so he cannot find them? He will think she is keeping them in her drawer as usual, so she will hide them under her bed instead.

### He thinks that I think...

Once you start down this road, it is clear that there is more to it than someone else's different point of view. You can also know that other people can do what you are doing – take someone else's view into consideration. I know that he will think that... becomes I know that he will think that I will think that.... This gives much wider possibilities for predicting what others think and do and understanding other people's feelings and actions. It is this juggling of predictions about deception and lies which is so enthralling in whodunit? books and films.

*Shortly before your child's second birthday, she recognizes that she is the little girl in the mirror.*

# Pretending and imitating

*Babies mimic actions from early in life, but imitation and role-playing take a leap forward after the first year*

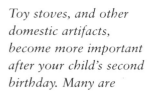

Although grimaces and grins have an obvious inherited component (even deaf and blind children smile and look angry), the development of mature facial expressions seem to depend on seeing other people making them. The expressions of those who have been blind from birth are different from those who can see. Although tiny children can copy, the real expansion of learning by imitation does not happen until around the child's first birthday.

## Early copying

Some time around her first birthday a child may pick up a toy cup and put it to her lips. It is hard to say at this stage whether she is using action to depict a word ("This is a cup") or pretending to drink. Toward her second birthday such actions are much more clearly imitations of your intentions rather than a slavish copying of your

*Toy stoves, and other domestic artifacts, become more important after your child's second birthday. Many are simple to improvise: paint a box white and draw the rings on top. Either cut a door open or simply paint it on.*

*The action of drinking from a cup is initially a way to communicate: without being able to say the word for cup, your child uses the action associated with it to define it. As she grows, such actions become increasingly imitative.*

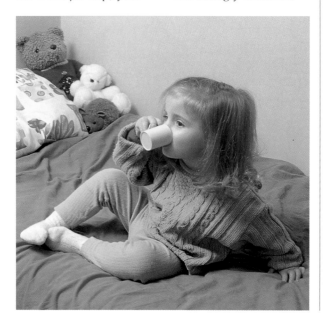

body movements. Your child may, for example, give her teddy a "drink" from the cup or take the animals for a ride in the back of her truck. In their second and third years children do what they see adults doing. They trot behind you with their toy vacuum cleaners and lawn mowers, they cook on their toy stove, say what you say, stand how you stand and altogether enjoy being like you.

## Imitation to acting out roles

There is not a clear-cut distinction between imitation and fantasy. In their second year children copy from others, and some of these activities have strong elements of fantasy. Feeding a doll from a spoon may be copying, but the food that your child gives her doll is entirely in her head, because the spoon she puts to the doll's lips is empty.

As she grows these actions become more elaborate until, at the age of about four and a half, there is a clear story line that is negotiated with other players. Ask her a question about Batman when she is dressed as a lion and she may tell you quite straightforwardly that lions do not know anything about Batman. Language clearly has some role here, and the elaboration of pretend play mirrors the development of language abilities. There is, however, more to it. The child's pretend play starts with the mundane, anchored in the copying of domestic activities, and moves to the fantastic, which requires acting out roles and taking on other identities. These abilities require knowledge of "self" and "others."

### Pretending to be someone else

At first children do not pretend to be Mommy in the kitchen. They are a mommy because they are doing what mommies do. Only later do they take on the role of "Mommy" and switch between Katie mode and Mommy mode. When she is herself she tells you she will fetch her coat in a minute, then turns, switches to Mommy mode and tells her dolls that she has to go out soon and they should all be good while she is away. This ability to switch between fantasy and reality clearly requires the knowledge that others have separate experiences, thoughts and feelings.

### Pretending and knowing

Early imitation and fantasy can be seen as developing the skills needed to understand the idea of self. Children dress up, and parents act as if they are now someone else – but the child still feels like "me." Played over and over again such games help the child to consider the possibility of being someone else and the idea of being herself.

### Story lines

The story lines for early pretend play tend to be mundane. If all the children in the game need shared knowledge to play, it is almost inevitable that games are about domestic activities. As the child's ability to tell stories improves, the scripts can move out of the domestic arena. But the need to explain the script to others usually means that preschoolers play games based on common knowledge. The entry ticket to shared games is among the most valuable contributions of TV at this age (see also pp. 171–72).

### Little worlds

Sometimes a child is Batman, at others a godlike figure in charge of a little world. Often these little worlds are complete. Children are engrossed in the world but do not play a role in it. This sort of play starts early – the child takes her plastic ducks to the glass pond to swim – or "vrooms" her cars down imaginary roads. It becomes more elaborate, and as the child's ability to tell stories develops she constructs whole scenarios that she plays through. Most people continue to pretend (by reading, acting or watching films and plays) into adulthood; fewer engage in games with little worlds.

*Train sets give children the ability to create a pretend world and elaborate it: where the train will stop, where the passengers step on and off, whether the bus will meet the train, how many trees there are on the street.*

# Caring about others
*A child's family is her first model of loving, caring behavior*

Babies are born to love. They gaze into parents' eyes and smile and their faces light up when you enter the room. You don't have to do much to gain such devotion. Babies adore people because adults are their source of care; the love of a baby is readily bestowed on anyone who is around. This love must be nurtured because it is the foundation of later relationships. Tiny children love their parents regardless of whether those caregivers deserve it. But while the need to give and take love remains, such blind attachment will not necessarily be offered again.

As children grow up the way they treat other people is based on watching and modeling the loving and caring behavior of those around them. A child's family are the first models, but influences beyond the family also play a role. A child can be loving in spite of uncaring parents if she has a good model outside the immediate nuclear family, but naturally such positive attitudes to people are more difficult to learn. Other children may suffer such negative experiences outside the family that the fragile first model of caring and loving she learned from her family is overruled by the reality of the world she finds herself in.

### Wanting to love
A child who feels loved wants to care for others. Most small children do feel secure in their love, so, apart from the odd "off" day, most preschoolers are kind, helpful, thoughtful and affectionate individuals. They may be possessive about their belongings, but they are ready to share. Such caring and cooperation can wear a little thin as they grow older. Once children move from the cooperative home base into the more competitive culture of school, they tend to show more rivalry and be less considerate.

### Like parent like child
By the time a child is two she learns by watching and imitating what others do. Such lessons include the way the child expresses emotions, interacts with other people or gets her own way in a battle

*A child who knows from the start that she is loved and valued for who she is finds it easier to learn caring behavior than one brought up in a manipulative,* *unemotional or violent environment. A loving grandparent or other caregiver may go some way toward compensating for negative parenting.*

of wills. Children growing up in warm and open households tend to be correspondingly warm and open. Those with manipulative parents develop devious skills. And studies of the correlation between parental violence and aggressive children have found that those who grow up in households in which control is exerted by hitting and shouting are likely to learn this mode of interaction with others. This is not to say that the occasional slap turns a child into a bully or makes her take out her aggression on other children. It does not. It is the consistent pattern of interaction within the family, and between relatives and the rest of the adult world, that the child imitates.

### Demands and counter demands

The demands parents and caregivers impose are mirrored by the claims children make on them and on their peer group. Such demands can be both positive and negative. Most caregivers control children through a combination of the two. Children do the same in their interactions with others: they make some requests and also some attempts at preventive action.

If you expect your child to obey you without question she will expect other children to comply with her or, alternatively, expect to be bossed around by her peers. Tyrants (parents or children) are rarely popular, nor are those who can be entirely manipulated. Whether they become bullies or victims, such children are often isolated. They do not find the balance between dependence and independence, essential for normal relationships.

### Learning to live in the real world

Often in a child's life someone is in control, telling her what to do and when to do it. At other times the way people act toward each other is difficult to understand. Why does Mommy get cross with Daddy? Why is Daddy watching football and not me? Why is the baby-sitter looking after Susie instead of me? Such thoughts are easier to cope with if she can play them through with her dolls.

### Take time off to watch

You can learn a lot from watching your child play games that involve relationships, whether these are with other children or with substitutes such as teddies and dolls. If you see yourself in what she plays – and you may well – it may not be flattering. Do not interfere. Children cannot see matters in shades of gray. Thinking of extremes is a way to understand the middle ground. Your child's play is based on a truth, but also explores the extremes. The extremes worry her most.

### Gender games

As children learn about other people's lives they also learn about people's gender roles. Since their view of the world is black and white, the gender roles children adopt in play are stereotyped. Girls sit their teddies in neat classroom rows and organize them. Boys crash them in cars and hurl them down the stairs in battle. They are merely playing it as they see it, choosing the role that fits themselves. At night, or when upset or tired, both boys and girls lovingly cuddle their teddies. This hard-soft role-play is typical of boys just as "I'm in charge" games are typical of girls. A child's world usually has women in charge. Not only are daytime caregivers almost always women, so are the staff at playschool and the people they meet in shops. Boys looking to see what makes them exlusively male grab role models where they can: from films, TV and their peers, areas where "aggressive" role models dominate.

*You may seldom raise your voice to your son or say that he is naughty, but you will probably find him doing both to his dolls and teddies at some time in his childhood. By playing through "the time Mommy was upset," he will come to understand all the other times when you weren't angry.*

# Real people, imaginary people

*Games and activities to stretch the imagination and enhance your child's social skills*

The line between reality and make-believe becomes gradually clearer as your child grows. Her interactions with more and more people on many different levels help her to fine-tune her understanding of who she is.

## Meeting strangers

Provide as many opportunities for social interaction as you can. These are the people she will model in her games.

Your child can carry the money to buy an ice cream, point out what she wants and ask the storekeeper for it.

She can deposit birthday money into a bank account. She can choose her books at the library and take them to the counter.

She can buy her comic at the newstand.

She can say hello to the supermarket cashier.

## Meeting children

Children have to meet their own age group if they are to make friends, but it can be a daunting experience for a child who is not used to it. Take a trip to the park and watch the children. Adults find out about each other by asking questions, but preschoolers usually start by saying what they have.

*I've got a new coat.*

*I've got a new book.*

*I'm having a sandwich for lunch*

Practice these opening lines with your child. Small children like to play through make believe games of shopping, phone calls and meeting people.

## What would happen?

Here is an imaginative game for the over fours. What would happen:

... *if clouds were on long strings like kites?*

... *if everyone was as small as a pin?*

... *if children grew giant and grown-ups shrank?*

... *if all the buses went backward?*

... *if all the traffic lights stayed red?*

... *if all the trees turned into chocolate?*

It is more interesting if you avoid the usual fairy-tale scenarios of magic carpets and talking animals. If the game leads to real questions answer them fully.

## TROUBLESHOOTING

**When it comes to presents, my daughter always wants another doll. We have tried buying her train sets and construction kits, but they just stay on the shelf. I love my children but think there is more to women's lives than child care. Do you think she is reacting against me working? Is there any way to wean her off doll play onto something more constructive?**

Does she dress her dolls? If so, she is using fine finger movements and fitting things together exactly as she would do if she were building with Lego. Does she talk to her dolls and answer for them? If so, she practices conversation. Does she role-play with them? Organizing them into classrooms, hotels and schools lets her tell herself stories, remember events and play through the roles of being herself and others. There is a great deal more than "being Mommy" in most girls' doll play. There is also nothing wrong with playing "being Mommy." Mothers are important people for small children. It is natural for her to see this as your primary role. The games she plays are about her life now. They have little relevance to her later lifestyle.

## Puppet play and telling stories

Puppets can have conversations with each other. They can tell fantastic stories. They can tell lies and make people laugh. They can play through pantomime favorites; they can fight. Puppets are real creatures who can have conversations with the audience and say things no one else could.

Finger puppets are inexpensive and kits are also available. But finger puppets are easy to make out of felt, or you could cut the fingers out of old cotton, leather or plastic gloves. With some beads for eyes and a little wool for hair you can make a whole range of characters both human and animal. Alternatively, you could leave the fingers on the glove and simply sew on the "extras" to make each finger into a different character.

You can make a glove puppet from a sock. Put four fingers in the toe end and the thumb in the heel. Again you can add buttons and beads for eyes and wool for hair. Create a stick puppet by pushing an old-style pot scrubber through a plastic sponge or foam ball. The mop makes the hair and the ball or sponge the face.

## Making a picture book about me

Every family has its own history, and every story is worth a book. Re-create your child's early life in a picture book. Choose the small events of her

### WHAT YOUR CHILD LEARNS

**• Meeting strangers**
Strangers help your child to form role models of the world and improve her ability to interact with it.

**• What would happen**
This encourages your child's imagination.

**• Puppet play and telling stories**
When she has finger puppets on her hands, a child can be someone else for a time, playing out scenarios that can't be enacted in real life.

**• Making a picture book**
This helps your child to remember events, and reinforces that she is now the same little girl who had the adventures in the story. Children develop their sense of who they are by looking at, reading and listening to family stories told time and time again.

baby years, a striking occasion or something more mundane, such as going to visit Grandma or a day at the beach. You could include anecdotes, such as how Mommy and Daddy met. Give it a title page. It is thrilling to read that it is a story about her before the tale unfolds.

## Telling stories to herself

If a child hears stories she will start to tell them as soon as she is able to talk. Often she relates them as she plays, in her bath or in her bed at night. Sometimes she may tell stories to you. The subject matter can be a guide to her worries, her interests or both: cars crash, disasters happen and fantastic events occur. These stories help her to weave the web that connects her to the events of the past, present and future.

## Reading to your child

Cuddled up next to the people you love most and listening to a story is one of the most wonderful ways to wind down at the end of the day. Young children are happy to hear the same stories again and again; older ones enjoy a "chapter book" read over a period of a week or two. Even children who can read enjoy the ritual of a story told.

# Pretending activities

*Being someone else, or changing her situation, can help your child to understand reality*

Pretending is good for children; through being someone else they act out worries or concerns, try out situations to see if they like them and work through problems that seem insoluble given their limited vocabulary and understanding. All you need to do is provide a few props.

## Outdoor play areas

Most parents cannot provide a permanent playroom to play games in, but here are some possibilities:

A tree house if you have a suitable tree.

A small tent for an occasional treat.

Put a blanket over the clothesline or a branch and hold it out and down with house bricks.

Make a secret corner in the bushes – put a drop cloth down if it is wet.

Mark off an area between the house and fence with a few chairs – a blanket helps to define the area.

Use the garden shed as long as it is safe.

Curtain off a corner of the garage.

## A box full of hats

A hat can change the whole personality. A child needs nothing more than a hat to take on a different character.

A sailor hat turns her into a sailor.

A police officer's hat enables her to direct the traffic or chase a suspect.

With an army hat she can fight a war.

A wedding veil makes her a bride.

A baseball cap or a straw hat with flowers and a veil is just for wearing as she goes about her day.

### GUN PLAY?

If all the boys around him have toy guns your son will want one and, if you refuse, he will probably turn every stick and piece of Lego into a gun. You then need to decide whether it is better to continue to say "no" to guns. It is sometimes argued that once a child is fixated with gunplay, refusing him a toy firearm may simply fuel the obsession. You could equally argue that if all parents refused to give in, the obsession would stop. My experience is that both these are true. My eldest son grew up in an area where most boys had guns and he was obsessed with shootouts. Until I bought him a gun he turned everything that was shaped remotely like it into one. Having a toy gun seemed to decrease not increase his gun play. By the time my younger son was a preschooler we lived in an area where boys did not have guns. Although his elder brother's toy gun was still in the toy chest he did not play with it.

Research suggests that children do not become more aggressive by playing gunfights, and watching them play war games indicates that they are fun and involve no more real aggression than a game of football. The inclusion of guns and bombs in many boys' role-play toys may be more of a problem. War toys are part of a wider culture that depicts men as belligerent and guns as a fairly normal trapping of the male role.

My personal view is that accepting killing as a normal part of a man's world could be dangerous. But there is not a great deal of evidence on this, and whether or not withdrawing all war toys would halt the rise of aggression in society is unclear.

## A dressing-up box

Preschoolers often go to the dressing-up box for inspiration. They do not have a game in mind; they dress up and play whatever seems appropriate. If they find a length of netting they are a bride. If they find glasses and a briefcase they go off to work. If there is a Batman cloak they play Batman. Sometimes they dress up just because it looks glamorous or monstrous. Silver shoes, sequined tops and glass beads are always popular, as are hats, cloaks and suits of armor. Older children may want outfits that depict characters more accurately. At this stage you may decide to buy some costumes. Until then the best source is your own castoffs.

## A miniature home

Playing with a dolls' house is playing "mothers and fathers" in a different way from acting out the roles. Because everything is on such a small scale she can handle and control the situation: she decides what people do and what the house should look like. She can sit dolls in a chair and forget all about them or take them for a ride in the car. She can be caring or neglectful, nasty or kind. Preschoolers often prefer houses to be the homes of animal families. If she does not play with the house you have built for her, moving in a family of bears could change matters.

### WHAT YOUR CHILD LEARNS

**• A box full of hats; a dressing-up box**
Apart from being great fun, stimulating and creative, acting out roles helps a child learn to see the world from someone else's perspective, explore other people's lifestyles and live out her fantasies and fears.

**• A miniature home**
This lets your child work through any recent emotional landmarks, for instance, if she was reprimanded or particularly praised at nursery, within an environment that is secure and hers to control. Outdoor play spaces also help her to feel secure.

## Being me being you

Children like to play through their experiences of other people's lives. Often a few props are all that is needed to start the game. An office, for example, needs a word processor, a telephone, a stapler, lots of paper, some stamping pads, paper clips and pens. Other locations to consider are a bank, a workshop, a store (clothes, shoes or supermarket), a ticket office.

# Something awful is happening!
*Helping your child come to terms with fear of the unknown*

When adults have fears that are debilitating, psychologists use a variety of techniques to teach them how to cope. Many of these are based on the premise that fear and relaxation are incompatible. If people can learn to feel relaxed when faced with the fear-provoking objects and situations, they will not feel frightened, or will at least be able to stop terror spiraling out of control. It is a technique that all children use. Play is by its nature a relaxing and fun activity. A child who is afraid cannot play. One way he can deal with his fears is to introduce them into his games at times when he is feeling happy and relaxed, especially when he is with his friends. This is why children who scream about weird creatures under their beds at night often play monsters or draw pictures of them the next day.

## Monster meetings

Monsters are near the top of most children's lists of fears. A meeting of the worst monsters in town should calm them down. You will need some paper plates, some lengths of elastic and some felt-tip pens to make the plates into monster masks, plus a few children to have fun being scary.

Attach the elastic to the side of the plates. Then put the mask on and decide where to make the eye holes. Remove, then cut these out. The children can now either draw their own monster faces or color in one you have drawn for them. When they have all finished they can put on the masks and do a monster dance.

## What happens when you die

Everybody dies. Sooner or later all children realize this and begin to worry about it. Often these anxieties center around what will happen to them if you die. Explaining that this will not happen for a long time is not always reassuring, because children find it hard to understand what life could possibly be like without a parent to care for them. Games about death may seem morbid but they are often a child's way of coming to terms with the idea. These are not games you can easily introduce to a child. If the idea bothers him he will talk about it and play it through in his own way. Remember the child needs to combine relaxation and security with his fears. So cuddle up close when you talk to him.

Many people feel that owning and looking after small, short-lived pets like hamsters help children learn that death is sad but ultimately something that can be coped with.

## Moving

In the excitement of moving into a new home it is easy to forget how much security is based on having familiar objects around. Your child may be excited about his new room and his new school – but the reality can be daunting. Parents are always exceedingly busy after the move, and it may seem to the child that he has gained a new bedroom but now receives less of you. To pretend to move, you need moving crates (supermarket boxes will do), newspaper as wrapping paper, toys to wrap, a crayon to mark the boxes and some of your old clothes.

## Going into the hospital

If you know that your child is going into the hospital, you can prepare her by reading books, telling stories and talking through what will happen. Not all such stays are planned, however, and many children find themselves in the hospital without any preparation. Although these days parents are usually allowed to stay with their children, being in a strange place, having a painful illness or injury, having to take strange-tasting medicine and undergo necessary treatments make hospitals places that generate fears. This is the case whether the child is the patient, a visitor or the one left worrying at home. Children deal with this by playing hospital. While one child is a genuine patient, seeing the other playing at "dying in the hospital" can be alarming. But it is just a child playing out these worries – as the patient will when he goes home.

### Imagine how it would be . . .

Sit and cuddle and talk. Share wishes about how it would be …
*If we could send baby back.*
*If Daddy would come home.*
*If Granddad wasn't sick.*
*If Hamster hadn't died.*

### WHAT YOUR CHILD LEARNS

Talking, playing and acting out fears and situations that make him unhappy is the only way your child can deal with his anxieties. Don't try to prevent him facing unpleasant facts. He needs to know that life doesn't always go as planned. But while he relaxes next to you he cannot be truly afraid, even if what you are talking about is frightening.

## A NEW BABY

Most parents tend to exaggerate the benefits of a new baby. The baby and your child may become friends somewhere down the line, but at first they may not be in the least amicable. On the contrary, to your child the baby is stealing all the attention from you and from visitors that he believes to be his due. After the first three months it is much easier to persuade a child that a baby sister is a plus. In the first days it is just something strange and disruptive. The younger the child, the more dependent he will be on his now-distracted parents and the more difficult he will find it to understand what is happening to him.

### Preparing for the baby

• Bring a present: if a baby comes bearing small gifts, your child may feel the day is special for him too.
• Buy a new doll and a buggy: if she can imitate you and play the role of mommy she will understand better.
• Making a fuss: if people make a fuss over the child, he will be less jealous of all the attention that the baby is receiving.
• Coming to see the big boy: if visitors come to see him, he will continue to feel special.
• Being in first place: sometimes everyone needs to be number one; the baby has to wait every now and then while older brother has his story.

# 11 *Learning to be social*

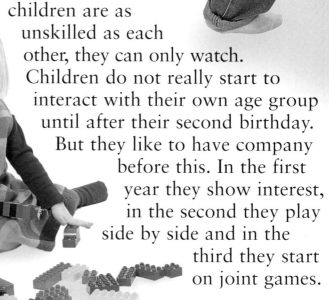

It is much harder to interact with peers than with adults. Grown-ups are skilled listeners and interpreters. You know what he wants from the way that he stands – even if his words do not make his needs clear. Parents anticipate children's needs, make allowances and fill in their words. Older children, especially siblings, may manage some of these. But children who do not know your son must take him at face value. When two children are as unskilled as each other, they can only watch. Children do not really start to interact with their own age group until after their second birthday. But they like to have company before this. In the first year they show interest, in the second they play side by side and in the third they start on joint games.

# Milestones in social skills

## HOW SOCIAL SKILLS DEVELOP

**6-12 months**
- He likes to look at other babies.
- He loves the company of other children.
- He joins in with activities which are centered around him.

**1-1½ years**
- He plays next to (parallel with) other children, offering toys but not playing together.

**1½-2 years**
- Most children still do not play together, although siblings may.
- Parallel play is common.
- He loves being with other children.

**2-3 years**
- He begins to play with other children.
- He also begins to quarrel.
- He may not share toys and can become possessive and uncooperative.
- Children who have little social experience will still not be able to play.
- His conversations with other children increase.

**3-4 years**
- He plays more complex and imaginative games.
- He teases and taunts siblings.
- He makes and breaks friends easily.
- He copies other children.

**4-6 years**
- As he reaches school age his friendships become firmer.
- Boys may begin to play in bigger groups than girls.
- He is more independent; children do not all do the same thing and can take on separate roles in complex games.

| **HOW YOU CAN TELL** | **HOW YOU CAN HELP** |
|---|---|

- Your baby loves to see other children.
- Siblings can make him laugh.

- He loves the company of children; make sure that he has it.

- He happily sits side by side with other children.

- Ask friends with children his age over to play. If there are older children who think he is a pet let them play too, especially if he does not have siblings.

- He may allow toys to be snatched from him.
- He smiles at other children and says occasional words but does not have a true conversation.
- Toward his second birthday he begins to talk to and play with siblings.

- Visit parent and baby groups so he grows used to being with other children.
- Try not to anticipate all of his needs.

- Games are simple, friendships fleeting and explanations minimal but he plays, interacts and has friendships.
- He rushes to other children when he reaches the nursery.
- He squabbles and fights and often refuses to share his toys.

- Before friends come to play decide which toys can be shared and put the rest away.
- Try to wait for him to ask and encourage him to explain his needs: the most successful social games let children do the same thing.

- Friendships become stronger, but he still falls out and squabbles with other children.
- He plays more elaborate games but can take on only simple roles.
- He can follow instructions but cannot dictate a complex story line as older children can, or switch easily between pretend and reality.

- Children of this age need plenty of company of their own age. If he does not go to a nursery try to arrange this for him. Give children space for rough-and-tumble play and exuberance.

- He explains games to other children.
- He describes other children as "best friends."
- He indicates to others when to "pretend" and when something is "real."

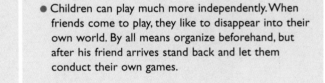

- Children can play much more independently. When friends come to play, they like to disappear into their own world. By all means organize beforehand, but after his friend arrives stand back and let them conduct their own games.

# Making friends

*How friendship develops between babies and children as they build on their early social skills*

Babies love people and interact with them, but their conversational skills are limited. They smile, but if you choose not to begin a conversation, that is as far as it goes. They gurgle and babble but are not able to keep a conversation going unless an adult (or older child) takes on the major role. So, although a baby loves the company of other babies, he cannot interact with them.

### Little pets

Older children love to play with babies, and babies dote on them. No one can make a baby laugh quite as loudly as a sibling. This is an important element in the bond between both children. That a child is so obviously adored by the baby makes up for some of the attention that has been taken from him. The fact that a toddler is not as adept as his parents in interacting socially means that the baby learns certain skills earlier. For example, he learns from other children that he should laugh and shout if he is having fun.

### Nice to see you

Until they are about two years old, children do not interact or play together unless they know each other well. They do not have the

conversational skills to initiate and maintain a chat with someone who is not able to guess or interpret their intentions. Children like to be together and are tolerant of each other. They may say a few words, offer and grab toys, but rarely get upset. Even if one child hits another, they soon settle to play next to each other again.

### Beginning to interact

Some time after their second birthday most children begin to interact and play together. Games are simple at first. They may for example gather in the home corner at playgroup and play together at the stove. Conversations, too, are simple, and children often do exactly the same. By now they are less tolerant of each other. They may not share, and if a toy is grabbed from them, they protest. They may hit, kick and bite each other too. This is all part of learning how to interact and cause a reaction.

### Quarrels and fights

Children do not usually quarrel unless they know each other extremely well. When a strange child hits them or grabs one of their toys, they are more likely to protest and snatch the toy back than quarrel. Real fighting and arguing is a sign that the children are closely involved with each other and does not happen until friendships begin to develop. But once children can make friends, intimacy and quarrels go

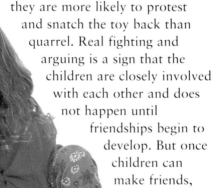

*A favorite sibling can elicit many more responses from a baby than even a parent can. Through watching their older brothers and sisters, and being included in their games, babies rapidly develop their social skills.*

*Children learn through imitating adults and older siblings, so, even when they start to play alongside their own age group, they may copy what their neighbor is doing. A tower may be built with constant reference to how the next child is making it or a doll tucked up using the same words and gestures.*

hand in hand. Fights are most common between siblings. When children are not competing for attention the atmosphere is always calmer. An argumentative child at home may be an angel when at playschool.

## Making friends

When children first interact they show few preferences for one child over another. They are happy to play alongside, and later with, anyone who will join in with them. Gradually, however, friendships develop. These can be fleeting. Although some children seem to be inseparable for weeks and months at a time, in most cases friends can come and go rapidly. At nursery two- to three-year-olds often play in large groups and are happy to sit with a group and do the same as everyone else. Later, when the roles in pretend games are more clearly defined, the play group shrinks. Less popular children can be excluded.

## How friendships develop

Children make friends as adults do. If they are competent they approach strangers with an opening line; those who are less skilled hover around the game until someone comes up to them. At the stage when groups of children form around an activity, entry into the group is relatively easy. If the children are constructing towers the child waiting simply fetches his own blocks and starts to build. There may be a verbal exchange to give out some news, comment or offer help. Even when two- to three-year-old children are playing imaginative games it is fairly easy for another child to join by going up to the group and doing what they do.

Later this becomes much more difficult. When everyone is engaged in domestic activities an extra body is neither here nor there. When children have different roles, any child entering the game must be given a part that is acceptable to him or her and to the rest of the players.

## Popular children

Research suggests that popular children are:
• Friendly: children like those who draw them into a game
• Outgoing: gregarious children are more popular than shy ones; children who always talk and never listen are not popular
• Bright: intelligence helps a child catch on quickly and explain details to others
• Skilled: specific talents are always admired
• Attractive: the more physically appealing the child, the more he is liked by his peers

Other factors that matter are:
• Family position: younger children are more popular than firstborn
• Size: being among the tallest is popular, being very tall is not; plump children are less popular
• Name: a liked name matters, especially for boys

Characteristics that deter friends are:
• Bossiness: aggressive, bullying, spiteful, mean and domineering children are unpopular, as are those who hold grudges
• Predictability: moodiness and manipulation are disliked; children like to know what to expect

# Brothers and sisters

*First role models are the family and a child with siblings has a head start in finding his place in the world*

Younger siblings' social skills are well-honed by a lifetime of practice. They learn early in life how to nitpick, irritate, manipulate, maneuver and get their siblings into trouble while taking on an innocent demeanor. They have a lifetime of practice with equals (or almost equals). Skilled in the home, they move out to the world knowing when to give way and when to take advantage. Because they are not their firstborn, parents tend to love them more for themselves than for their own ambitions.

Second and third children know there are many competitions they cannot win. An older brother is going to win simply because he is more physically and intellectually developed. The big ideas, the crazy notions in history, generally come from younger children. Both Galileo and Darwin were younger sons, while Sigmund Freud grew up in a household that included his young uncles. Elder children tend to be more conformist.

## Children and parents

When children outnumber the adults in the household, the focus of the family moves away from the grown-ups toward the children. What the children like and need becomes more important. A first child may be expected to keep his toys upstairs and to watch the TV channels his parents choose, but when there are more children than adults such rules are worn down. Vacations become children-centered, visits to theme parks, zoos and cartoon-type films more frequent. Meals are more child-friendly.

Although children play power games with one another, they are on much more equal terms than the only child who has to play such games with his parents. The skill of controlling other children is important when it comes to making and keeping friends, which is perhaps why younger siblings are more popular at school.

## One-child families

Only children grow up to be well-balanced individuals and are more likely to succeed in their careers. Among any list of famous people – politicians, writers, business tycoons, scientists – there is more than a fair share of only children. The fact that they are more likely to be conformist, strong-willed, secure, capable and responsible probably has something to do with this. They get on well with adults, which may also contribute. That they sometimes lack spontaneity, tact and patience is of less importance when success is measured in the marketplace.

## I know you so well

Even if you have lived apart for years, your brother or sister can slip easily back into your life. Siblings share each others' secrets and experiences and approach to the world. Closeness needs no

*When a child has siblings, the views of the majority often prevail, and attitudes to life in general may be more child-centered.*

*Sibling competitiveness is strongest among brothers, and least pronounced between a brother and a sister. Quarrels reflect this, as do closeness and love.*

*Younger children are less driven adults than firstborn, more spontaneous, patient, adaptable, easygoing, relaxed and well-balanced. They also tend to be more popular.*

questions; fallings out can be extreme. Siblings rarely need detailed explanations to understand what the other means. They can laugh as no others do, and just a word can set them off again. When they are friends they are the best of pals. Brothers and sisters know each other too well for any trick or deception to succeed for long. Whatever skills children have in hiding their feelings or intentions, cajoling, manipulating and covering up are honed in these early interactions with their siblings.

## Competition

Siblings love, support and share but they also compete for the attention of their caregivers. Siblings know to the nearest crumb which slice of cake is the biggest, to the nearest penny which present cost most. Or they think they do. Children constantly monitor whether they are receiving more of their parent's time and attention or whether a sibling has an advantage. This is a competition that no parent can ever win.

• Treat children uniquely rather than equally: "You are my own special Florence"; "You are the best Sam in the world."

• Give according to need: buy Florence a new dress when she requires one; buy Sam some new felt-tip pens when his have dried out.

• Accept their feelings and frustrations: "I know you wish Florence would not be so mean. Why

not use your new pens to draw a picture of how you feel ... that does look very angry."

• If you give a child a role he will play it: "Mark, why are you such a bully?" means he gets attention by playing this part and his sister is labeled as the victim, a role in which she can see there are advantages.

# Boys and girls

*Gender is apparent at birth, but it still takes a child time to understand the permanence and significance of being male or female*

Whether your child is a boy or girl depends on his or her chromosomal makeup. The characteristics associated with being a boy or girl may be built-in, or they may be the result of the roles society tends to assign to gender.

### Why is a girl a girl?

A girl is a girl because she has two X chromosomes, one from her mother and one from her father. About six weeks after conception a small structure in the fetus starts to grow into an ovary, and somewhat later (about 12 weeks after conception) a structure called the Mullerian duct develops into female internal genitalia. The unisex external genitalia that developed in the first weeks after conception turn into female genitals. Girls' brains form in female ways (the left cortex is a little thicker, the connection between left and right side a little bigger) and develop so that at puberty they will release hormones in a cyclical pattern. Most of these changes happen because nature tends to make females. This is the way development is programmed. All babies would turn into girls if some mechanism did not make them stop doing so and become boys instead.

*All-male team sports are one of the last bastions defining what being a boy is all about. In such* *ball games, boys can shout instructions, play with friends and be generally "manlike."*

### Why is a boy a boy?

A boy is a boy because he has an X chromosome inherited from his mother and a Y from his father. An instruction on this Y chromosome tells the small structure that in girls turns into an ovary to become the testes instead. The testes produce the male hormone testosterone and this tells a structure called the Wolffian duct to become the male internal genitalia and the unisex external genitalia to become a penis and scrotum. Another hormone stops the female Mullerian duct becoming the female internal genitalia. Testosterone makes the right side of the brain grow bigger, and causes the sex hormones to be released in a random pattern.

### The feelings of boys and girls

It is not clear if these biological facts explain why girls generally feel like girls or boys feel like boys. Some people believe that the hormones that change the body also make children feel a sense of identity as a boy or a girl. Others think it is more a question of how children are raised. Probably it is a little of both.

### Knowing he is a boy

By the time they can answer the question, girls and boys know which gender they are and what each sex looks like. Even though they know what they are, they do not know they were always the same gender and always will be. If a boy has a little sister he may think he was a girl when he was a baby, and he may believe he will be a mother when he grows up.

Just as children do not recognize themselves in the mirror or in photographs until they are 21–22 months old, so they do not grasp the concept of their younger selves until they are about three or four years old. It is only at this stage that they can understand that they will continue to be what they are now.

Even when children have developed a gender identity (I am a boy) and a gender consistency (I always was and always will be a male) they may still feel that if they dress in the wrong clothes and play with the wrong toys they could slip into being the other sex. It does not make much sense to adults, who can look at matters in an abstract and logical way. Neither abstraction nor logic are a small child's strong points. Until children are about six, they act as if they believe that the slightest lack of vigilance will hurtle them into the wrong gender class. This is why appearances matter so much, especially for boys.

## Stereotyped toys

Identity is how you feel; role is what you do. Gender identity is part of a child's sense of self. A strong gender identity is vital for well-being, success and personal happiness. When you look at how boys and girls play, bear in mind that although gender identity and roles are related they are not the same. The gender-stereotyped toys children crave may throw them into stereotyped roles. But the fact that such toys have increased in popularity as gender roles in society have become less distinct should make parents wary of thinking that they have much to do with the child learning about men's and women's part in society.

*If a boy today wants to know what it is to be a man how does he learn? If his father cooks dinner and his mother goes to work and they both dress him and take him to the baby-sitter what is he to conclude? The clear-cut qualities of gender are packaged in fashion dolls. Children's fascination with such toys has more to do with identity than role play.*

## Gender roles

Defined by society, gender roles can and do change. When observing your child's gender role stereotypes, keep in mind that preschool children are not able to think in shades of gray. Androgyny (the idea that everyone has both masculine and feminine traits) is not a concept they understand, but it is one they enact. The boy who wrestles with his brother and plays Batman all morning is gentle with his baby sister and takes his teddy bear to bed. The girl who plays with her dolls can be aggressive and bossy toward them. Children learn the reality of men and women from those around them. If parents and friends are free to show their androgynous natures, children will grow up with similar freedoms.

*As men become more involved in caring for their children, traditionally the preserve of women, boys have more difficulty in understanding what being male means. Playing cops and robbers or team sports helps boys to find an identity.*

# Silly games for parties and beaches

*Games to play when there are plenty of children who want to let off steam*

These games can be adapted to be played indoors or out, and with any number of children. You may have to give younger children "chances" if they are playing with several older ones.

### Pin the tail on the donkey

Draw a large donkey without a tail. It should be at least 10–12 inches (20–30 cm) long. Make a tail out of wool. The child must pin the tail on the donkey. The challenge is that the child is blindfolded and turned around twice before attempting the pinning. Use Velcro or a little tape to fix the tail.

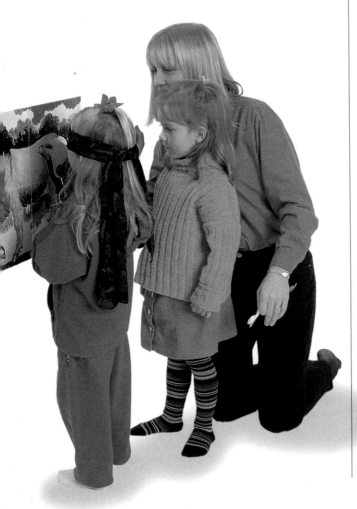

### Musical chairs

Everyone runs around a group of chairs (one less than there are children). When the music stops they sit down. When it starts again they run around. They can, of course, also dodge and bump and fall down laughing. You can adapt musical chairs for smaller children by using cushions on the floor, rather than chairs.

### Pass the hat

You will need as many silly hats as you have children. The music plays and when it stops the hats pass around. This may be enough to make the children giggle – or you could add a silly action that goes with each hat. Hats might include some made of newspaper, large brown envelopes and underwear as well as clown hats, wedding veils and doilies. If you have any costumy hats, so much the better.

### Pairs

Everyone has a picture pinned to his or her back. Pictures form pairs: there might be a glove and a hand, a sock and a shoe, a dog and a bone, a cat and a mouse. Without looking at their own picture children have to find their "pair."

### Red light, green light, one, two, three

One player – the caller – stands at the base and everyone else moves a certain distance away. The caller then hides her face and everyone else starts to creep up on her as she shouts "Red light, green light…" quickly or slowly. The aim is to touch the person on base without being seen moving. The caller can turn when she's finished reciting the phrase. The players can't guess how long that will take, and anyone she sees moving goes back to the start line.

### Can you hear me mother?

Children play this game in pairs. Each has a rolled up piece of newspaper. They hook their left legs together. When the starter says "Go," one child shouts "Can you hear me mother?" and the other

## WHAT YOUR CHILD LEARNS

All these games are good ways to let off steam, in relatively controlled circumstances (most need an adult to be referee). In addition:

### • Musical chairs
This teaches your child to listen for when the music stops. Like drop the handkerchief, it helps his physical coordination as he makes for the cushion.

### • Red light, green light, one, two, three
Players who fare best at this game can move quietly; stopping as soon as the caller does helps their coordination.

player shouts "No" and tries to get out of the way as the caller hits him once with the newspaper. Then the roles reverse. Players must remain joined at the knee.

### Drop the handkerchief

Children sit in a circle. One player walks around the outside carrying a handkerchief. He drops this behind another. This player must pick it up and try to catch the first player before he grabs the vacant place. Everyone must run clockwise around the circle. All players must look straight ahead until they can see or are told that the handkerchief has been dropped.

### Waiting for the tide

This is a game for tidal beaches and one that only the sea can win. The idea is to build a castle in a spot below the high tide mark and wait for the tide to knock it down. The fortifications hold the smallest children. The adults and the older children work to keep the castle and its fortifications in place for as long as possible.

# Whatever the weather

*Fun games do not have to be confined to warm, sunny days*

You can teach your child about the weather by playing games that work only in certain weather conditions. This also makes them special to talk about later.

### Games for sunshine

#### Rolling down grassy slopes
Why children like to make themselves dizzy is unclear but they do. All you need is a dry grassy slope and a bunch of children. They lie sideways onto the hill and start to roll. It is wise to move any stones out of their path, because the children can gather speed.

#### Turning windmills
This is another dizzy game. The child stands with arms outstretched and whirls around until she is so dizzy she falls over. This is more fun to play when there are other children staggering about too.

#### A human sundial
This needs a sunny spot. A south facing patio or driveway would be ideal (or you could play on the beach). The child stands on a fixed spot and at exactly 12 o'clock the position of her shadow is marked. The position at two other times (ideally one in the morning and another in the afternoon) is also marked. Draw a circle between these three points and work out the times the shadow will fall between them. The full shadow will give only a rough time. A more accurate time can be obtained by holding a stick (or a plastic sword) against his nose so that it stretches above the line of his head. Numbers can be painted onto concrete or nails knocked into tarmac to mark the time for future reference.

#### Sprinklers
Nothing is more conducive to glee than a garden sprinkler, half a dozen children and a warm, sunny day. Just strip the children to their underwear, turn on the sprinkler and let them run in and out. Have some large fluffy towels handy in case any of them feels cold.

#### Mirrors
Small plastic mirrors can be bought from pet shops. On sunny days these can be used to send reflections onto walls, fences and buildings. Prisms and crystals are even more impressive.

### Games for wind

#### A message in a bottle
An offshore wind and a falling tide quickly carry bottles with messages away. They may come back on the next tide, be thrown up on the next beach or be carried away to faraway lands and distant times. You may never hear of them again. You will need a bottle, some paper and a waterproof marker. Write your name, address and the place you are throwing the bottle into the sea. Add any message you want. Then seal the bottle (a cork plus duct tape is best) and throw.

## TROUBLESHOOTING

**When other children come around to play Paul becomes mean and selfish and refuses to share, even if we're all out in the backyard. If other children try to take one of his toys he loses control and has a tantrum. How can I prevent him losing all his friends?**

Discuss with him beforehand which toys should be put away and which he is willing to let his friends use. It will also help if you organize activities that do not need any toys, which is much easier outdoors. Remind him before his friends arrive that he has agreed to share. If you see he's upset, distract him. If he looks possessive, remind him what you have both agreed to.

### Standing in the wind
Find a high spot on a windy day and stand facing the wind. Or find a beach where the waves are crashing and the wind almost blows you away.

### Catch a falling leaf
Visits to the park on windy autumn days mean leaves to chase. It doesn't matter if the child does not catch one. She can still carry one home.

### Games for rain
· · · · · · · · · · · · · · · · · · · · · · · · · · · · · · · · · ·

### Tracing raindrops
This is a game for a wet day when you are all trapped in the house. Each person picks a spot of rain and follows it down the windowpane. You could have races or see which drops go farthest.

### Pooh sticks
For this game you need a bridge over flowing water and a pile of sticks. It is most exciting when the river is swollen with rain. Throw the sticks in on the upriver side of the bridge, and watch for them on the downriver side. (This is not a game for a busy road.)

### Games for snow
· · · · · · · · · · · · · · · · · · · · · · · · · · · · · · · · · ·

### A family slide
Sleds are fine once a snowy hill has been packed down well, but until then a drop cloth is much more fun. It also helps prepare the sled run. Put down the drop cloth, all climb on and edge it forward. Being a little out of control is part of the fun.

### The biggest snowball
Even small amounts of snow can be gathered up into large balls as long as it is damp and sticky. Start with a small ball and keep rolling.

### Snowmen
Snowballs can be made into snowmen, women, children, dogs and cats. If there is enough time and snow you could make a whole family or spend your energies on making one stylish and beautiful person. You can give him a traditional carrot nose and a scarf, or model a head of curls and give her a sunhat and a pair of dark glasses.

### Footsteps
There is something about fresh snow that beckons people to stamp in it – whatever their age.

## WHAT YOUR CHILD LEARNS

**• Changing seasons**
Watching the weather change from season to season introduces your child to the idea of the natural cycles and rhythms of life. It also gives him some reference points: his birthday is in summer; it may snow at Christmas or Hanukkah; leaves fall in autumn.

**• Basic science**
Many of these games introduce scientific concepts: snow is different from rain; the Sun makes shadows; mirrors reflect light; the wind blows things away.

# Becoming a self-starter

Independence gives children confidence and self-esteem. "I can" always sounds better than "I can't," especially when everyone else is able to do it. There are times when every child wants the dependency of babyhood – usually when her caregiver is busy and she needs attention, or when she is out of sorts and unhappy – but most of the time children grab at any independence when it is offered. To be independent a child must be able to carry out the basics of caring for herself – eating, dressing, using the toilet, washing. More important, she must be able to motivate herself into action, whatever the task. A child who can put on her pants but does not do so until told is still dependent on you. If you let this type of dependency (put that away, don't touch, do you need the toilet, eat your broccoli) permeate every action, life away from you will be hard for your child. Neither her teachers nor her peers have the time to organize her every action.

# Milestones in becoming independent

## THE ROAD TO INDEPENDENCE

### 9-12 months
- She should be able to sleep without you holding her hand.
- She should be able to play when you leave the room for a moment.
- She should be able to feed herself with her fingers and hold a sucking cup.

### 12-18 months
- She should be able to play alone.
- She should be able to use a cup and feed herself messily.

### 18-24 months
- She should be beginning to wash herself and use a toothbrush (you will probably still have to do a follow-up cleaning).
- She should be a little more skilled at feeding herself (although still messy).
- She may be ready for toilet training.
- She should be starting to dress herself, but can manage only pull-on clothes.
- She should be able to play without always being organized.

### 2-3 years
- By the age of three, most children should be clean and dry by day, and able to take themselves to the toilet (or ask to be taken) without always being reminded. (When busy they may still need reminding.)
- She should be able to dress and undress herself in pull-on clothes and put on a coat, but will still need help with buttons, zippers, shoelaces or anything tight.
- Eating should be neater, but she will not be able to manage a knife.
- She should clear away her toys and be able to play in the yard.

### 3-4 years
- At four years old, she should be able to wash herself and clean her teeth, dress and undress, eat fairly neatly, drink from a cup and take out and put away toys.
- Under supervision she should be able to carry out an activity from start to finish.
- She should use language to express needs and feelings.

### 4-6 years
- She should be able to organize her own play.
- She should be able to carry through an activity without waiting for praise and direction (although praise never goes amiss).
- She should be able to sit quietly and cope for extended periods without her main caregiver.
- She should be able to dress herself completely, bathe herself, clean her teeth and use a knife to spread and cut (some meat may still be difficult).
- She should be ready to spend large parts of the day without you and able to share attention with 20–30 other children and thrive.

## HOW YOU CAN HELP

- Do not sit with your child while she drops off to sleep.
- If you leave the room during the day, come back soon and greet her warmly so she has confidence that you will return.
- Let her try to eat by herself even though she makes a mess.
- Praise, praise and praise again.
- Cuddle her warmly.

- Praise her for trying.
- Laugh off mess.
- Adopt a stone face toward the bad and the babyish.
- Don't wait for her to succeed: show your pleasure for every little step along the way.
- Cuddle her warmly.

- "You are clever!," "What a big girl you are!," "That is difficult, I'm very proud of how hard you try" should figure large in your vocabulary.
- Criticism should be confined to behaviors, never to children ("That's a silly thing to do" not "You're being stupid").
- Always make sure the praise outweighs criticism ("That's a very clean face, but there's a tiny bit you've missed here").
- Cuddle her warmly and tell her you love her.

- Laugh off errors if she has made an effort ("Oh dear, we need a toilet with legs to run down the stairs. That would be funny, wouldn't it?").
- Reminders are still necessary, but allow her to take some responsibility and always praise her when she does.
- Accept her frustrations when things do not go as they should.
- Show her how to express frustrations without losing control ("Those socks would make anyone mad. Stamp on them to show me how mad you feel. That much? I hope they'll behave better next time").
- Make chores into games: a special "cleaning up" record can turn the chore into a race.
- It goes without saying that she still needs to be cuddled often and know she's loved.

- Be the coach on the bench and an entire troop of cheerleaders but don't rush in before she needs help.
- Continue to love, praise and appreciate effort.
- Curb criticism and confine it to the behavior rather than the child. Remember she is a good person behaving badly.
- Let her know you make mistakes: "Silly Mommy" and "Silly Daddy" should feature largely.
- Tell her and show her that you love her.

- Expect competence but help where help is needed.
- Do not rush in before she has had time to try; wait for her to ask and then coach her to take one further step. Praise her when she does.
- Hold back and let her carry through an activity without waiting for praise and direction at every stage.
- Give attention for behavior that will put her in good stead at school: sitting quietly, getting on with activities, asking for help, expressing problems, being helpful, paying attention and listening.
- Ignore attention-seeking activities which will label her as difficult: antisocial behavior, disruption, temper tantrums, aggression, skipping from activity to activity and not listening.
- Keep cuddling her and make it clear that you love her.

# Coping and working alone

*School demands that children can work for extended periods without constant direction and feedback*

Starting school means a child must cope for a large part of the day without the one-on-one interaction he has known at home. If he is to slip happily between home and school your child must be able to fit into a much larger group and be capable of continuing an activity when he is not the center of attention. He must have the social competence to ask for what he needs, the personal confidence to try even when something is difficult and the ego to withstand criticism.

At a practical level he must be able to work by himself, focus attention, listen, understand and sit still for extended periods. A secure child copes better on all these fronts, especially if he has been encouraged to be independent.

### Intermittent schedules

If you are training a dog to sit you say "Good boy" every time he does it. Children are basically the same. When a child first learns to do something he needs consistent rewards. The consistency helps him to understand what he should do, and tells him that you are pleased. But

if you keep on rewarding the child every single time, he will perform to gain your praise rather than completing a task to feel competent or take pleasure in the activity.

Before they start school children need to be able to cope with, and get used to, intermittent praise. The more the child works by himself the more he needs to learn to praise himself. Show him how. Encourage him to pat himself on the back and tell himself "I did really well." There is no motivation to do this if you always rush in; your child has to learn that gratification is often delayed.

### Listen to what children say

Actions speak louder than words. Look at him when he speaks to you and lean toward him so that he knows what he says is of interest to you. Never deny what he says is true, or that his experiences aren't real. Naming a feeling makes it better not worse. Sometimes adults should control their feelings and protect their children from them. But if you always disguise your emotions, children do not know that others also feel angry,

*The ability to sit and work or read alone is fundamental to school work. Encouraging your child to indulge in quiet activities at some time of the day is an ideal way to prepare for this aspect of school life.*

*No teacher can cope with 30 children chatting and moving around at will. The ability to request permission to move and wait to be asked to contribute is essential.*

upset and scared. Knowing makes it easier to cope. If he is upset, sympathize. Sympathy encourages him to expel negative feelings from his system, which is always better than trying to pretend they were never there. Even adults find this difficult. Express what the child feels because this helps him to clarify his emotions. Going out into the wide world is a scary prospect.

### Keep trying

However you say it, make the message of perseverance clear. If at first you don't succeed, try, try again. While he is in your care you can always help your child. It is often easier than letting him struggle. But always jumping in prevents him from learning and discourages him from tackling any difficult challenges.

### I'm busy

If you teach a child that you are always prepared to drop everything for him, he will expect others to do the same. Sooner or later a child has to learn that everyone has a right to come first sometimes, and everyone has to take a turn in coming last. While it would not be right to tell a child constantly that you are too busy for him, it is equally wrong never to tell a child this. True independence depends on everyone having rights.

### Self-confidence and security

Security is the bedrock of independence. A securely attached child knows that as his parent or caregiver you are there for him, but also that if you go away you will return. Most of all, security is knowing that whatever he does or doesn't do, love is without question. His parents love him for himself alone.

### Dependence and independence

The love of a tiny child is unquestioning. It is difficult to accept that it cannot continue like this forever, especially if you have not known a great deal of love in your own life. But the love that initially makes children thrive can become stifling unless you accept that it must grow and change. You do not love your child less because you allow independence; you love more, and less selfishly.

### The right time and the right place

Children like repetition; it makes them feel secure. They like to hear the same story over and over again and wear the same T-shirt for a week. This conformity makes it easier to plan the day. You can have messy time at 11 o'clock every morning, and go shopping after lunch. More than that, routine is a source of security. Children like to know what is happening to them. Even though you let them know today's plan, they may forget. An unchanging daily regime is easier to remember and makes them feel secure.

### Activity and inactivity

There is nothing that is guaranteed to make a child more unpopular than running around the classroom when he is supposed to be working. Dividing the day into quiet and noisy periods will help him learn to let off steam when the opportunity arises, and settle quietly again when he has to do so.

# Getting dressed
*Being able to put on her own clothes makes your child independent*

Part of the independence that getting dressed brings is managing to go to the toilet by herself and put on her coat and shoes at playschool. Not being able to manage makes her look like a baby in front of her friends. In the long run the fact that she can dress herself cuts down a parent's work, but in the short term it can be frustrating for both parents and child. Socks and tantrums have an affinity, and shoes that go on the wrong foot are common. In the morning rush it is often easier to scoop her up and dress her yourself. This is sometimes necessary, but don't do it every morning: she will not learn unless she practices.

Loose clothes make it easier. Jeans with zippers, shirts and dresses with buttons and skirts and trousers with bibs may look fashionable, but they are difficult for small inexperienced hands to deal with, as are shoe buckles and laces. While she is learning to dress herself, choose elastic and Velcro whenever there is an option.

## Putting on underpants

*The right choice:* pants that have an interesting pattern on the front and clearly marked leg holes.
*The problems:* getting both legs in one hole; getting the legs in the body hole.
*How to do it:* lay the pants out on the floor. Sit the child at the top end. Make sure the feet are poking out of the leg holes before pulling pants up.

## Putting on socks

*The right choice:* socks without heels would be ideal; failing this, oft for something stretchy where the base of the foot and the top of the sock where the toes go are different.
*The problems:* mixing up the heel and toe end.
*How to do it:* put the socks down on the floor with the heels facing each other. Fold the top of the sock over the heel. Show the child how to slip her foot into the sock and check that the heel is on the bottom before pulling the sock right up, but without scrunching up her toes.

## Putting on pants

*The right choice:* loose with elastic waists. No zipper.
*The problems:* zippers, buttons and bibs. Tight pants and putting both legs in the same side.
*How to do it:* lay the pants out the right way round with the seat rolled down to the crotch. Show the child how to put in both legs before pulling the seat up.

## Putting on T-shirts and tops

*The right choice:* a T-shirt with a clear pattern on the front and a plain back; a large neck also helps. Avoid tops with back fasteners.

*The problems:* knowing which is the right way around; doing up fasteners.

*How to do it:* lay it out so that the picture, if it has one, is hidden and the neck is farthest away. Show her how to burrow in from the bottom, push her arms through the armholes and pull the top over her head. Teach her to fasten any buttons. T-shirt dresses and jumpers can be put on in the same way.

## Putting on skirts

*The right choice:* those with elastic waists.

*The problems:* bibs, buttons, zippers.

*How to do it:* lay it on the floor. Slip legs in from the waist. Stand up and pull it up.

## Putting on shoes

*The right choice:* elasticated shoes or ones that fasten with a Velcro strap; avoid buckles and shoe-laces until your child can manage shoes well. Likewise, boots should not have fastenings.

*The problems:* getting them on the wrong feet.

*How to do it:* children sit with their knees out and their feet together, which means the fasteners – the interesting parts – should go underneath. Explain the fastener has to hide, and put the shoes out in the right orientation. With boots, put them right way around on the floor at the bottom of the stairs. Let the child step into them.

## Putting on coats (shirts and sweaters)

*The right choice:* toggles are the easiest fasteners.

*The problems:* both arms in, right way around.

*How to do it:* put the coat on the floor button side up. Show the child how to slip her arms into the sleeves and swing the coat on.

## Putting on gloves

*The right choice:* mittens.

*The problems:* find correct hand and thumb hole.

*How to do it:* mittens attached to the sleeves of her coat with elastic are in the right place for each hand. A mark on the front helps orientation.

# Learning through helping

*Domestic tasks may be chores to you but to your child helping is playing*

Children do not understand the difference between work and play; all that matters to them is whether a task is fun. You may find washing dishes a chore, but to a three-year-old it can be a wonderful game. Like schoolwork, helping activities should have a structure and an aim. They encourage children to plan. "Helping" involves a sequence of activities that start at a beginning and work toward an end. Noise makes children "go," so music may help with tasks that can be worked through a set time sequence, such as picking up toys. However, music may well be a distraction when it is necessary for the child to stop and think.

## Cleaning activities

From a very young age your child is likely to follow you around with a mini-broom or lawn mower, imitating your actions. At first such activities are simply imitation, but later your child will be delighted if you offer her the chance to do "housework" for real.

Children and water make an excellent combination. Let your child stand at the sink, put on a waterproof apron on to protect her clothes, and do not have the water too hot. Her own tea set after a doll's tea party is an obvious item to clean, but any "grown up" china that is

not too dirty or expensive and any cutlery that is not too sharp are all suitable for a child to wash and dry.

Polishing is another activity children love, but most polishes have a strong smell and may not be suitable for a small child to use. Similarly, many love cleaning windows, but window cleaners are too harsh. Dusting, however, is ideal for children. Encourage both boys and girls to dust the furniture.

## Putting away toys

If there is a single situation that is liable to cause a bad temper, it is getting children to tidy up after themselves. Start early, make it clear that you expect them to help and always praise them at the end.

Make a game of this by using music. Start by describing the task, using such phrases as "puzzle in the box," "teddies in the chest." Keep the list short for the youngest children – you can always add to it. It's a good idea to set a time, otherwise your child may be distracted along the way. Use such phrases as "Can we pick all these up before the music stops?" Build up the excitement by using such tricks as "Are you ready? Steady? Just a second … Go!"

Small children have more difficulty stopping than starting. Noise excites them and all the "go" parts of the brain are switched on. (This is why shouting at a small child rarely works.) For this task, however, being on "go" really helps.

## Helping at mealtimes

Cooking (see pp. 214–15) is loved by all children, but there are lots of other ways they can help you with food preparation if you don't have time for cooking. Let the children help make sandwiches, perhaps buttering the bread, slicing banana or placing sliced ham or cheese on the bread. If you do any slicing that needs a sharp knife, your child should be able to do the rest.

Setting the table and clearing it away when the meal is finished are also tasks that your child can help with. Setting the table is a perfect matching game: each person needs one plate, one fork, one knife and one cup, for example.

## Helping with the shopping

Every parent knows how important is it for children to be able to draw, even though the earliest results may look like scribble. It is, however, difficult to remember that they should also be encouraged to write. Elements of both drawing and writing are present in your child's earliest artworks (see pp. 82–3). Encourage writing simultaneously with your encouragement of drawing. Your child does not have to write real words, but give her a piece of paper and let her write a shopping list. Point out any letter-like shapes: "Lily, I see you have made an M there. Does that mean we need margarine or marshmallows?" Write a simple list for your child, perhaps with drawings alongside the words so that she can find some items on the shelves.

Supermarkets, in particular, are full of all sorts of interesting letters and numbers for an observant child to identify. Looking for small details in the environment in this way helps to build your child's ability to concentrate.

Once you are home, putting away some of the shopping teaches your child many skills. Learning to sort things into groups and subgroups is a way of understanding what they have in common. Give your child the time she needs to put the shopping away at her own pace.

## WHAT YOUR CHILD LEARNS

All these activities teach your child that working together, like playing together, is good fun – an essential attitude to take to school.

### • Clearing up the toys
This teaches your child to be helpful and to please others as she enjoys herself. Social interaction is at the very root of early learning skills. Working together enables children to predict what others will say and do. Working at a complete task like this is excellent practice for school, where almost everything your child does has a beginning, middle and an end.

### • Helping with the shopping
Shopping sharpens a child's observation skills and eye for detail, both important prereading skills. Sorting out purchases in order to put them away helps her to understand number concepts.

### • Cleaning activities
This builds a child's self-esteem since you trust her with a grown-up task.

### • Helping at mealtimes
These activities help sorting and matching skills, which are the foundation of mathematical skills.

# Cooking
*Give your child the opportunity to create a finished dish*

These are just a few of the many recipes you and your child can make together in the kitchen. Be guided by your child's likes and dislikes and try not to mind if you make the same dishes again and again.

## Making pizza

A pizza is one of the easiest meals to prepare with a child. The crust can be made from bread dough, biscuit or soda bread dough, a mix or, alternatively, buy a crust from the supermarket. You can even use the crust section from a round loaf or a chunk of French bread. If you make the dough let your child do the measuring and mixing. A big bowl is a good idea, even if you are making only a small quantity. Biscuit and soda bread doughs do not need to be left to rise. Bread dough can be left to rise in the airing cupboard.

### Biscuit dough
8 oz (225 g) all-purpose flour
½ tsp (2.5 g) salt
¼–½ pt (125–250 ml) milk or yoghurt
2 tsp (10 g) sugar
2 oz (50 g) butter

### Soda bread dough
2 tsp (10 g) baking powder
½ tsp (2.5 g) salt
1 oz (30 g) cheddar cheese
snipped chives, optional
1 tsp (5 g) sugar
¼–½ pt (125–250 ml) milk or buttermilk

Mix everything together to make a stiff dough. Divide into four and roll out on a floured board. Cut into circles, using a plate as a guide.

## Decorating and making faces on pizza

The crust of the pizza is traditionally covered with tomato sauce, but pesto, garlic butter or olive oil with garlic and herbs are options. Cut shapes for eyes, nose and mouth from ham, sausage, vegetables, peppers or olives, then let the child put these on the pizza. Make hair from grated cheese. Alternatively, the child could pile on his favorite fillings, then put the face on top. Cook in a very hot oven (475°F / 220°C) for 10–15 minutes.

## An apple pastry for snack-time

Apple pastries can be made from ready-made pastry. Let your child roll out the pastry and show him how to cut it into 6-inch (15-cm) squares. Peel and slice the apples and let your child cut these into small sections. Mix with raisins and cinnamon (if desired) and put a couple of spoonfuls onto one-half of the pastry. Add sugar to the middle of the apple and cover with more apple (if sugar comes into contact with pastry it goes soggy): you need about 1 oz (30 g) for each 1 lb (450 g) apples. Paint the edges of the pastry

## WHAT YOUR CHILD LEARNS

Children like to be helpful, and helping with cooking (and shopping) not only allows them to do so but also teaches them a whole variety of skills.

### • Observation of detail
This is important whether he is looking for a particular type of food, such as beans, or the brand you normally have (letters, words).

### • Independence
Choosing what to buy or what to eat makes your child feel independent and enhances his self-esteem.

### • Hand control
Sifting and spooning ingredients are excellent ways to practice hand skills.

### • Wrist control
Stirring and beating improve wrist control.

### • Mathematical skills
Weighing and measuring teach an understanding of mathematics.

### • Working toward an end
Much of cooking is about working toward something: a cake, pastry, the dinner, something for Grandma.

with milk. Fold over to make an oblong. Seal and crimp with a fork. Glaze with egg yolk and bake in a hot oven (400°F / 200°C) for about 20 minutes until golden brown. Test with a knife. If the fruit is not yet soft, return to a lower oven rack for another 15 minutes.

If baking apples are not available use tart dessert apples such as Granny Smiths; add a squeeze of lemon and much less sugar.

### Animal toast

Let your child butter two slices of bread. Use animal-shaped cookie cutters to cut two shapes from each slice. Cut similar shapes from a piece of ham or sausage (slice the meat into strips if this is easier). Grate some cheese. Let the child make two open sandwiches using the cheese and ham. Pop these under the broiler. Add eyes (snipped spring onions) and whiskers (chives) after cooking.

### Fancy jelly

All children love stirring gelatin mixes, and you can make a simple and wholesome one with fruit juice and gelatin (vegetarian is available). You need about ¼ oz (20 g) gelatin to 1 pt (500 ml) juice, or follow the packet instructions. Dissolve the gelatin in a little of the hot liquid. Cool, then let the child stir this into the fruit juice. Add grapes: cut these in half and he can remove the seeds.

### Making truffles for Grandma

3 tbsp (45 g) unsweetened cocoa
2 oz (50 g) unsalted butter
1 oz (30 g) brandy or coffee or a little vanilla
8 fl oz (250 ml) heavy cream
8 oz (250 g) good quality plain chocolate, grated in a
    warmed bowl
Pitcher of hot water

Give your child the bowl of grated chocolate. Heat the cream in the microwave at 100 percent for two minutes 30 seconds. Pour over the chocolate and let your child stir until it is dissolved. Add the butter and the flavoring and stir again (warm the butter slightly if it is very hard). Chill the mixture in the fridge for two hours.

Fill a saucer with the cocoa. Scoop a ball of the chocolate mix from the basin and add to the cocoa. Let your child roll this briefly in the cocoa. Repeat until all the mixture is used. You will need to dip the scoop in hot water between balls. Store the truffles in a box dusted with cocoa powder.

# Gardening
*Introducing your child to a love of growing things*

Even if you are not a keen gardener yourself, try to give your child access to this life-enriching hobby.

## An instant garden

Even when there is no time to grow plants, children can make a garden from scraps and pieces they collect. Start with a seed tray or a shallow box. Put in a layer of soil. Your child can transplant some plants into this and decorate with flowers, pebbles, a small mirror, bits of broken tile or anything else that catches his eye. This garden is not meant to last, so it does not matter that the flowers will fade.

## Nice to eat

Children like to be able to eat what they sow: Radishes are ready in a matter of weeks. Mung beans – once they sprout they can be eaten. Tomatoes take longer, but have the advantage that they are both hungry and thirsty. There is always something that needs to be done.

## TROUBLESHOOTING

**What is reasonable to expect of a four-year-old? My partner says that our son (who is just four) is old enough to keep his room neat, clean himself up after he's been in the yard and put his toys away. I think this is unreasonable.**

It depends on what your partner means by keeping his room neat. It is reasonable to expect a preschool child to keep his room relatively neat, but not immaculate. If he has help, direction and encouragement he can clear up his toys, but expecting him always to remember to is unreasonable. It is easier if he has a special place for each item rather than a general toy cabinet.

You can expect him to stay clean for a short period of time, but not all day or if he has been playing in the yard or at playschool. If he has "good" and "play" clothes the message is clear.

If you always do everything for children they will be messy. After all, if they don't have to do the work, why should they bother?

Strawberries are good – grow them in a special pot.

## A more lasting garden

Bedding plants are ideal for a child's garden. They retain some of the mystery of watching the garden grow and change, without the long wait that is all too common with many seeds. They can provide interest over a very long period. If you do not have room for your child to have a section of garden of her own, consider letting her have a large tub. Fill this with potting compost and make sure that the pot retains as much water as possible. Help your child with the first two or three plants then leave her to plant the rest. It is sometimes difficult to get the small plants out of the packages without damaging them, so it is advisable to do this for a small child. It is a good idea to have a mix of plants so that some come into bloom when others have finished flowering. If you add a small conifer you have year-round color.

## Growing trees from seeds and pips

Lots of fruit seeds and pips will sprout if covered in potting compost and kept warm and damp. The easiest way to do this is to put them in a small pot, dampen the soil and then enclose the top of the pot with a plastic bag. Water that evaporates can then roll back onto the soil. Try orange, lemon, lime, grapefruit and melon pips, paw paw, passion fruit, and kiwi fruit seeds. Avocado stones will sprout but need to be half immersed in water (jars sold for growing hyacinth bulbs in water work well). You could also try mango stones.

## Mr. Grass head

Fill an old nylon stocking with soil-less compost. Tie it so as to make a head. Draw in a face and plant grass seed on the top of the head to grow into hair. Trim as necessary.

## A tree for me

Let the child choose a tree. One with flowers and fruit or one with interesting leaves and flowers at different seasons would be nice. Let her help you plant it. She can watch it grow as she grows.

## PLANTS TO GROW AND GROW

For adults, part of the joy of gardening is planning how it will look and watching plants slowly grow. Children are less patient: they like plants that grow quickly.

**• Sunflower**
These grow more than six feet in a few months. The seeds can be planted directly in the ground or into small pots. Seedlings can be potted on.

**• Nasturtium**
Climbing varieties can grow all over the fence and will flower right up to the first frosts.

**• Canary creeper**
A pretty yellow flower with long clambering stems. It is somewhat delicate and so will need to be started in pots indoors.

**• Black-eyed Susan**
A pretty annual climber. Needs to be started off indoors.

**• Banana**
These will not fruit outside in colder climates. But they will grow outside during the summer months. The seeds take a long time to germinate, but they grow at breakneck speed.

# *Head start for school*

One moment he is a baby, the next your child is ready for school. Starting school makes demands that parents cannot back down on: children have to go to school and they have to go every day. Your child will be away from you for the entire day, competing with his peers for his teacher's attention. He will have to cope with a noisy playground and children who may not be considerate or friendly; he will have to sit still, be quiet and work without constant attention or praise. It is a tall order. The more you can prepare your child for school the better he will cope. He does not need to be able to read, write and add before he starts school, but it will help if he can sustain an activity without adult guidance, sit without fidgeting, control a pencil and handle the bustle of a roomful of strangers.

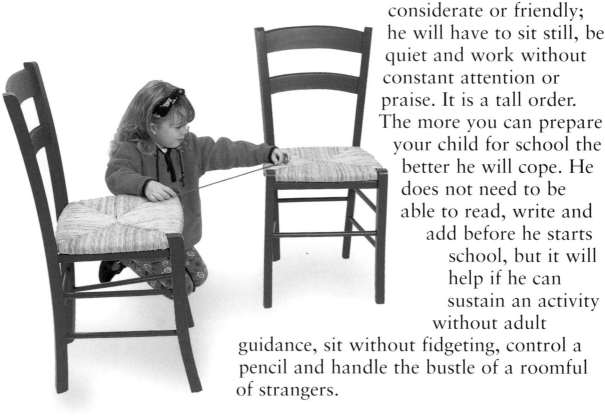

**Milestones in preparing for school**

| WHAT YOUR CHILD NEEDS TO DO | HOW YOU CAN HELP | |
|---|---|---|
| ● **Survive away from his loved ones**<br>Parents can often go into school for the first few days, but sooner or later they have to leave. A child who needs you to be with him to feel secure will be lost. | Substitute caregivers who love the child give him the confidence that he can cope without you. He may not be able to take a comfort object into school but having one teaches the child how to "psych" himself up to cope. A special word or activity can act like a comfort object to psych him up. | |
| ● **Cope with strangers**<br>Even if he has a few friends the school is full of strangers. | Psyching himself up helps here, too, but it needs practice. Children have to know how to approach other children and that strangers become friends. There is no substitute for experience. A daily visit to the park and joining various group activities are the best preparation. | |
| ● **Survive in a crowd**<br>Playgrounds can be alarming. They are often noisy and most children are not only bigger than he is, but they also race about. | Take a trip on public transportation, presenting it as a treat, to show him that crowds can be exciting rather than frightening, even when people are bigger than you. If your child goes from home to car and back again he may never experience the bustle of the playground. | |
| ● **Not crumple if criticized**<br>Even if his teachers do not criticize him, other children will. Such criticisms may be well founded or just mean and spiteful. A child who crumples is fun to bully. | Children need praise because this gives them self-esteem. Children whose self-esteem is fragile collapse easily. Even with high esteem children need to be taught techniques to cope with criticism. Whatever anyone else thinks he is your special boy. Whatever anyone else thinks your love for him is as high as the sky and twice as wide. | |
| ● **Work with intermittent praise**<br>However much they would like to, few teachers have the time to give every child constant praise for each step they take along the way. | By the time he starts school he should not need constant encouragement. But he still needs plenty of praise and to know you are proud of his achievements. | |
| ● **Work by himself**<br>Sooner or later children have to learn how to work alone. | There is little point in setting a room aside for play if you are never in there with him. Children like to play under grown-ups' feet. Weaning him from always playing with you should be gradual. | |
| ● **Settle down and sit still**<br>All children have to learn to listen in silence once they start school. Those who do not do so may learn that disruption gains them lots of attention which is a "skill" few teachers or parents want them to learn. | Reading stories, watching videos, traveling in the car, helping with the housework, playing in the bath or at the sink, sitting and building or helping with the cooking should be in the daily repertoire. But punctuate these with some noisy games for the fidgety child. If he learns he can scream and shout and run around in "noisy time" he should be able to wait to let off steam until school recess. | |
| ● **Express his needs verbally**<br>Parents can usually read their child's expressions and body postures and anticipate his needs. Teachers cannot do this; nor can other children. To function in school he needs to be able to express himself in words. | Wait for him to ask even if you know what he wants. Encourage him to tell you about his day even if you shared it with him. Consult him and take note of his requests. | |
| ● **Have the prerequisite skills**<br>Not all children have every component skill in place when they start school, but they will feel more competent if they do. Starting from an "I can" attitude is always better than beginning with the thought "I can't." | Help him to work by himself, finish what he starts, look carefully and take note of small details. Encourage him to learn how to control a pencil and familiarize him with the written word and the concept of numbers. | |

## ACTIVITIES THAT MAY HELP

- Playing out in the yard or in a room by himself.
- Going to a nursery or playgroup.
- Going to play in another child's house or yard.
- Being left with baby-sitters or substitute caregivers.

- Going to the park and playing in the sandbox or kiddie pool.
- Attending mother and baby groups and, later, playgroups.
- Talking to people when he is out with his caregiver.

- Going to the swimming pool.
- Experiencing crowded and noisy places such as train stations and busy shopping malls.
- Playing alongside children on an apparatus at the park.

- Having high self-esteem.
- Having self-control.
- Being able to psych himself up.

- Playing in a room a little distance from his parents.
- Playing out in the yard.
- Having his finished picture put on the wall rather than praised line by line.

- Being expected to fetch his own toys, amuse himself then put them away.
- Being expected to wash and dress himself.
- Knowing how to switch on his tape player so he can listen to a story.

- Sitting at the table to eat.
- Waiting his turn.
- Usually completing what he has started.
- Playing games which require concentration such as building, drawing or playing with playdough.

- Expecting him to say what he wants, and allowing him to do so.
- Saying in words rather than tears or bad behavior that he needs attention. Let him know he can say "I need a cuddle Mom." One way to convey this is to tell him you need a cuddle when you are feeling low.

- Knowing how to use a pencil and being able to control his hand.
- Knowing how to look for detail.
- Being familiar with the concepts of reading and numbers even if he cannot recognize letters or count.
- Understanding what work is.

# In the classroom

*A major point about school is that your child is working for himself in a competitive environment*

Small children know how to learn. They approach the new task with enthusiasm and try to work the problem out, or they watch their caregivers and copy them. They expect praise. Having gleaned a rough idea of what to do, they practice and practice until they get it just right. Tiny children think learning is fun and adults agree with them (adults call children's learning play). Small children are cooperative and helpful and those that are well looked after expect the same of other people. With siblings, an element of competition creeps into this tranquil world, as it does for any child who has had to share his caregiver's attention with others (which all children do to some extent). However, the competition at home is rarely on a scale to compare with that found every day in the school classroom.

As in the home a child can attract notice for being good – or bad. If he needs regular attention from a caregiver he will do whichever is easiest. The best techniques for gaining a teacher's attention are to work hard, to sit and daydream, to chatter constantly or to be disruptive. The more attention the child needs the more likely he is to choose one of the last three options.

## Less help than at home

The 20:1 child/adult ratio of the typical classroom means that children receive less encouragement or gentle nudging in the right direction than they did at home. Learning becomes more dependent on listening and working without the attention of a caregiver. Children who have learned how to praise themselves thrive in this environment. Those who still need coaxing from an adult because they cannot praise themselves have difficulties.

Life inevitably becomes more competitive when 20 children all do the same thing and some

*While most children learn quickly that their peers may be better at some aspects of schoolwork and worse at others, the fact that sports and other "fun" activities are also occasions for competition can come as a shock.*

always do better than others. Not all children can be among the best all the time, and the realization that he will never be head of the class can be a shock – especially for a firstborn. Coming to terms with not excelling at schoolwork can be difficult, especially if he learns that there are other ways (being the noisiest, most disruptive, naughtiest child) to adopt center stage.

### Coping with the crowd

Children need to have experience of being "one of the crowd" before they start school. Preschool playgroups, nursery schools or even swimming and trampoline classes are the best introduction. If your child finds school difficult you may need to find a group that is less concerned with success and failure. Learning self-sufficiency is another solution.

### Reinforcement schedules

Those who study learning in rats know that if you give a rat a lump of sugar every time it does what you want it to do, it stops behaving in the correct way almost as soon as the sugar is withdrawn. If it is on an intermittent schedule of reinforcement, it learns to work without consistent rewards. The same applies to children – bear it in mind as your child approaches school age. If he is used to an intermittent schedule of praise, he should thrive.

The most consistent behavior comes from schedules that reward the child after a variable interval. Sometimes praise him when he starts. At other times wait to express approval until he is part way through his activity, near the end or when he has finished.

### Self-motivation

The key to coping with school is to learn how to motivate and reinforce yourself. A child who can praise his own work is not reliant on a teacher's approval. A child who can plough through his exercise without having every detail explained also puts himself in line for praise and success. "Getting on with it" while others struggle is a competition won – even if the results of his activities are not among the best.

*Teachers cannot give constant praise to all the children in their care. But a reward system of stars and badges is a powerful motivating force for your child to work diligently. He'll find it easier if, before he starts school, he is already used to playing creatively and working alone for short periods without praise at every step.*

### Growing used to working

Once children start school they are expected to settle down and work for extended periods of time. They are not allowed to jump from activity to activity and have to complete the tasks given to them. For many children this is the most difficult aspect of starting school. If you always let your child stop when he is fed up you will never instill the necessary perseverance. It is a matter of compromising between only ever having one piece of paper to draw on and being able to throw out 10 drawings before he gets started. Tidying up after himself is a reasonable expectation to place on a four- to five-year-old and encourages him to work toward an end and finish what he started.

### Retaining the pleasure of finding out

Small children love to explore and discover. When they first enter school most children are wide-eyed and ready to learn. Not all of them continue to find learning such fun. Competition is fine if you are among the best but disheartening if your best efforts still result in failure. A poor start is also likely if children are not prepared for learning: if, for example, they cannot sit still or work by themselves. The best way to ensure your child enjoys learning is to encourage him to take pleasure in discovering how things work. An inquisitive mind always wants to find out why.

# Nature and science

*Finding something out for themselves gives children a huge amount of enjoyment and satisfaction*

When children find an activity fun, they relish it. If you can reinforce the enjoyment of her toddler years in making discoveries about the world as your child nears school, you will help her retain her enthusiasm for work.

### Blue celery

Mix some blue ink or food coloring with water and put it in a jam jar. Take a stick of celery and put it in the jar. As the celery absorbs water, sections also take up the dye. Cut across the stem to see how it travels up.

### Catching insects

The easiest way to catch a large number of insects is to place a white sheet under a small bush and then beat the bush with a broom. It is astonishing just how many insects live in one bush. Gather them up. Put them in a jar together with a few leaves from the bush. Watch them for an hour or two then let them go.

### Watching small animals move

You will need a piece of clear Plexiglas 20–30 by 12–20 inches (50–75 by 30–50 cm) and two supports. A couple of cushions or four bricks will do. The child needs to be able to poke her head under the Plexiglas. Place various small animals on the Plexiglas and let your child watch how they move. A good selection includes earthworms, millipedes, slugs, snails, beetles and grass snakes.

### Looking inside a seed

You will need a big seed such as a fresh bean or a pea. First take the thick protective outer coat away. You will find that the seed has two halves. Open these carefully to see the tiny root and shoot at one end. This is what grows into the plant. The two thick sections are the seed leaves, which are full of food to make the plant grow. If you eat the food instead it makes you grow.

### Looking at nature

Buy a book on wildflowers, trees or fungi, with large, clear and colored illustrations, then set off and explore. A magnifying glass is a useful addition to your kit.

## Footprints

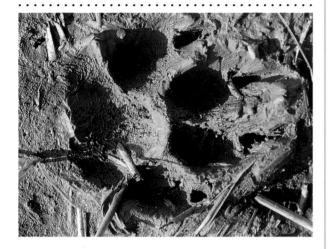

Many animals feed at night. If there is snow on the ground they often have to travel some distance before they find food. If you go out early enough you can trace the night's activity by the footprints in the new snow.

In wet weather, animals leave footprints in the mud. Make a circle of stiff cardboard around the print, pour in some plaster of Paris and let it set. Your child will have a cast of the print.

## Roosting birds

Birds often live in big noisy groups. They spend their days together feeding, and in the evenings come home to roost in gangs. This can be dramatic to watch. The easiest birds to watch in cities are pigeons and starlings and, in the countryside, crows. The time to watch is before dusk on an autumn or winter evening.

## Clever squirrels

Squirrels are skilled at walking tightropes and climbing poles. Take a paper cup and make a hole in the bottom. Pass a string through this and tie a knot on the outside. Fill the cup with a mixture of melted lard, seeds, grains and breakfast cereals. A few raisins are also good. To make the "cake" just melt a block of lard (it does not need to be hot). You need to use the hard type not the whipped variety sold for baking. Coat the other ingredients with the lard and pour the mixture into a paper cup. Pull the string up through the middle. Put this in the fridge to set.

Hang the cup from the clothesline or the branch of a tree. As birds and squirrels eat the contents you can cut the cup down, exposing more lard and seeds. If you hang the pudding in the middle of a long line, squirrels will be forced into walking the tightrope to reach it.

## WHAT YOUR CHILD LEARNS

Most city dwellers do not have the introduction to nature that children who grow up in the country take for granted. But "nature" activities teach even a city child about the living world.

### • Observation
The ability to look for small details and differences, in how small animals move, for example, is a key skill in reading and understanding math.

### • Group work
Watching herds of animals and how they live together broadens your child's ability to understand how social groups interact.

### • Finding out
Children who retain the idea that finding out is fun are likely to have happier school careers, regardless of academic success.

# Prewriting skills

*Your child does not have to be able to write before he starts school, but with a little encouragement he is likely to have the underlying skills*

## Realistic squiggles

If children are encouraged to make little squiggles to name their paintings they will. Rather than saying "Is this a house?", try "Is that the house and this the story about the house?" The child may also sit down and do his writing. A small book or piece of paper is a good way to inspire this. Study his writing – as you do his pictures – and look for sections that resemble real letters.
"I can see you have made a letter *l* here."
"Is that a letter *u* – it looks like one."
"What a lot of *m* letters you have here."
A child who is reinforced in this way will want to make more of the same, just as such rewards as asking if a picture of dots in a circle is a face encourages your child to draw people.

## Making his lists

Children may not see adults writing often, but there are contexts when most put pen to paper. Perhaps the most common are filling in forms, writing checks, taking notes and making lists. These are all occasions when he can write too.

### TROUBLESHOOTING

**How do I make my son William do as he is told? Whenever I make a request he just ignores me. I have to nag and nag to get anything done. I dread to think what will happen when he starts school.**

First, stop nagging. If it's important tell him once and expect him to behave. If it is not important leave it. Be firm but reasonable. Describe the problem, give information and say what you expect. *Your things are all over the table. It's dinner time. Can you start to put them away, please? I'll help when I have finished this.* If he delays add: *If you will not clear up I will have to put those pens away until Wednesday.* If he still does not act remind him with one word. *Dinner.* Then act. *I see you have chosen not to play with your pens until Wednesday.* Put the pens out of reach. If he protests explain it was his choice.

• Collect forms from the post office and bank for him to fill in.
• Give him some paper to write his list before you go shopping.
• Give him a little book of Post-it notes to take down messages.

## Connect the dots

Preschoolers find big connect-the-dot puzzles difficult. But they can manage the numbers 1 to 10, especially if you write them out in order at the top of the page. Ten dots are enough to draw a kite flying in the sky, a mug or a pan.

Letters can also be formed from dots. These may not need to be numbered; you could simply show the direction he should use when forming the letter with an arrow.

## Mazes

Draw a simple maze for your child. This could involve a couple of lines crossing with a balloon on each. The child colors in the balloons and then follows the line of the string using the same colored pencil.

### Looking and finding

Encourage your child to look for letters in what he writes. He will need help at first but will soon learn to pick out the most obvious. Once he can do this, you will find that he begins to write these over and over again. When he can do all the ones he has generated himself, he may ask you for a new letter. Show him one. In this way you can expand his repertoire. Do not bother about how carefully he forms his letters. At this stage all that is important is that he understands what writing is – and likes to do it.

### Making "words" and spelling

As soon as he can write letters, try reading out what he has written: "Rrru – that sounds a bit like a dog!"; "Nnmp – that's a hard one to say!"; "Up – wow that's a real word you have there!"

Once he realizes that he can make real words he may want to do so. Show him how to make any letters he does not yet know and spell words for him if he asks. If he wants to carry on "scribble writing" that is fine. The name of this game is wanting to write – not perfecting the skill.

### Well-formed letters

In order to form letters clearly a child needs to have good pen control. Not only must he put lines where he needs them, but he has to do so in a certain order. There are a number of activities that can enhance this skill.

## WHAT YOUR CHILD LEARNS

### • Sitting still
It is hard to write when you are running around, so all these activities encourage your child to sit still.

### • Attention to detail
Looking for the next number or the next directional arrow encourages your child to pay attention to detail.

### • Wrist and finger control
The children who have the least difficulty learning how to write are those whose hand skills are the best developed. Practice helps enormously.

### • Vocabulary
A child who knows the names of the letters of the alphabet and can recognize some of them has a head start with reading and writing.

### Coloring books

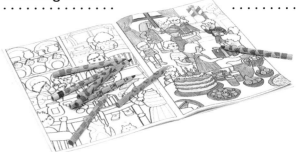

Coloring books provide lots of practice in pencil control, and they are cheap enough to buy with pocket money. Colored pencils and fine felt-tip pens are easier to use than crayons or paints.

### Tracing

You can buy good quality tracing paper at stationery shops. Using a soft pencil also helps, as this erases more easily. Tracing is an excellent way to practice pencil control. The pictures your child traces should be simple. What could be better than tracing letters?

### Writing his name

Children like to write their names on their work. If you always do this your child will want to copy you as soon as he is able to form his letters.

# Prereading skills 1

*The necessary preliminaries before your child learns to read*

In order to learn to read a child must recognize that a certain pattern of letters represents a particular sound. There are a number of elements to this skill and each needs to be practiced. The first element is understanding that the squiggles on the page represent words. The second is that these words are specific (that is, that a book always tells the same story, and a word is always written in the same way). The third is that the way the squiggles are placed on the page matters (we read from left to right and from the top of the page to the bottom).

### Following with a finger

The most obvious way to tell a child that the words you are saying are printed on the page is to read to him from a book. If your child has a number of different books she will soon learn that if she wants to hear a particular story she needs to select a specific book. This lesson can be reinforced by following the lines you are reading with your finger.

### Hunt the thimble

This is a simple game that requires your child to make a careful search of an area. The child goes out of the room while you hide a small object (it does not have to be a thimble but it needs to be

small: a button or a coin would do). The child then comes into the room and begins to search. The farther away she is, the colder you tell her it is. The nearer she comes the warmer she is. When she is extremely close she is hot. If several children play, the winner could receive a little prize.

### Comic books

Comic books lay out the sequence of pictures in the same way that words are laid out on the page, so sitting and reading comics and comic books helps your child to practice using the structure of the written page.

### Making a comic book

Making a comic book is simple. You need to take a series of photographs that can be placed in order quite easily. So you might, for example, tell the story of a trip to the park. Putting her coat on might be the first picture, followed by leaving the house, walking up the road, entering the park and going on the swing. Arrange these photos comic-book fashion on the page. If you have eight you can make two pages. Write a sentence under each photograph.

## Left to right

Reinforce page layout in as many areas as possible, not just reading. For instance, it helps to lay out her clothes each morning so she selects them from left to right: sweater, pants, T-shirt, jeans, socks, shoes.

## Looking for daisies

This is another simple searching game that can be played in the garden or when out for a walk. It could also be adapted for plenty of other situations. The task is a simple one. You search for one item and when you have spotted it you simply shout out "I see a daisy." What can you look for apart from daisies? Pigeons, flies, acorns, the letter B, certain makes of car, square objects, things beginning with C, round things, plants with reddish leaves. There are many possibilities and the game can be made as easy or as difficult as your child likes.

## Puzzles

Most good toy shops have a wide range of games that are excellent practice for observational skills. Any game that encourages a child to observe the pictures or words closely

is excellent practice. The visual side of reading is all about recognizing small differences in the shape of written words. The more practice she has at this the more simple she will find the task. Jigsaws are an ideal learning tool in this respect.

## Matching shapes and pictures

This is a simple puzzle type game. The idea is to draw for the child a picture that contains a number of different hidden shapes – circles, triangles and squares. The child then has to find these. The game is made easier by cutting out the shapes and asking the child to place the cut-outs on top of the shape in the picture. It is excellent for observational skills.

### WHAT YOUR CHILD LEARNS

All these activities teach children two important prereading skills.

**• Shape recognition**
The ability to recognize shapes and differentiate between them is fundamental to reading.

**• Sequencing**
Words are comprised of sequences of letters and sounds. A child who understands this has grasped a fundamental prereading skill.

# Prereading skills 2

*Building on the basics to give your child the foundations that will lead to learning to read*

The second step for a prereader is to associate the written word with the sounds he hears. There are two elements that need to be practiced here. The first is that your child must be aware that small variations in shape can make large differences in sound and huge changes in meaning. The second is that words are made up of little sounds and these are represented by letter groups. Both tasks involve attention to detail.

### Listening for the sounds

To read we need to translate the sounds we hear into symbols. So cat has to be broken down into three sounds c–a–t. This is difficult for small children to do and they need practice. One way to practice is to listen to poems and songs that use rhyme. Reading poems to a child can help him to hear the sounds.

### Making the rhyme

One person says a word and the next person says one that rhymes with it. Then the next person finds a rhyme and so on until no one can think of any more. This game can be made more challenging for older players by not allowing words to be used in alphabetical order and making each player repeat all the words that have already been found: a cat; a gnat cat; a flat gnat cat; a fat flat gnat cat; a hat fat flat gnat cat.

### I spy

Whoever is starting the game chooses an object he can see and lets the rest of the players know the first letter. So if he is thinking of a cup he would say "I spy with my little eye something beginning with C." The child then has to guess what the object is. If he is close you can say "warm"; if not, you can say "cold," although you can play without this information. The person who guesses correctly has the next turn.

### Labels on the door

This is not so much a game as a decoration. Write out a number of words in lowercase letters and place these on the objects they name. (For metal surfaces such as the fridge, magnets are ideal.) Choose words that have different shapes. The best contrasts come from choosing one word with an upward stroke at the end, such as "wall," another with an upward stroke at the beginning like "door" and contrasting longer shapes like "window," or "cupboard." The word "drawer" is shaped like a drawer and "bed" looks a little like a bed. Start with about six and add to them later. After the child has looked at them for a few days, can he say what they are if you write them out for him in a book? If he finds this hard at first, color code the words so he has another clue.

### I packed my case and in it I put...

This can be played in a number of ways. Children must think of words beginning with a certain sound or letter, or they might use letters in alphabetical order (as they start to understand sequencing), or they can just present the words. They could try to remember all the words that have gone before: a shoe; a shoe and a sock; a shoe, a sock and a sea lion; a shoe, a sock, a sea lion and a submarine.

## Looking for letters

This is a simple game that can be played whenever you are out and about. The task is to find certain letters among those on advertisements, store and road signs and street names. *S* for "snake" is an easy one, so is the first letter of his name; *M* for "mommy" and *D* for daddy; *T* for "teddy" and any of his brothers' and sisters' initials.

A variation on "looking for letters" on a car journey (or a bus ride) is to look for letters on license plates. This time you have to look for the letters in alphabetic order or, if that is too difficult for the child, in the order of the letters in his name.

## Looking for his words

This is a variation on the letter game that looks for certain words. Finding one word in a sea of sentences on the page gives children great

## WHAT YOUR CHILD LEARNS

### • Labels on the door
When your child goes to nursery school, there is likely to be a peg with his name on it. It helps if he can recognize this. Labeling also introduces the child to the idea that all objects have names that are composed of different letters.

### • Making the rhyme
These games are a great introduction to the idea that strings of letters that are spelled similarly are often pronounced in the same way. Understanding this concept means that a child does not have to learn each new word he encounters. It also helps him "hum" the little sounds that make up words. This encourages him to "spell out" and read.

### • Looking for letters and words
All children like the challenge and triumph of finding things. Looking for words and letters gives the satisfaction of a job done. It teaches your child the names and shapes of words and letters and encourages him to pay attention to detail.

confidence. All my children believed they could read once they could pick out "the" and "is." You can rely on there being at least one of these on every page.

# Premath skills

*Laying the foundations for an understanding of the way numbers work*

No teacher will expect your child to have grasped all the concepts of arithmetic before she starts school, but it will help if she has some understanding of what numbers mean.

## Connections

Draw a number of objects in one column and a series of related objects in another. The child has to connect the two. The drawings might be:

| | |
|---|---|
| Egg | Glove |
| Hand | Egg carton |
| Cup | Shoe |
| Sock | Saucer |

## A collection of caps

Collect the tops from bottles and tubes of all kinds and put them in a box. Sort them by whether or not they can be used to build a tower and by size, shape and color. Can they be put into pairs? Which ones fit inside others?

## Counting the spoons

Children like something to count, but since they tend to give the wrong answer it is a good idea to start with an object that does not involve large numbers. Teaspoons are good, since few people have more than 20 of them.

## Big feet

You will need remnants of carpet or padding and a pair of old slippers or sandals. Cut out two foot shapes that are exactly 12 inches (25 cm) long. Glue them to the bottom of an old pair of flip-flop sandals or slippers. Alternatively, make two holes in each foot shape and thread a ribbon through so they can be tied to the child's foot. The child can now measure all kinds of areas. How big is the yard? How long is the family room? How wide is the bed? You could also construct a standard 2-inch (5-cm) finger or a standard 4-inch (10-cm) hand.

## Connect two

This works on a similar principle to "Big feet." Cut various lengths of string in pairs. Then place a number of objects different "string lengths" apart and let your child match the distances between them with the matching length of string.

She can also add together the different lengths to see how they form a longer string.

### Sorting buttons

These can be collected by cutting them off old clothes or buying new ones. Just put them all in a can. Your child can sort the ones that are the same; sort the ones that are the same except for size; sort the ones that are the same except for color; sort those with two holes from those with four; sort the plastic from the metal; arrange them in stripes, in patterns and by size. This also works with beads.

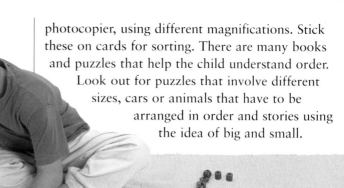

photocopier, using different magnifications. Stick these on cards for sorting. There are many books and puzzles that help the child understand order. Look out for puzzles that involve different sizes, cars or animals that have to be arranged in order and stories using the idea of big and small.

### The threeness of three

To understand numbers children have to see what three eggs, three plates, three spoons and three cups have in common. The easiest way to do this is to match each item to something she understands. So three might be one for Daddy, one for Mommy and one for Mandy. Or it might be one for this hand, one for that hand and one left over.

### Candy math

One piece of candy for Mommy and one for Tessa: one, two. If Mommy gives her piece to Tessa she has one, two. One and another one make two. If Tessa has two pieces and she eats one, she has only one left. Two take away one is one.

Keep it simple. Just add and take away one at a time until the child is clear about the concept. Then try adding and taking away two. If you progress slowly she will do well. If you try to rush you will simply confuse her.

### Putting things in order

Counting is a rhyme. Understanding what that rhyme means involves grasping that two adjacent numbers are formed by adding one to the previous number. Part of this comprehension involves the idea that things can be put in order. Copy a set of simple outline drawings on a

### Putting the groceries away

Next time you do major grocery shopping – you need plenty of variety for this to work well – let your child help you to put it away. While she is helping, she is learning many premath skills.

## WHAT YOUR CHILD LEARNS

### • Connections
This will help your child to understand how to match two objects.

### • Connect two; big feet
These lay the foundation for measuring and for understanding the basis of multiplication.

### • Threeness of three
By introducing the idea of what "three" or "four" means in terms she can understand, you give your child the foundation of all number work.

### • Putting the groceries away
Knowing where everything goes – matching objects to cupboards – is a mathematical skill, so too is putting the objects that go in one place away one after the other. If you suggest she group items, this will help. She will start to understand volume if she stacks cans and packages to make the best use of space. Stacking four small cans so they are the same height as two big ones helps her understanding of multiplication.

# Index

# Acknowledgments

l= left, r = right, t = top, c = center, b = bottom

1–4l Laura Wickenden, 4r Sandra Lousada/Collections; 5–6t Laura Wickenden, 6b P.Barton/The Stock Market;
7 Laura Wickenden; 8t George Contorakes/The Stock Market, 8b Laura Wickenden; 9–28t Laura Wickenden;
28b Ian West/Bubbles; 29t Laura Wickenden; 29b The Stock Market; 30/31 Elizabeth Whiting & Associates;
32–33t Laura Wickenden, 33b Ian West/Bubbles; 34–35 The Stock Market; Laura Wickenden; 37t Steve Bavister/Robert Harding
Picture Library, 37b Laura Wickenden; 38–39 Laura Wickenden; 40 Sandra Lousada/Collections; 41 Andre Gallant/The Image Bank;
42–47 Laura Wickenden; 48 Robert Harding Picture Library; 49l Elizabeth Whiting & Associates, 49r Angela Hampton/Bubbles;
50–51t Laura Wickenden, 51b Loisjoy Thurston/Bubbles; 53–60 Laura Wickenden; 61t Robert Harding Picture Library,
61c & b Laura Wickenden; 62–64 Laura Wickenden; 65t Susanna Price/Bubbles, 65b Laura Wickenden; 66–70l Laura Wickenden,
70r Susanna Price/Bubbles; 71–73 Laura Wickenden; 74 Loisjoy Thurston/Bubbles; 75–79 Laura Wickenden;
80 Julia Yelland/Laura Wickenden; 81t Laura Wickenden, 81b The Stock Market; 82 Laura Wickenden;
83t Julia Yelland/Laura Wickenden, 83b Eliza Sleeman; 84l Jack Sleeman, 84r Eliza Sleeman; 85tl Jack Sleeman;
85tr, 85bl, 85br Julia Yelland/Laura Wickenden; 86–97 Laura Wickenden; 98t Sandra Lousada/Collections, 98b Andrew Sydenham;
99l Laura Wickenden, 99r Andrew Sydenham; 100 The Stock Market; 101 Laura Wickenden; 102 Susanna Price/Bubbles;
103 Loisjoy Thurston/Bubbles; 104–105t Laura Wickenden, 105b Loisjoy Thurston/Bubbles; 106–108 Laura Wickenden;
109t Jennie Woodcock/Bubbles, 109b Laura Wickenden; 110l Laura Wickenden, 110r Geoff Du Feu/Bubbles;
111–114 Laura Wickenden; 115 The Stock Market; 116–117 Laura Wickenden; 118 Frans Rombout/Bubbles; 119 Laura Wickenden;
120 Jennie Woodcock/Bubbles; 121 Loisjoy Thurston/Bubbles; 122 Laura Wickenden; 124t Anthea Sieveking/Collections,
124b Laura Wickenden; 125–127 Laura Wickenden; 128 Loisjoy Thurston/Bubbles; 129 Laura Wickenden;
130 Anthea Sieveking/Collections; 131–134t Laura Wickenden, 134b Anthea Sieveking/Collections; 135t Jennie Woodcock/Bubbles,
135b Laura Wickenden; 136 Laura Wickenden; 137t Andrew Sydenham; 137b Laura Wickenden; 138–140 Laura Wickenden;
141l The Stock Market, 141r Robert Harding Picture Library; 142l Laura Wickenden, 142r Frans Rombout/Bubbles;
143 Laura Wickenden; 144–145 Laura Wickenden; 146l Anthea Sieveking/Collections; 146r Laura Wickenden; 147 Ian West/Bubbles;
148–152 Laura Wickenden; 153t Robert Harding Picture Library; 153b–156 Laura Wickenden; 157t David Young Wolff/
Tony Stone Images; 157b Jennie Woodcock/Bubbles; 158 Jeff Cadge/The Image Bank; 159–162 Laura Wickenden;
163l Robert Harding Picture Library; 163r John Walmsley; 164l Laura Wickenden; 164r Jennie Woodcock/Bubbles;
165–166 Laura Wickenden; 167 Andre Gallant/The Image Bank; 168l E.T. Archive; 168r The Maas Gallery, London/
The Bridgeman Art Library; 169l Bob Thomas/Tony Stone Images; 169r Laura Wickenden; 170 Chris Steele-Perkins/ Magnum Photos;
171–172 Laura Wickenden; 173tl The Image Bank; 173tr Chris Beetles Ltd, London/The Bridgeman Art Library;
173b Sandra Lousada/Collections; 174–176t Laura Wickenden; 176b–177l Ray Moller; 177r–180 Laura Wickenden;
181 Sandra Lousada/Collections; 182 Andrew Sydenham; 183 Laura Wickenden; 184 Ian West/Bubbles; 185 Laura Wickenden;
186 Jacqui Farrow/Bubbles; 187l Andrew Sydenham; 187r–188 Laura Wickenden; 189 Robert Harding Picture Library;
190–192 Laura Wickenden; 193t Anthea Sieveking/Collections, 193c Laura Wickenden, 193b Robert Harding Picture Library;
194–195 Laura Wickenden; 196 Ian West/Bubbles; 197t Richard Yard/Bubbles, 197b Ken Fisher/Tony Stone Images;
198 Christian Liewig/Tony Stone Images; 199–202 Laura Wickenden; 203 Terje Rakke/The Image Bank; 204–206 Laura Wickenden;
207t Robert Harding Picture Library, 207b Laura Wickenden; 208 The Stock Market; 209 John Walmsley; 210–216 Laura Wickenden;
217 Chas Wilder; 218–219 Laura Wickenden; 221t John Walmsley; 221c & b Laura Wickenden; 222 John Walmsley;
223–224l Laura Wickenden, 224r The Stock Market; 225 David Thompson/Oxford Scientific Films; 226–230 Laura Wickenden;
231 Quadrant Picture Library; 232–233 Laura Wickenden

The publishers would also like to thank Galt Educational for the loan of the toys featured throughout this book.

PROJECT EDITOR **Anne Yelland**
EDITOR **Anna Fischel**
ART EDITOR **Allan Mole**
EDITORIAL DIRECTOR **Sophie Collins**
ART DIRECTOR **Sean Keogh**
PICTURE RESEARCH **Zilda Tandy**
EDITORIAL COORDINATOR **Becca Clunes**
INDEXER **Laura Hicks**
PRODUCTION **Nikki Ingram**